ADVANCED STUDIES IN
UNDERSTANDING
YOURSELF

ADVANCED STUDIES IN
UNDERSTANDING YOURSELF

*The Masters of the East unlock the mystery
of being and the psychology of the soul*

Commentaries by
ELIZABETH CLARE PROPHET
on the Spiritual Classic Understanding Yourself

SUMMIT UNIVERSITY PRESS®
Gardiner, Montana

For information, contact
The Summit Lighthouse, 63 Summit Way, Gardiner, MT 59030 USA
Tel: 1-800-245-5445 or 1 406-848-9500
info@SummitUniversityPress.com
www.SummitLighthouse.org

Library of Congress Catalog Card Number: 2013952711
ISBN: 978-1-60988-226-6 (softbound)
ISBN: 978-1-60988-238-9 (eBook)

SUMMIT UNIVERSITY 🕉 PRESS®

Contents

Decrees and Mantras

Foreword

The true science of psychology is the study of the soul. In reality this study requires an awareness beyond the circumstances and momentums of our present life. It includes an understanding of karmic patterns from this and previous lives, of the preexistence of the soul in other dimensions. From this vantage point we recognize that each soul has a unique destiny and reason for being here in the schoolroom of life called planet Earth.

In the beginning of our soul's evolution, we were given the gift of free will. For many lifetimes and thousands of years we have charted our course through the use and misuse of that supreme opportunity. In some ways we have remade ourselves—not in the original image in which we were made, but after a new image, self-created.

So today we find ourselves far from our original source and the eternal freedom, light and love we once knew. We desire to return home. Therefore we must begin the process of the re-creation of self. We must remake ourselves after the real image we once knew—what has been called the mighty work of the ages.

Many others have walked this path before us. They returned home. They ascended to the heart of God, to the Source from which they came, the great sphere of light that is their own highest Self. They are known today as ascended masters.

They invite us to walk in their footsteps. They teach us how to unravel the bonds of limitation we have created, whether consciously or in ignorance, in this or previous lives. They tell us that our present circumstances represent the outworking of all our experiences in Spirit and matter. If we would transcend them, we must change our psychology and change our karma. They show us the way.

Some years ago, three masters from the East—Meru, Lanto and Kuthumi—delivered a series of letters on the psychology of the soul. They spoke of karma and destiny, of how to overcome the limitations of the lesser self. They spoke of the universal disease of human unhappiness and how to overcome it. They spoke of opening the door to the superconscious mind.

These teachings were recorded by Mark Prophet, messenger for the ascended masters, and later published in a book titled *Understanding Yourself.* In 1975 Elizabeth Clare Prophet, Mark's successor as leader of The Summit Lighthouse, gave a series of commentaries on these letters. These lectures were delivered to a small group of students who had come to study the masters' teachings at Summit University.

Delivered under the direct inspiration of the masters who dictated the original releases, Mrs. Prophet's commentary on *Understanding Yourself* reveals the more esoteric meaning of the masters' words as well as the practical application of their teaching to daily life. The result is a profound exploration of the higher science of psychology and the path of true soul liberation.

THE EDITORS

CHAPTER ONE

THE STUDY
OF THE SOUL

In the name of the Christ, in the name of the Holy Spirit, we invoke the presence of beloved Hilarion. We call for the light of the healing ray, for the healing of the consciousness of mankind. Let it be upon each heart, each mind for the quickening of the impulse of the Creator's consciousness. We thank thee and accept it done this hour in the name of the Father, the Mother, the Son and the Holy Spirit, Amen.

Commentary on Chapter 1, Part 1

Kuthumi, Lord Lanto and Meru are the masters of illumination giving this course, which is based on their 1969 series of dictations "Understanding Yourself." This series appears simple on the surface but it is extremely profound, far more profound than that which will seem profound in the texts on psychology we will also be discussing.

When we look into the works of Freud and Jung, we find that many terms that are part of our everyday language are taken from their writings. Most of us use the word *ego,* but we don't realize the connotation it has in Freud's works. We may use the word *id* or talk about complexes or psychoses or schizophrenia, but all these terms just have a vague meaning for us without the depth and breadth they should have.

We do need to understand how the world has attempted to define the mechanizations of the ego and the personality. However, there is a danger of succumbing to the fascination of the human personality. Observing the human personality can become an endless fascination. If we are on that path, we can spend lifetime after lifetime exploring the labyrinthian caves of the subconscious, the ghosts, the patterns, the past events and the negative substance that is there.

So we have to be extremely careful as we enter into this study and analysis. We have to bear in mind, at all times, that the flame of the Holy Spirit is able to transmute and consume on contact these records in the subconscious with their cause and core.

The Soul and the Ego

Some study of psychology is indeed vital because it helps us to know ourselves. "Man, know thyself"[1] means we must indeed know the pseudo image as well as the real image, the synthetic mind as well as the real. A study of psychology exposes the whys and wherefores of our actions. It breaks down the ego into its parts so that we can see what it is. We can examine it and we can be aware of what is acting, and so we are no longer deceived by our ego.

The word *psychology* itself is formed from the Greek word *psyche,* meaning "soul," and *-ology,* which means "the study of." Psychology, then, ought to be the study of the soul. But as I have reviewed these books on psychology for the last month, I have come to the conclusion that modern psychology has become a study of the human ego with the ramifications of the negative patterns of past karma.

Actually, it was not Freud who discovered the ego. It was the apostle Paul who named it. He said, "The carnal mind is enmity against God." He talked about the natural man and the spiritual man and the warring within his members. The things that he would do he did not. The things that he wanted to accomplish he could not because of this warring within.[2]

So Paul defined the carnal nature, which Freud called the ego, and this is what needs to be replaced with the Christ nature—not suppressed, but replaced. If we only suppress the carnal mind, its momentums and the energies of the lower nature, it will result in an explosion.

If you deprive yourself or your children of all the necessary functions of the physical body, the emotional body, the mental body, the etheric body—if you try to just stamp them out, if there is inculcated in you a shame of the expression of this aspect of self—there is such a warp of your being that when it comes time for the real personality of God to act in you, there are so many complexes and problems that God *cannot* act. The Divine Ego has no matrix, no platform through which it can function.

The ascended masters want us to lead normal lives because the spiritual life in itself seems so abnormal that they want the norm as the foundation. That way, what is normal can be a partial fulfillment of the needs of the natural man, so the natural man is not totally insane or totally falling apart by the time he comes to the path of the ascension.

There is a middle way, a golden mean, a path for us to follow. And we have to be careful that we don't try to completely wipe out some of the normal experiences that serve as a buffer to sustain the finite consciousness while it is evolving.

Take the situation with children. If you completely cut them off from the world—you don't let them hear music, you don't let them go to the movies, you don't let them associate with other people—they will become warped and very ineffective at being on the path of the ascended masters. You have to inculcate in them the correct principles of life. You have to bring them into alignment and attunement with the Christ consciousness. But you have to have a certain amount of trust in the real consciousness of God *in them* to allow them to go into the world to have experiences and to know that they will tether to Reality.

Guy Ballard (Saint Germain's messenger in the early twentieth century) used to go see a Western now and then. Mark Prophet used to do the same. There are certain things that people do that help maintain the integration and sanity of the four lower bodies while the flame is rising in the center. Balance is so important.

Wedges in the Mental Body

Some people come to the feet of the masters with such intense emotional problems that they can scarcely tether to the teachings or to a path of discipline. However, there is no question in my mind that the paths of both East and West, of Buddhists, of Christians, of various religions, the mystical path or the path of the monastery, are calculated to take care of all problems—emotional, mental, physical, whatever they may be—if the path is followed.

I have found without exception that individuals who have very deep-seated mental and emotional problems have them as the result of rebellion, which comes on the four o'clock line of our cosmic clock.* Rebellion is a wedge in the mental body. The wedge in the mental body creates a division within the mental body itself and also a division between the mind and the emotions. Rebellion against living the laws of God causes the individual to be divided against himself, and a house divided against itself cannot stand.[3] That division is the serving of both God and mammon that drives people to insanity.

Now, I have observed people coming to the masters'

---

*In a number of these commentaries, Mrs. Prophet refers to the science of the cosmic clock. An awareness of this universal spiritual law allows us to chart the cycles of our lives—of returning karma, both positive and negative, and of the spiritual initiations that are key for the evolution of the soul. For a brief introduction to the principles of the clock, see pp. 365–68.

teachings who have small problems—not big ones, but certain problems that must be dealt with if they are going to be effective on the world scene. I have also come to see that the bigger our organization grows, the more the masters' teachings attract those who have some form of mental illness or who aren't making it in the world because of their mental or emotional problems, so they are seeking religion. That is good. The masters have the whole answer, the complete answer, but it requires the surrender of that momentum of rebellion.

Rebellion (the negative quality on the four o'clock line) has a polarity with selfishness, self-centeredness, and the tendency toward self-preservation (the misuse of the ten o'clock line). And Morya said that when beginning on the Path, the cardinal principle of the chela, the student, is to obey the statement of the Master: "He who seeks to save his life shall lose it; he who loses his life for my sake shall find it again."[4]

Losing one's life for the sake of the Christ means laying down the carnal mind and exalting the Christ within. That is done on the ten o'clock line, which is in polarity with the four. When a person is in rebellion, he is in a state of rebellion against his own inner reality, against the laws of his own inner being. He thinks he's rebelling against the world, against injustice, against a host of things. Actually, he's cutting off his nose to spite his face. He is going contrary to the law of his own real identity and is consequently splitting himself apart from that identity, refusing to conform to it, refusing to come into alignment with it, and this creates the wedges which I so often see in people's auras.

The wedge comes in at an oblique angle and goes right through the mental body, the mental forcefield. And the consciousness is just like a phonograph record. When the record is playing, the needle of the Christ mind is attempting to deliver the pattern, the geometry of wholeness, and the needle goes round and round and then it hits the wedge. And each time it hits it, there is a click and a jump, and then it continues around.

Each time people who have these wedges in any of the four lower bodies come to a certain test or a certain point in their lives where it's time to rally their forces and really manifest a victory—maybe the victory is over a momentum of procrastination or disorganization or some form of internal chaos or confusion—they don't make it because they don't have the thrust to get through this substance.

Transmutation is the answer, driving the energies of the sacred fire in to consume the wedge. When we learn to isolate these wedges, to understand what they are, where they came from and what they are doing there, we begin to have an exact knowledge of how to direct concentrated spirals of the sacred fire into our consciousness for the removal of the cause and core of these conditions.

Now, when people go into meditation, very often they will get "answers." They'll say, "Well, I got this from my mighty I AM Presence. I got this from my Christ Self."* Or they'll say, "I don't think this is the right quarter for me to be in Summit University. I got that in meditation." Without wishing to insult the intelligence or the integrity or the ability of the individual to make that communion, and without seeming presumptuous, I do have to inform the individual that he is not contacting his Christ Self. He is contacting a wedge of concentrated energy which represents the stronghold of the ego.

---

*The I AM Presence is the individualized presence of God; the Christ Self is the individual Christ consciousness. See p. 361.

The ego wants to retain its identity. It does not want to be replaced by the Christ mind. So any removal of these

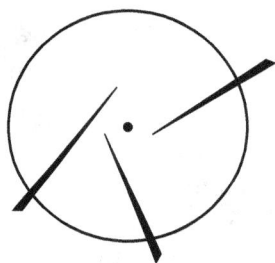

Wedges in the mental body

dark wedges is a terrific threat to the ego. In meditation the individual does not get beyond his own aura or his four lower bodies to contact the higher way. He can't even make contact with the Christ Self because he can't plow through all the density. So he contacts a wedge of rebellion and the carnal mind and the forces outside of himself that tie into these wedges—forces in family, in friends, in the world momentum of the mass consciousness.

All of this is the pushing and pulling of the consciousness and the lower nature talking to his consciousness with all kinds of objections: "No, you shouldn't be at Summit University. It's not time for you to go. You need more preparation. You can't make it. You don't have the proper educational background. You should be somewhere else doing something else."

The resistance of the carnal mind at the hour when its death knell sounds is overpowering. This is why there have been retreats and monasteries and teachers through the ages. Being together with a group of individuals who have made a pact to be overcomers, to put aside that aspect of consciousness, to put on the Christ, reinforces your momentum and your determination to do so. "Come let us reason together, saith the Lord."[5]

Now, to the extent that we read Freud and Jung and some other modern psychologists and understand how these wedges were created, what they are doing, how the ego evolves out of the id and the superego out of the ego, all for the sustaining of the desires of the id, we realize that there are very complex machinations that go on in our consciousness to promote the lower desires and the lower subconscious in order to sustain them. Once you find out what these machinations are and hold them up in front of you like your underwear on a clothesline, you see the result for what it is—a pseudo image—and it's easy to be objective and watchful and identify it.

Remember in *Peter Pan*[6] how Peter had to find his shadow? That's what it is—it's your shadow self. Jung actually calls it the "shadow," the portion of the self that is the not-self yet is very much the governing factor of the self.

We see, then, that this process of exchanging the human ego for the Divine Ego can be done with what the masters have called "Christly aplomb." That implies a tremendous dexterity, an astuteness, a great ability, a deftness. When we study the great masters and what they did in their final incarnations, we see that on the one hand, they lived normal lives that allowed the natural expression of the human aspect of self to evolve. On the other hand, their souls were being transformed.

For example, Thomas Moore, the Irish poet, was married with children and so was Sir Thomas More. Both men were embodiments of El Morya. Even Joseph and Mary—Saint Germain and Mother Mary—raised a family, and yet she was at the hour of her ascension. Going through the steps of doing what is normal placates all the hundreds and thousands of years of momentum so that you don't totally destroy the platform of evolution. Consequently the ascended masters advise us to be normal. It's good for you and it's good for the world's image of the ascended masters. Find people where they are. Accept them as they are.

Understand that people have needs, that if you tell them they can't do this, they can't do that, they can't do this, they can't do that, pretty soon they're "can't-ed" right out of existence. And of course, they deny the religion that preaches such things. The path of austerity carried to its end destroys the ego before it's ready to be replaced, before it's ready to give up, before it's ready to say die.

Psychology Books

We study psychology so that the Christ consciousness can reveal to us the nature of the soul, the soul that has descended into matter, "the fallen potential," as Morya calls it in *Climb the Highest Mountain.*[7]

In order to understand modern psychology and where it's going, we will be reading *A Primer of Freudian Psychology,* written by Calvin Hall.[8] It tells us exactly what Freud thought, what he did, how he started out, how he outlined his diagram of the human consciousness.

Calvin Hall also wrote *A Primer of Jungian Psychology.*[9] Jung started out with Freud then broke with him when they had disagreements. He has a different diagram of the personality. This book gives you Jung's background and his structure of the personality.

I have a great respect for Jung. I feel that he was inspired by the ascended masters. As far as Freud is concerned, I think he was in much greater darkness, that he explored the depths of the electronic belt and didn't get himself out of the electronic belt.* Nevertheless, Jung and Freud are the

---

*The electronic belt is a kettledrum-shaped vortex of energy surrounding an individual's four lower bodies, extending downward from the waist to beneath the feet. Referred to as the realm of the subconscious and the unconscious, the electronic belt contains the cause, effect, record and memory of untransmuted negative karma from all embodiments.

key figures in psychology. And to intelligently discuss the ascended masters' answers to psychology with any students who have had even a basic course in this study, you have to know this material.

When I read these books to prepare for the class, I had to lower my vibration so much to read them that I got a headache. So there is obviously a much lower vibration in these works than in the masters' teachings on the subject.

One book that I think is absolutely marvelous is *The Undiscovered Self*,[10] by Jung. I want you to read Jung because I feel that he parallels the masters' thought. He wrote this in the fifties as a commentary on what was happening in the conflict between Communism and the free world and the empowering of the state—the state becoming all-powerful—and what this does to the individual, how the individual is destroyed.

Then there is a simple book about how to deal with yourself and others, *How to Be Your Own Best Friend*.[11] It's the kind of book that might be something you could offer to someone who can't take anything more difficult.

We are going to hang everything we read in the psychology books on the *Pearls of Wisdom* series "Understanding Yourself." We are going to get the ascended masters' interpretation of everything we study so we can approach this course from the level of the Christ mind, not from the fascination of the human mind with itself—which is a very dangerous thing.

Self-Knowledge

Now we will take up the first *Pearl of Wisdom*, by beloved Kuthumi, titled "To All Who Would Know Themselves." The question we must ask here is "What is self-knowledge?"

As I noted earlier, self-knowledge must be the knowledge of the Real Image and the knowledge of the synthetic image. You can read the two chapters that cover this in *Climb the Highest Mountain*[12] so that you know what your synthetic image is and what your Real Image is. Then when you are hearing all these theories of psychology you can discern the difference between the two as you analyze yourself.

To All Who Would Know Themselves:
Self is interwoven with consciousness, and consciousness is the doorway to reality. In an impure state, consciousness puts out the light; in a pure state, it radiates light.

The impure state puts out the light because it blocks the light. It puts out the light because it absorbs the light. Just as a dark color will absorb light and white will reflect it, you will find that the impurities within you will absorb the light you receive, pollute that light and direct it into the subconscious channels or ruts of consciousness that you have already established.

This is why people who are really sick—mentally ill— will come in and give decrees in a fanatical way.* The fanatical decrees they give will only serve to reinforce the patterns of their own fanaticism because the light of decrees is pure energy. A certain amount of it will go into the cups of consciousness or the patterns the person already has within his subconscious. Therefore, decreeing by itself is not the answer.

You have to study to show yourself approved.[13] Showing

---

*Decrees are a dynamic form of spoken prayer used by students of the ascended masters to direct God's light into individual and world conditions.

yourself approved means that your consciousness becomes more and more like God, so that when you do decree, the light will amplify what is good.

Now, this is true in every area of life. It is true of our moral codes, our ethics. We can go for a long time in the teachings and not feel it is wrong to lie once in a while, to cheat here and there to get along. So what happens in such instances is an impure consciousness absorbs the light unto itself.

There is a process of evolution that definitely occurs with the light. The light will evolve your consciousness of its own accord, but it may take ten or more embodiments without a teacher to tell you right from wrong. Once you have a teacher, you understand right from wrong. You begin to consciously make the correction. You substitute a right pattern for a wrong pattern. A right pattern is a right matrix, and when you have substituted a right matrix, the light starts filling and reinforcing that matrix. You become strong in it, and you put off a portion of the carnal mind and put on a portion of the Christ mind.

That's why we have Summit University—to teach you the Law and the way and the correct use of the sacred fire. When you have that understanding, step by step you make internal corrections. As you make them, the old patterns give way to new patterns. It's the same concept that Jesus taught with the breaking of the old wine bottles—you don't pour new wine into old bottles.[14] You don't pour the new wine of the Holy Spirit into the old patterns of consciousness, because those patterns may break and cause you great problems, or you may simply reinforce those patterns.

Motives Must Be Examined

Now we understand what Kuthumi is talking about in this first paragraph: what happens in an impure state and what happens in a pure state. This is one reason why some people feel spiritual radiation and some people don't. The people who don't feel radiation have imperfections that block the light. These blocks may be absorbing and stealing some of that light energy for the reinforcement of impure motives.

Motives must be examined and reexamined because they steal an enormous quantity of energy from us. Many motives are subconscious: the motive to push the ego, the motive for sex, the motive to control other people through sex, the motives of greed, of acquisition, of success. All these are at subconscious levels.

You may not even admit to your outer self that you have these motives. But such motives and momentums at subconscious levels are so strong that they may be stealing nine-tenths of your energy. You may have only one-tenth left to function on. Your energy may be going into pockets of hatred, of ancient resentments that you have sustained at lower levels of consciousness that you aren't even aware of in this life.

That's the nature of an impure consciousness—and it puts out the light. That's the consciousness we need to define and transmute. The masters tell us it's not necessary to totally define it in order to transmute it, thank God. We don't want to have to see all of it. We want it to go into the flame. But somehow there is a point of consciousness where we are aware of what's going into the flame, and there is also the resistance of that impure consciousness to going into the flame, to being transmuted. That is where we have problems. That is where we have the pulling in the opposite direction and the warring in our members.

Sometimes at the last moment when we are about to transmute a momentum, a pattern of desire, we take it back to ourselves and we don't let it go into the flame. We gobble it right back down and put it in the subconscious. We'll snitch that piece of chocolate, or we'll eat another helping of something we shouldn't be eating. And we miss an opportunity to abstain and therefore overcome and let the flame flow through.

But that's all right—we'll get another chance to give up the chocolate. We can't condemn ourselves and flail ourselves for our imperfections. That's a very unhealthy state of mind.

The Cultivation of Light

The admonishment "Let your light so shine before men, that they may see your good works, and glorify your Father which is in heaven"[15] is both blessing and reproof—a blessing to those who follow it and a reproof to those who do it not. But the purposes of life are not to reprove; they are to cultivate qualities of reality. The appearance world is a world of illusion. Yet it seems real, and to some even the idiosyncrasies of the human personality take on a form of reality.

Whenever you see the word *cultivate*, you should associate it in your mind with the word *culture*. The culture of the Divine Mother is the cultivation of light.*

---

*The inner meaning of *culture* derives from "*cult-*" or cultivation, and "*-ure*" from Ur of the Chaldees, an ancient city of light mentioned in the Bible (Gen. 11:28). Culture (*cult-ur*), then, is using God's energy for the cultivation of light.

Kuthumi speaks of the cultivation of reality. When you think of a cultivated plant, you are thinking of a plant that is special, that is a hybrid, like a special rose. You don't think of a wildflower. Someone who is cultured is someone who is refined, who has sensitivity, who appreciates good art, good music, who has good manners. Having good manners comes from a sense of doing the right thing that makes someone else comfortable. It is the flame of the Holy Spirit. It's not rote or a ritual of habit patterns that somebody thought up. It really comes out of what makes people comfortable.

We want ascended master students to be cultured. We want you to cultivate light and the appreciation of light. To do this, you need a refinement of your sensitivities. You need a refinement of your soul faculties. You can gain this refinement simply by constantly attuning to other people and doing what makes them feel comfortable, "letting your light shine that they may see your good works and glorify your Father which is in heaven."

How many times when you do something good does somebody come up to you and say, "Praise God!"? They usually say, "You've done a great job" or "You're wonderful" or "You're beautiful" or "You're really smart." When you let your light shine so that men see your good works and *glorify your Father,* if you can make yourself a pane of transparent glass so somebody can acknowledge you did something great but God did it through you—that's doing something. Usually you have to remind people, "All glory goes to God."

The appearance world and the human personality are the illusions, and that is what we have to eliminate as we cultivate reality. So many idiosyncrasies of the human personality take on a form of reality that sometimes it's really hard to tell the difference. We have to cultivate a sense of reality and what qualities of God are real in order to use that as a measuring rod against what we are doing and what we are manifesting.

Shattering Illusions

Our subject, understanding yourself, is a broad one. We would softly yet skillfully pull the thread of man's consciousness through the eye that opens into the world of crystal clarity. From the standpoint of the human, how sad it is that illusions must be shattered. But we deem it far wiser and less painful to shatter them by the skillful use of spiritual discernment than to have them broken by the impact of the higher law as the law brings to the doorstep of each man a return of the energies he has sent out.

Unfortunately, most of us do not know what our illusions are. This is why we come to the feet of the ascended masters. Those who are rebellious against the law of their own being, who refuse to come into conformity with that law, will usually rebel against the teacher who becomes the personification of the Law. They rebel in a moment when only the teacher can discern what is acting and isolate that illusion so that the person can surrender it, can challenge that aspect of his ego. In that very moment the student will say, "I challenge the teacher. I don't believe the teacher is telling me the truth. I don't believe the teacher is qualified. I'm going to search for another teacher."

Out of all the students who have come to Summit University, we've only had a few who have done this. They have come to a point in the quarter where they could have surrendered a whole block of their human consciousness. But it was such a traumatic experience—they could not part with this aspect of themselves—that they had to blame me or the ascended masters.

Usually the ascended masters don't get blamed because they are always held in the place of absolute perfection, where they can do no wrong. Obviously the ascended masters understand the challenge "I'm right and the teacher is wrong." And the student who does not wish to give up his human consciousness will conclude that he is right, but I am wrong because I am not yet perfected. Because I still have a human consciousness, which he can clearly see for what it is, he can then reject that moment when the shattering of the illusion is necessary.

When shattering illusions, you don't get to see the reality of what the illusion is a perversion of until the illusion itself is shattered. So you need to take on faith that a certain illusion has to be shattered. It takes courage. It's like walking across a very narrow bridge that crosses a deep, deep, deep chasm to get to the master's retreat. Of course that's an illusion that is created to see if you would really risk losing yourself in order to get to the master. It's the illusion on the old occult path of journeying to the master's retreat, which is far away, high in the mountains, and having to go through all kinds of terrible hardships to get there.

The whole question is this: If the teacher tells you that you have an illusion, are you willing to accept it is an illusion on the word of the teacher? Then, are you willing to shatter it or have it shattered in order to get to the Reality you really are?

Well, no one is going to force any shattering of your human consciousness that you're not ready to accept. During this course you have a maximum opportunity to get the maximum illusions shattered. If there are some that you would withhold, you withhold them, and you go out the door with them and probably won't have an opportunity to have them shattered for quite some time, because the shattering of such deep-seated illusions is like major surgery.

The ascended masters will come in and using our invocations they will withdraw these illusions from you. But it's a very delicate operation on your consciousness. It has to be done in a forcefield of light, in a focus where there is control, where there are no invading entities, demons or fallen ones that are going to cause you to become insane through that experience.*

The shattering of illusions is an extremely important part of the work of the ascended masters. An example of the perversion of this is the communist practice where a group sits around in a circle and everybody criticizes everybody after they have finished a group project or worked together on something.[16] Another example is one of those psychology sessions where one person is totally picked apart—almost like the one little bantam chicken that gets into the crowd of the older hens and is completely picked apart until there aren't even any feathers left. The picking apart of the human consciousness by the human consciousness is totally destructive.

What we do here at Summit University is done from the level of the Christ mind in the oneness of the Christ

---

*The forcefield of light in this case was the Keepers of the Flame Motherhouse in Santa Barbara, California, where the teachings on "Understanding Yourself" were delivered during a twelve-week residential session of Summit University. The focus was maintained by the daily decrees of the students and the staff of the center. The spiritual work referred to here can also be accomplished by those living and serving outside such a center. Its effectiveness depends on the level of spiritual forcefield they maintain through a daily focus on the masters and their teachings as well as consistent application of the science of the spoken Word.

mind—amalgamating the momentum of our causal bodies,* we challenge those energies that have stolen our real identity, our God-reality.

What is being accomplished here is preparing you for world service. The masters are going to come with the greatest amount of transmutation possible for you so that you can leave this place and be of some worth in reaching humanity with the light. The increments of your karma are what keep you from world service. When your karma is heavy, you cannot become a world teacher or leader.

The crystal clarity of the Christ consciousness—this is where the ascended masters who are giving this course would lead us. They would pull the thread of our consciousness through the eye that opens into the world of crystal clarity. The crystal clear river flowing as the water of life is the flow of your own energy of the Mother.[17] The crystal ray is a ray that is used in connection with the healing ray, the green ray. And the third eye is the eye that opens into the world of crystal clarity.

Now I would like to conclude today's lecture with an invocation.

> *In the name of the Christ, in the name of the Holy Spirit, I call forth the light of the crystal ray and of the emerald ray from the causal body of each student. I call forth the light from the heart of Hilarion. I call to Pallas Athena, the Goddess of Truth. I call for cosmic momentums and cosmic dispensations to send forth the blazing light of Reality. I call for the matrix of God-reality, of the*

---

*The causal body is the body of First Cause; seven concentric spheres of light and consciousness surrounding the individual God Presence in the planes of Spirit. The causal body is the storehouse of every good and perfect thing that is a part of our true identity. See the Chart of Your Divine Self, page 361.

Christ Self of each one to be superimposed and intensified in the aura of each student. I call now for the tying of the heart chakra of each student to the master Hilarion. I call for that cord of the emerald ray to intensify the quest for truth. I call for the light of truth to intensify. I call for the blazing forth of the energies of the heart for the clearing of the heart chakra, the clearing of the third eye as the open door to Reality.

Blaze forth the light! Blaze forth the light! Blaze forth the light! Blaze forth the light! Burn through and let God's will be done. In the name of Jesus the Christ, I call for the sealing of the third eye, the heart and the hand of each soul in the way of the ascended master consciousness. In the name of the Father, the Mother, the Son and of the Holy Spirit, we accept it done this hour, in full power.

January 13, 1975

CHAPTER TWO

THE SEARCH
FOR THE FRIEND

In the name of the Christ, in the name of the Holy Spirit, we call forth the flame of living truth, the full power of the sacred fire from the heart of beloved Hilarion, Pallas Athena, the Maha Chohan. We call for the ring-pass-not around this forcefield, the sealing of the third eye of each one, the purging of the third-eye center by the full power of the crystal flowing stream of God's consciousness.

Blaze forth thy light! Let thy will be done in us. Let the diamond-shining mind of God draw into our consciousness now the full power, wisdom and love of Christ-discrimination that we might see and know and be the fullness of living truth. In the name of the Father, the Son and the Holy Spirit, Amen.

Commentary on Chapter 1, Part 2

We are taking up the *Pearl* of beloved Kuthumi where we left off.

> Let us journey through the night of human reason. As we pass through the undergrowth of the wilderness, suddenly a light appears! 'Tis a light set upon a hill.[1] An old castle is perceived dimly through the mist, yet the feeble beam by contrast is a glowing filament of hope. Someone is there. Someone lives whose consciousness will smile with joy at our approach. The hope the heart holds to hear the word "friend" is very great. We approach with some degree of caution yet with the awareness that all may be well and that a warm reception can be anticipated.

This concept of the castle and the light and that someone is at home, someone is waiting to welcome us, is a universal pattern in the subconscious. It is the focal point for our yearning to have a home, to have friendship, to find our place. Every man's home is his castle. We have a mansion in the Father's house which is our causal body. It is a dwelling place like the retreats of the ascended masters. *

---

*The retreats of the ascended masters—temples and cities of light—are located in the heaven-world, the etheric plane. We may visit these retreats during spiritual meditation or while our bodies sleep at night.

We feel there isn't quite a place on earth we can call our home. "The foxes have holes, and the birds have nests, but the son of man does not have a place to lay his head."[2] Wherever we go, we still feel it's temporary, we are on a journey, we are pilgrims. It is a journey of the soul through planes of consciousness, and this course, Understanding Yourself, is to analyze what happens to the soul as it makes this journey.

The soul is looking in the planes of matter for the fulfillment of what it recollects from the planes of Spirit. When it does not find here all that it anticipates, there comes the shock, the trauma, the splitting of consciousness and the beginning of the fears, the doubts, the sense of separation, the schism, all of which results in the psychological problems that people have.

The image of the castle, then, is this archetype, and it keeps appearing, again and again. Everyone is enchanted with the fairy-tale stories where there is a castle. Everyone is enchanted with visiting castles in Europe or going to the Hearst Castle at San Simeon and conjuring up, from deep within, this sense that we all have a castle somewhere.

The concept of the castle is reminiscent of the mansion of which Jesus spoke: "In my Father's house are many mansions."[3] The mansion refers to the causal body. And the causal body equates with the retreat on the etheric plane where you are most at home. It is either a retreat that has been founded by you and your twin flame* at inner levels or, if you have not yet evolved to the point where this has

---

*Twin flames are two souls who were created together and who were conceived out of the same white fire body, the fiery ovoid of the I AM Presence. They are one in Spirit. Whereas twin flames share a common spiritual origin, soul mates share a complementary calling in life. They are partners and co-workers on life's journey.

been accomplished, it is the retreat where you have taken your course before your incarnations, such as the retreat of the God and Goddess Meru or of Lord Himalaya.

The Memory of Etheric Retreats

As your soul lives in the etheric envelope between embodiments, you have felt at home in the master's retreat because it was like a compartment of your own real identity. When we make a home, when we have a family, we are always striving to reproduce this mansion, this focal point of the retreat. We are always trying to reproduce the inner experience.

Now, some people live in mansions and some people live in shacks. Some are in shacks because of the economic trap they find themselves in, with increasing taxation and their supply being taken away by those who control the world's money and who have put a very heavy yoke and burden upon mankind. Aside from that (and discounting the injustices in the distribution of wealth on the planet), many times you will find that those who live in hovels or shacks are people who have never made it through the astral plane.

When they passed on in a previous life, they did not have the momentum of light to go into the etheric body or into the etheric plane, so they remained floating in the muck of the astral. They live in a shack because they are outpicturing only what they know. All they have to remember, all they have as the model to draw upon and design from in their present life is their previous experience on the astral plane. And they have probably been going back and forth from the astral to the physical for thousands of years. Their memory of the mansion of the Father's house, of the causal body, of the inner retreats, is covered over by these layers of effluvia that are just like the "dead sea" off New York City where the pollution has accumulated and formed a substance like gray mayonnaise.

These people just go back and forth between the astral plane and the physical. They don't reach the mental plane—they have little mental development—and they never reach the etheric planes of light. This is the dilemma of many of the world's people. In many, many civilizations—in parts of South America, in Asia, in Africa, where there is very little drive to improve their lot, very little momentum for culture, for beauty, and so forth—you find that these evolutions are not penetrating to the etheric plane. They are not reaching the influence of the Venusians in the Grecian temples that are on the etheric plane in the retreats of the Brotherhood.

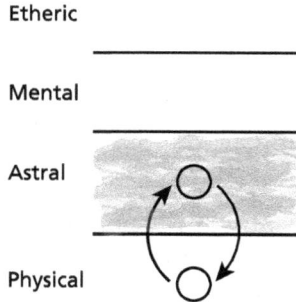

Etheric

Mental

Astral

Physical

Many individuals never reach higher planes between embodiments. They reembody having only reached the astral plane, which has been polluted by mankind's negative emotional energies.

In the United States you find a group of people who as a whole, as a nation, have had enough momentum to reach mental and etheric planes between embodiments, to retain the memory of science, of invention, of beauty, of high standards, of cleanliness. And they have come back with the drive and the determination to outpicture in matter what they have seen on the etheric plane.

So the standard of living is high in America, not because we are spoiled, not because we have such an abundance. There is more to it than that. Let's cast aside for a moment the world's hatred, condemnation and jealousy of America and her people. Let's realize that that isn't coming because of our material wealth. That energy comes to the United States because of the abundance of light that is here. It is the demons and the fallen ones, in their anger toward the light that is here, who incite the jealousy and the condemnation. And right while there is the condemnation, the jealousy and the hatred, there is the undermining of the nation by those very same forces who want to take over America and have it for themselves.

America is "a new nation, conceived in liberty, dedicated to the proposition that all men are created equal."[4] America is the archetype of every man's castle. It is the place prepared, the wilderness place where the Woman, the Divine Mother, comes forth to give birth to the Manchild.[5] That is an archetype in everyone's subconscious—the archetype of the image of the Mother and the image of the Christ Child being born. No matter how it is distorted, it is always there.

America, then, is the convocation ground for the souls upon the planet who make it to the etheric plane between embodiments. They have been brought together to outpicture the archetype of a golden-age civilization. The golden-age civilization itself is another matrix that everybody has in his subconscious. It is the memory of an ancient past. Everyone has it, but the ones who make it to the etheric temples between embodiments have it more on the surface. The others have it buried under astral muck.

So here in America is the supreme and the final opportunity to bring forth a new-age culture. And here we sit as the remnant of lightbearers with the key—the knowledge of the key, according to the ascended masters' teachings— whereby every man, woman and child can unlock the fire of the heart to bring forth the golden age. It is the nucleus of those who get this teaching and master it and practice it that will turn the tide of the economy and of the corruption in government, of the takeover by the international bankers, and so forth.

The Sickness of Society

This all relates to our psychology because we cannot stop in our study of psychology with the analysis of the individual. We must see that the problems of the psyche, of the soul, are problems that have already reached national and international proportions.

We live in a nation whose collective consciousness is sick. We live on a planet whose collective consciousness is sick. We find that the seriousness of the mental and emotional problems is far greater than the physical outcropping of these problems, which manifest as heart disease and especially cancer, the cancer that eats away the body of the Mother. Cancer is the perversion of the Mother flame in the astrological sign of Cancer—the grasping, greedy substance of consciousness, the hatred we find typical of the disease, the malaise of the age.

I read an article yesterday evening about a woman in Ventura. Seven days ago she was driving her car in the mountains on a section called route 33. She had a cramp in her leg, so she parked the car by the side of the cliff to get the cramp out of her leg. She pressed the accelerator instead of the brake and the car leaped over the embankment, rolled over many times and came to a stop down a deep gorge.

She was able to remove herself from the car by wrapping herself in a floor mat and getting through the glass of the window. When she got out, she found that she could not move her legs because they had been injured. In trying to move them she rolled over and fell another 350 feet below the 250 feet to which the car had rolled. She was pinned there for four days and nights, with temperatures reaching twenty-five degrees at night.

On her fourth day of no food and no water a man who was walking his dog came by. She cried out for help. He heard her and asked what was the matter. She told him what had happened. His answer to her was, "I'm sorry, I can't help you. I don't want to get involved." Then he added, "Any dame driving on highway 33, who has no more brains than to drive on a dangerous curving road like that, deserves all she gets," and he walked off.

She was pinned another two days, went through two more days of lying there. Finally on Sunday afternoon after our services and our invocations and the light we call forth here in Santa Barbara, some boys went hunting and heard her cries, called the police and she was rescued.

Now, the attitude of this man who didn't want to get involved is so frightening. "It's frightening to everyone," the doctor and other people commented. This is the sign of the sickness of the age. It's the sign of the Luciferian consciousness of those beings that we call soulless, who were created by the Luciferians and are without conscience, without a threefold flame in the heart. They are the test-tube babies of Atlantis who have come down through the ages and multiplied, who live in and among humanity as the bad seed, as the sons of Belial. They are the wicked that are referred to in the Bible.

When you understand what the potential in America is and how the rats are eating away and have been eating away at this granary for two hundred years, when you realize that all of the churches, all of the teachings, all of the positive thinking, all of the mind control and all of the science that we have been able to bring forth has not touched upon the unlocking of the fires of the soul, the flame of the heart, you come down to the realization that there isn't anything but the ascended masters' teachings that can save this hemisphere.

When I speak about America, I am thinking from the North to the South Pole, including all of Canada and Central and South America. But I realize that there is such a division of hatred that has been projected between these areas in our hemisphere that unless we focalize a victory in these United States, we will not have the momentum or the thrust of light, of consciousness, to roll back the darkness, to push back the schism in Canada, in Central America and in South America.

So no matter how we look at saving the world or helping humanity, it all comes back to the individual and to the nation. We have to start right where I AM* and we have to conquer, and then we have to move out from there.

A Conspiracy against the Light

There is a conspiracy against this nation. It is organized by the fallen ones on inner planes, the dark forces led by the head of the false hierarchy, who is Lucifer, and whole echelons of

---

*I.e., right here, where God is present in me. "I AM" is the name of God revealed to Moses (Exod. 3:14).

lieutenants on down.[6] It is their determination to take over the nation and destroy the opportunity for the releasing of the light from the heart chakras of the American people.

America is the heart chakra of the world. The focal point for the release of the heart energies is in this nation and in our hearts. It is the focal point for the Christ consciousness. The way to destroy the light and the lightbearers, then, is to destroy the platform out from under the lightbearers—in other words, to bomb the castle. There's a raid on our castle. That is what we are getting at.

I want to give you the vision of widening the area of your consciousness so you understand that your awareness of selfhood must include your awareness of America, first as the United States and then as the hemisphere and finally as the entire planet. In other words, we are not an island. None of us can be an island in our individual path. If we try to be, we will find that the island will be torpedoed out from under us.

Unless we master and take dominion over the platform of our evolution—which is the planet itself—we may no longer have the opportunity for evolution. There is nowhere we can run to hide. There is no place we can really go on the planet and be safe for very long. Maybe we will be safe, but what will happen to our children and their children? The planet is so small that there is no place to go.

So we need to be on the offensive, not the defensive. We have to launch an offensive of light on the planet. From the point of balance within, we have to thrust forth the energies of light and take dominion of the entire atom of the planet, the molecule, the cell of the planet with its teaming millions. These millions need to be conquered by the light of the I AM Presence.

Everyone has an individualized I AM Presence. But God is one. Therefore the I AM Presence is one, and yet it is individualized. If you understand this concept you can see how the I AM Presence of the whole group is one I AM Presence because God is one God. Therefore the I AM Presence of the planet is one, yet it is always individualized. You always retain your individualized I AM Presence.

What I am getting at is this: If your God and my God is the same God, then that same God has the same authority to conquer the human consciousness within you and me. So if I say, *"In the name of the Christ, I call forth the light of the I AM Presence to take dominion over the human consciousness,"* the response comes from the I AM Presence of all and goes into the human creation of all. So we answer the fiat to take dominion over the earth[7] by our contact with the one God who is the master of the one collective subconscious.

The True Friend

And so we come first to the golden rule, "Do unto others as you would have them do unto you,"[8] and we hold in our hands the chain of affinities that links many embodiments to the present one. Many times the skeins of recognition have been unraveled in a momentary thread of contact. A touch long forgotten sparks a human relationship as souls contact the bitter and the sweet of passing experience. Place this motif against the light in the castle window and realize how men search the past in their longing for a good reception, for friendship, for decency, and for a sense of belonging.

From our earliest memories as children when we have gone out into the world—thrust from our comfortable, cozy home where we were the favored one into that place where we were equal among our peers—the longing and the search has been for a friend. The longing for the friend is also a pattern, an archetype. It is the longing for communion with the Christ Self.

The Christ Self is the true friend of us all. We walk and talk with the Christ Self as our dearest friend, who understands us completely, who favors our own reality, who understands how to mediate between the perfection to which we aspire and the imperfection we manifest, the friend who understands our problems and loves us just the same.

We can't see that Christ Self, so we look for that Christ Self in a friend. We find a friend. We place our hope and our trust and our love in that friend, and sometimes it is fulfilled and sometimes it is betrayed. Over the many times it is betrayed we develop a crust of cynicism and we cease to be able to totally trust anyone as a friend. We cease to be able to confide in a friend because we have been burned, we have been hurt. So a wall starts being built.

Unfortunately, our experiences in the world produce a wall that remains between our soul and our own Christ Self. Unfortunately, we take the experiences we have had with people as our criterion, and that replaces the concept of what would happen if we contacted the real friend. Every layer of cynicism we add separates us from the one, the true friend, until we have so many layers of human experience that we can no longer even conceive that there could be such a friend as the Christ Self. We no longer even think it is possible.

Beyond the Christ Self, of course, is the I AM Presence, as the *great* friend, the great regenerator of our life, and then all of the ascended masters, the ascended hosts of light who comprise our friends in heaven. Our memory of our friendship with these friends is eternal. We know that they are there. And the more we meditate upon these friends, the more we have the sense of walking and talking with the masters as the disciples did on the road to Emmaus.[9]

That walking and talking with Jesus, remember, occurred after his resurrection on Easter morning, showing us that the true ripening of friendship, of the friend that the masters can be, comes only after the individual's resurrection of the fullness of his Christ-potential. It also shows us that we ourselves can be the true friend only when we have resurrected the fullness of *our* Christ-identity. So friendship—and to be the friend—is the work of realizing the Christ Self within us and being the Christ to all.

A mature and well-balanced position to take regarding friends is to never expect too much, but to be grateful for small gifts, for a smile, for a word of good cheer—and if these are not forthcoming, to be grateful that we have friends so that we can be the Christ to them. The human consciousness is so undependable that there really isn't any point depending on it. If you have a friend, love the Christ, love the soul in the state of becoming, but depend on your inner Christ Self, your I AM Presence, the Christ Self of the friend and the ascended masters to supply you with the comfort and the love that you require.

You may think this is an obvious instruction. But I can assure you that you may be in the ministry or perhaps in the mission field abroad or another situation where you may be the only student of the ascended masters. You may be the only one of your nationality or your race or your faith. You may feel very much alone. You may look for the castle light and long to hear the word "friend." And you will be forti-fied by the realization that your Christ Self walks with you, that the Maha Chohan walks with you, that the ascended masters are your friends, so that you do not have the subconscious need to confide, to bare yourself and your problems to those who don't have the cup and the matrix of the true friend with a capital *F*.

When you are in the position of being the minister or the teacher, you find that those you are helping are not the ones to whom you ought to confide your problems, your shortcomings, your difficulties. It would be unethical. If you have a weakness of character that makes you constantly need to talk and confide in human beings, you might mar the image of the ascended master teachings, the image of the Christ that you are intending to portray.

In order to develop the confidence you need to have, you must talk to your Christ Self, talk to the masters. Guard your conversation so that you are not indulging your ego or your human consciousness or its sympathies by putting upon a new chela, a neophyte, the burden of your human creation, of your need to gossip and to carry on in a human way. We often think that's what friends are for, and that's right. But we have to know that the ascended masters are our friends, the Christ Self is our friend.

The mark of a chela who can be trusted is that he will keep his counsel to himself and prefer the ascended masters' friendship above all earthly friendship. And he will see in earthly friendship the opportunity to be the Christ unto others—not expect others to be the Christ unto him, but to be humbly grateful when they do manifest the Christ toward him. This is an important lesson for your own happiness.

The Danger of Gossip

When you know you have the real friend and you can confide in that friend, that real friend will take everything you say, especially when it's given in the form of prayer, and go forth to help the one who has the problem. You can keep your own counsel. You can be a pillar of fire in the midst of an organization. And you can be the difference between failure and victory by your attitude.

I want you to know that gossip is the greatest single cause of the destruction of ascended master activities over the centuries. Gossip destroyed the I AM movement.* It has destroyed every little nucleus of lightbearers almost since time began. So we might as well understand that it happens because the people involved have not really made contact with the friend—the friend who keeps the light in our castle.

"By thy words thou shalt be justified. By thy words thou shalt be condemned."[10] So let us value the spoken Word.† I have watched and the masters have watched how people who have failed to conquer their egos have betrayed the teacher and the teachings. But for them this was not enough. They had to go out and turn others against the teaching, against the opportunity for that supreme surrender. And once those words are spoken, they have such an impact and influence.

It is essential for you to understand what free will is and what gift lies in your hand. Every one of you could influence a million people in this lifetime, directly and indirectly, to bring them into alignment with the ascended masters. Every one of you could also influence a million people to be against

*Saint Germain founded the I AM Activity through his messengers Guy and Edna Ballard in the early 1930s.

†*Word* with a capital *W* signifies the dynamic, creative force of the universe, which releases the potential of God from Spirit to matter. "In the beginning was the Word."

their own I AM Presence and against the ascended masters. This makes you a focal point of God. You become a god when you realize what power is in your hands. Madmen on the planet have realized what power they wielded, men like Hitler, Karl Marx, Lenin. They have wielded enormous power for the control of man. But all of their power has been stolen energy, stolen light.

When you come right down to it, it is bringing people into contact with the I AM Presence and with the ascended masters that is important. In the final analysis, it's not important whether there are imperfections in myself or in the organization or in members of the organization. What is important is that the individual makes contact with the Great White Brotherhood.* The teachings are pure, and that is what is important. If we place the weight of our allegiance with the Great White Brotherhood, the masters and their teachings, we are not so moved when we see human frailty, because our organization doesn't rest on human frailty. People can rise and fall, but the teaching will remain. The Word will remain forever.

Sympathy and Compassion

The golden rule is "Do unto others as you would have them do unto you." I would like you to consider the concept of that golden rule in terms of human sympathy and divine compassion. No matter what you say or how you feel, you

---

*The Great White Brotherhood is the spiritual order of Western saints and Eastern adepts who have reunited with the Spirit of the living God and who comprise the heavenly hosts. The ascended masters of the Great White Brotherhood have risen in every age from every culture. The word "white" refers not to race but to the aura (halo) of white light surrounding their forms. The Brotherhood also includes in its ranks certain unascended chelas of the ascended masters. Jesus Christ revealed this heavenly order of saints "robed in white" to his servant John in Revelation.

would really rather have someone championing your Christ consciousness than your human consciousness. Even if it hurts, even if it is a terrible experience to have a friend tell you that you've got too much ego or you're lazy or this, that or the next thing, you will appreciate it because that friend is championing the Christ within you. He is defending your inner potential instead of feeling sorry for you and agreeing with the human consciousness.

Sympathy is agreement with imperfection. Sympathy equals "agreement with." Of course, if you have sympathy for the divine, you are agreeing with the divine. When we speak of sympathy in general, we are talking about agreeing with, defending or concealing the imperfections of ourselves or others. And when we do that we are breaking the golden rule.

Good deeds and the championing of the Christ consciousness are the links in the chain of divine friendships. When we look for a friend, we look for that friend through a chain of affinities that links many embodiments to the present one. And in that momentary thread of contact where you meet someone and that spark of an old tie is captured, you have found the friend. You have found someone with whom you have shared something very important—the contact with the Christ Self. Those are the friends who are important.

People come and go whom you have known before. People come and go with whom you have had violent experiences. Sometimes those relationships are very heavy, have very complex emotional ties, and sometimes they take years to unravel. But the real friends are the ones with whom you've had a sharing of God. When you find someone and you know that together you have perceived the infinite—sometime, somewhere, together you have perceived the stars—that is the friend you are really looking for because that is the friend who is the link to your Christ Self.

The bitter and the sweet of passing experience must pass into the flame so we can all approach the friendship that is in the Christ. We are here on earth for the transmutation of past experiences that have not been of the Christ. When you feel an overwhelming pull or magnetism that seems to be some kind of human pleasure between people but feels like a weight at the same time, you should pause and resist that downward sweep, that pull of emotions. Go into the chamber of your God Presence, your Christ Self and invoke Mighty Astrea and the violet flame* to remove the cause and core of the conditions of that human relationship that are not centered in the Christ.

Before you engage in a friendship with someone, if you take the time (it might take a week or several weeks) to give fervent decrees that will clean up the substance of past involvement and *then* you and this friend come together, you have the maximum potential of the Christ within yourself to offer for the balancing of karma. You find that then the friendship is renewed for the purpose of balance. And when the energies are balanced, the merging together of the Christ Self of each one can be for a mission for the Brotherhood, a mission of light and service or of doing some good deed in the course of the day for one's fellow man.

I might add that the same paper that had the article about the man who neglected the injured woman had an article about a fifteen-year-old boy. He was walking past a house in the middle of the night and saw smoke coming out of it, saw that the house was on fire. He leaped up to the

*For decrees to the violet flame and to Mighty Astrea, see pp. 101, 184.

front door, broke in, raced around, woke the people, saved their child, got them out of the house, got the garden hose and put out the fire.

So our faith is restored in our fellow man. I thought to myself, one of the differences between those two responses was age. The other person was probably an older man. This was a young boy. He was still in the idealism of his youth, in the energy of his Christ Self, and not cynical toward the world.

The Nature of True Friendship

Friendship, then, must be looked at not as a means whereby we control or possess others or are possessed or controlled by them. A friendship must not be a relationship where you use someone to be the instrument of your ego or to get something you want; nor should it be where you are thus used or allow yourself to be used and your energies to be dissipated.

A true friendship is a means whereby the Christ-potential is expanded, the Christ-potential is shared—where my Christ consciousness merging with your Christ consciousness brings together facets of God's consciousness that apart we would not have in their fullest development. By merging our attainment we begin to make a group mandala. And the group mandala is for the conquering of the planet with light—which we can't do alone so we do it together. Each of us is a great star of light, and the Christ consciousness in all these stars coming together means that by our united effort we can do more for God.

Every friendship has to be measured on this basis. When you come into the light, you have to ask yourself if you should continue relationships where you are being used or you are using the person who is your friend. There is an alter ego relationship acting when you can't get along without the other person because you don't really have an identity of your own, and somehow your identity is realized because they hang around with you. You can yell at them or they can yell at you or there is some sort of emotional tie-up where some aspect of the human consciousness is being continually fulfilled or stimulated. Those relationships are a drain. They are a drain on your divine plan. They deter you from your blueprint and from your mission.

You can ask the ascended masters to eliminate from your world all unwholesome relationships—all that are not of the light, that did not originate in the light—and to bring into your world all relationships based on the plane of the Christ consciousness. In order to do this, you have to see to it that you are acting from the level of the Christ, that you get over your pettiness, your jealousy, your using people or your dependence on people to do things for you which you ought to be doing yourself. So to *be* a friend, you have to rise to the level of the Christ consciousness. And to *have* a friend, you have to be the friend who is in the Christ mind.

The same holds true with relatives—especially relatives. You have to begin to cut the ties when their relationship to you is a karmic one where they use you. For example, you are a son or a daughter who has become the instrument of your parents' pride and what you do is vital to them because they can tell their friends about you, and if they can't say you're doing something acceptable to the world, they're having a fit because you have betrayed them and the family tradition.

You can be a much better friend to your mother and father, your uncles and aunts, your brothers and sisters and cousins if you have a tie to the heart on the plane of the Christ. We visualize the tie to the Christ as a figure-eight pattern. Instead of energies going through the cycles of the electronic belt and merging with the electronic-belt energies of the other person, you call to your mighty I AM Presence that all exchanges between you and your family member or your friend must pass through the cycle of the figure eight, through the threefold flame of the heart.

You

Your friend

**Visualize all interchanges between you
and others passing over the figure eight.**

The focal point of fire in the heart is the meeting ground. You determine that you don't want to engage in any interchange of energies unless it flows through the heart chakra and through the I AM Presence. What happens then is you probably wind up being more loving and kind to your family, but it is without human attachment, without human pull, without human control. That's the difference. You can do this so compassionately and with such kindness that your family doesn't realize that the old human consciousness has passed away and you are engaging in a relationship with the Christ.

You don't have to desert your families. You don't have to leave them behind. You can keep them in their place by this visualization of the figure-eight pattern so none of their energy comes to you to control you except it pass through your own Christ flame. You set up a boundary of consciousness. You allow nothing to pass into your world unless it has first been screened through the Christ consciousness.

We also need to think about friendships because the psyche and the psychology that we are considering really begin with our interactions with other parts of life. From the moment we are conceived we have karma, and that karma is the result of interaction, reaction, overreaction, underreaction with other parts of God's body. Coming to grips with our own identity and our relationship with other identities is our psychology, is our karma.

Once you get to the point of being the Christ, everything is going to fall into place. It's just like your eyes coming into focus and suddenly you see the detail of a cosmos because you are in alignment with the grids and forcefields of the cosmos. You're not off those grids; you're right at the point where the Christ is. The point of the nexus is always the point of the cross.

You can diagram any mandala you are involved in as a circle with intersecting lines throughout the circle. Wherever two lines meet there is a cross, there is a burst of light, there is an individualization of the Christ consciousness.

When you are not on the plane of the Christ, you are functioning somewhere off center, off that cross, somewhere on a line where there isn't the meeting of the energies of Alpha and Omega. The vertical bar of the cross is the

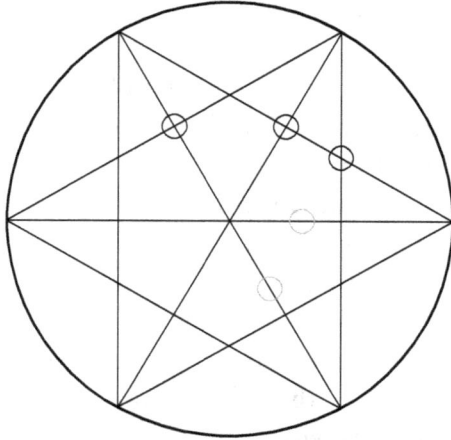

Every point of intersection of the grids and forcefields of the cosmos is a cross—the place of a burst of light, a manifestation of the Christ consciousness. When you are not in the plane of the Christ, you are off center from that point of the nexus.

descent of the energy of Alpha and the horizontal bar of the cross is the energy of Omega. The point in the center is you.

When you are not living in the Christ-center, when you are living in the human consciousness, you are so far off that all of life becomes an illusion, a miasma, a synthetic parade. There are the people you know, the people you mix with, the things you do, but it is all a sea that is out of focus. And to get it into focus you have to get back to being centered in the Christ.

I would suggest, as we are speaking of this centering, that you give the "Introit to the Holy Christ Self," that you meditate on becoming one with the flame in your heart and make that your point of contact with life.

Thank you.

January 14, 1975

INTROIT TO THE HOLY CHRIST SELF

In the name of the beloved mighty victorious Presence of God, I AM in me, my very own beloved Holy Christ Self and through the magnetic power of the sacred fire vested within the threefold flame of Love, Wisdom, and Power burning within my heart, I decree:

1. Holy Christ Self above me,
   Thou balance of my soul,
   Let thy blessed radiance
   Descend and make me Whole.

Refrain: Thy Flame within me ever blazes,
   Thy Peace about me ever raises,
   Thy Love protects and holds me,
   Thy dazzling Light enfolds me.
   I AM thy threefold radiance,
   I AM thy living Presence
   Expanding, expanding, expanding now.

2. Holy Christ Flame within me,
   Come, expand thy triune Light;
   Flood my being with the essence
   Of the pink, blue, gold, and white.

3. Holy lifeline to my Presence,
   Friend and brother ever dear,
   Let me keep thy holy vigil,
   Be thyself in action here.

And in full Faith I consciously accept this manifest, manifest, manifest! (3x)* right here and now with full Power, eternally sustained, all-powerfully active, ever expanding, and world enfolding until all are wholly ascended in the Light and free! Beloved I AM! Beloved I AM! Beloved I AM!

* Repeat three times.

CHAPTER THREE

THE SYNTHETIC IMAGE AND THE REAL IMAGE

In the name of the Christ, in the name of the Holy Spirit in each one, we call forth the light. Let the light blaze forth! Burn through! Blaze the light of ten thousand suns and shatter the forcefields of resistance to the Christ mind. In the name of Jesus the Christ, let the Christ Self of each one come forth. Blaze forth the light of the Christ Self and let the will of God, the love of God and the wisdom of God be made manifest now. In the name of the Father, the Mother, the Son and the Holy Spirit we accept it done this hour in full power. Amen.

Commentary on Chapter 1, Part 3

We have the image of the castle, the castle window, the light, the welcome word *friend*.

> Place this motif against the light in the castle window [the motif of human relationships, of past karma, present karma and future karma] and realize how men search the past in their longing for a good reception, for friendship, for decency, and for a sense of belonging.
>
> Ask yourself, Can the eternal Creator create without the hopeful thought of spiritual unity? Should unity be only spiritual or should it also enter into human affairs? Wherever the flame of life blazes, whoever is made conscious of the fact that he exists holds awareness of the unusual as well as the natural qualities of life. Sometimes these qualities change—the natural takes on the aspect of the unusual whereas the unusual may swing to the natural.

Unity is a principle which can only be realized if each individual first realizes the unity with his own Selfhood. To attain unity with the Self, one must understand the Self. In his third chapter in *The Chela and the Path*, beloved El Morya addresses chelas who would attain self-mastery.

He asks the question, "What is self-mastery?" In order to understand what self-mastery is, we must be able to define the Self, so he takes several chapters to define the Self.

His main point: You are what you are no matter what you think you are. That's very profound. It is the great fact of *eternal being*, that you are what you are. In the fiery core of your being, the voice of God speaks, "I AM WHO I AM." The human personality is composed of all the impressions and interactions with other parts of life and the record of the sense of separation from this fiery core. The human personality is what we *think* we are, the synthetic image. To move from the synthetic image to the Real Image is almost to grope in a totally dark room until the ascended masters light the candle of consciousness and show us the way out.

We proceed to discover the Real Self by faith. What else do we have? We have faith that the Real Self exists. We have intimations of the Real Self. And then we have absolute proof. What is the absolute proof? It is as simple as this— I will give you an example from my own life.

I went home late last night and found my smallest child had not slept and could not sleep. I decreed and decreed with her and she still would not sleep. So I thought, I will feed her, she must be hungry. So I fed her and she still was not sleeping. She was excited because it was to be her birthday at the stroke of twelve. She wanted to say good-bye to the two-year-old so she could say hello to the three-year-old—and she did. Still up. So by one o'clock I decided I would take her into bed with me, and finally, after all that wiggling they do in bed, she fell asleep. Then I had to maneuver carrying her to her bed. It was pitch dark and of course I couldn't see the way so I missed the bed. I bumped her head on the side of the crib and did everything one could possibly do to wake her up. Finally I said, "Mighty I AM Presence, put this child to sleep." And this torrent of radiation poured forth from my I AM Presence onto the child and she took the bumping in stride and asked for her blanket and went to sleep.

The proof that I'm speaking of is to speak the name "beloved mighty I AM Presence" and then to feel this torrent of white fire coming down in answer to your call. This isn't faith, it isn't hope and it isn't charity. It is absolute, positive, scientific proof. It is the fifth ray.*

You can make a call and instantaneously see the action. I'm sure this happens to you very often. It has happened to me for years and years. A single call to a single master made in the name of the Christ will produce immediate action and immediate reconciling of problems. When you have this kind of proof, the ridicule and the attempt to poke holes in a system or in a religious dogma or a doctrine cannot hold anything against your inner knowing of who this I AM THAT I AM is.

The spiritual unity I had with my Presence in that moment gave me absolute unity with the Presence of the child—an absolute unity of her Christ Self and my Christ Self. There is no other way to achieve unity with anyone. "Flesh and blood cannot inherit the kingdom of God."[1] A flesh-and-blood relationship, an outer relationship, no matter how close you may become, can never bring you into the centeredness of the I AM Presence and the light.

You can live with people for years and years and years and never really have any compatibility, any association, any attunement simply because the turning on of that light,

---

*The fifth ray is the ray of science, truth and precipitation. Its color is emerald green and the corresponding chakra is the third eye.

the call *"In the name of the I AM Presence let light flow, let unity flow, let our oneness resolve the problems"* has never been given, has never been spoken with authority.

There are times when you speak a fiat when you are absolutely at the end of all human recourse and human reason, when there is nothing left in the human that can offer a solution. The human consciousness feels bankrupt. You can't go anywhere else in this plane. But you are absolutely determined from within, with a fiery determination, that you will transcend the human. And in that moment, you make a fiat and the whole world can move a ninety-degree angle, your whole life can shift. *That* is unity.

I want everyone to feel that the light of your Presence will flow in answer to a fiat like that as quickly as it will flow to put a child to sleep. I don't want you to feel that *any* matter or momentum of the carnal mind multiplied by a million voices has the energy or power to defeat the I AM Presence. Your I AM Presence, all one, can change the planet. You must not feel hopelessness. You must not feel that you cannot tread in these areas.

Pick up your newspaper, read the headlines, hear the news and make those fiats. But make them from the standpoint of utter and total determination that the Christ Self in you is acting and nothing can turn back that energy. That energy goes forth just like an arrow. If you have ever seen a torpedo released from a submarine, it moves absolutely sure under water, it doesn't stop. A fiat is a torpedo of light. It hits its mark. And the masters need lightbearers who have conviction and who will make the calls, because those calls make the difference.

You can struggle for hours. You may decree and you may have a good decree momentum, but sometimes it takes a fiat, a command and a determination from within that nothing is going to stop the light that is released from your heart. That is unity.

The Power to Overcome Evil

We would point out that there is never an excuse, regardless of what men may do unto you, for your returning in kind an act of evil. At the same time we point out that this does not preclude the possibility of the individual, in the divine dignity of his being, avoiding subservience to human nonsense. Therefore, out of dignity and Christ awareness men can spread the balm of forgiveness to everyone they meet without becoming a victim of men's vicious energies.

The reason there is no excuse for returning in kind an act of evil is because you have such immediate access to light. It's like a giant water tower that's over you—you pull the cord and the water comes tumbling out. That's how accessible the energy of the I AM Presence is. If you can do that with just a flick of consciousness, a tuning in to the Presence and the uttering of a fiat, of course there is no excuse for trying to solve a human situation by human means.

An evil act is an *energy-veil* act. It's not just something dark and wicked and terrible that nobody would do anyway. *Evil* is *energy veil*. So anything that perpetuates the energy veil is returning in kind the veils of maya and only perpetuates this snarl of human energies. And it is a snarl. It is a snarl like a knot in yarn. It gets more and more tied up in knots until you can never untie it. Thank God, Archangel Michael has the sword to cut the Gordian knot. I don't know what we would do if we had to untangle the human consciousness.

The greatest weapon you have as a Christed being is to be willing to go all the way to the end, whether it's with a child, a husband, a wife, a relative or a friend. You have to be willing to let the carnal mind know that you will not compromise—as Morya says, "Let the chips fall where they may"—that you are not going to be subservient to anyone's human consciousness. When you let that be known, then you will rule your household, your own citadel of consciousness. And only then will you be able to keep the citadel of the community, the nation and the planet.

When you allow the forces of emotionalism, of fear, of the carnal mind to rail you and ride you and drive you into some kind of compromise, you are always in a weak position. For example, if you have someone close to you that you love very much but this person is challenging your freedom to worship God, your freedom to be the Christ—is stepping all over you or is entering into condemnation or all kinds of petty things—you have to be willing to take the ultimate stand which says, "Either you discontinue your human nonsense or you remove yourself from my life." If you plead and beg and cajole, you are giving the carnal mind power over you, and you will never be the master of your house.

You may never have to carry out the ultimate threat because the carnal mind may be sufficiently frightened by the fact that you've made the threat. But you have to show that you are willing to go through with it. You have to be willing to show the carnal mind that it has nothing, absolutely nothing to offer you, and that you will not be sold to it for any convenience, for any human pleasure, for anything on earth or in heaven. You will not fail that test. You are willing to walk out unless the individuals connected with your life will allow you to be free, to live in the flame, to worship as you see fit.

Somewhere, somehow along the Path we all have to make a choice like that. When those around us are not honorable—no matter how much we love them—we must be willing to surrender our human attachment. And when we fuse ourselves with the cosmic honor flame, we are championing their Real Self. We champion their Reality, hence we are one with that Reality. If they will forsake the carnal self and return to their own Reality, they will also know the oneness and the unity of which we speak.

Unfortunately, the compromise with honor has been the demise of many, many people in our society and the cause of people continually reembodying. It is subservience to someone's human consciousness. We have lost our identity because we have felt that we needed some aspect of their identity, and in our need we have failed to exalt Reality in ourselves and in the other person.

You will find that the carnal mind will back down in the face of the challenge of the Christ Self. If it doesn't back down in the immediate situation, you will nevertheless find that because you have championed the Christ, the Christ in you will ultimately triumph over your own carnal mind and the carnal mind of the mass consciousness.

So avoid subservience to human nonsense. In order to do that, you have to reclaim your Real Self. To reclaim your Real Self, you have to know what your Real Self is. To know what your Real Self is you must have living proof. To get that proof you have to experiment with the laws of God.

Whatever the situation is, to know your Real Self, you have to work with your Real Self and demand that living proof. Then you spread the balm of forgiveness and you feel that gentle rain of light coming from your Presence. You can do that without being victimized by men's vicious energies.

The Imitation of Christ

It is our intention to contribute to all who would follow in the footsteps of the masters the wisdom of God that
does not mock man's efforts to emulate his Creator. We
convey hope and the thread of contact. We convey a sense
of unity with the Brotherhood, but we alert everyone to the
great need for the construction of nobility of character in
imitation of the Divine.

God champions your right to imitate God, to become
God, to imitate the Christ. To make yourself equal with
Christ is not blasphemy.[2] It is the fulfilling of the law of
your being. All of the carnal consciousness of the planet will
attempt to take that from you. When you pursue the path
of the imitation of Christ, you will be labeled as one having
a martyr complex. That's a nice little intellectual term that
the psychologists have put forth to be sure that people are
embarrassed out of following the path of self-sacrifice.

A martyr is one who has laid down his life or lost his
life. I don't feel like a martyr—I never have. I think the word
martyr has a negative connotation. But in a sense we are all
martyrs for a cause because we are all willing to lay down
our life for the cause of truth.

The tricks that will be employed to take you from your
imitation of the Christ consciousness are condemnation,
belittlement, ridicule, family pride, family mesmerism,
worldly ambition. It is so easy to rationalize ambition and
tell oneself one is doing this in the name of the Christ. Then
one gets into the Machiavellian consciousness of the end
justifying the means. Since the end is the Christ consciousness, we justify any means, and of course the human mind
has many devious means.

Whenever you have an ego, you have to set up a defense mechanism of the ego, and that goes back and forth as a Ping-Pong ball between conceit and deceit.* The conceit, the pride of the ego, always has to be balanced by some form of deception—or so it thinks. The ego literally does believe that. It believes it has to be devious. And the heavier the carnal mind, the more deception you will find.

One grain of deception in your consciousness will mar the lens for the flow of the Holy Spirit. This is why I am after self-deception in this course. I am out to expose it in all of us. Exaggeration is self-deception. Sophistication is self-deception. There are all kinds of ways that we are self-deceived.

Any form of deceit is instantly a rejection of the Maha Chohan and the Holy Spirit. I have seen the Holy Spirit flee the presence of the chela who felt he had to lie to preserve his face, preserve his image, preserve the sense of his demeanor as a chela of the masters. It is the ego that thinks it has to do that. It uses all kinds of ruses. But the worst deceptions of all are the ones where we fool ourselves and we don't even know we are fooling ourselves.

The way you track down deception is to watch your speech, watch your thinking, and catch yourself. Are you saying a partial truth? Are you exaggerating for the sake of creating a nice, neat little story that is going to entertain someone or is going to build up your image?

Think about it, and just watch the flow of deceit patterns. When you see them just say, "Ah ha! I've got you." Hold up that little mouse by the tail and call to Astrea to encircle it and say, *"In the name of the Christ, in the name*

---

*Conceit, deceit, arrogance and ego are the misuses of the light on the three o'clock line, dishonesty, intrigue and treachery on the nine. See p. 368.

of my God-reality, blaze the flame of the Holy Spirit! Blaze the flame of the Holy Spirit! Blaze the flame of the Holy Spirit!" And be absolutely determined that those cloven tongues of fire are going to burn through that plane of consciousness and consume the record of that deception. It is not going to be there anymore. There is not going to be any aspect of the human consciousness that is going to be able to reproduce that energy of deception.

You will be amazed how a little determination and a little fire and a little use of the spoken Word can accelerate your attainment and your initiation. This is what the Path is all about: being determined to be perfect yet not worrying about being imperfect, not taking so seriously the fact that perhaps there are some imperfections around, because if we take them seriously, we believe they are real.

What we *are* taking seriously is the anchoring of the light, the thread of contact. There is a very fine filigree thread that goes from you to your I AM Presence. But the thread of contact we are speaking of here is the thread that connects you with the entire Spirit of the Great White Brotherhood. That thread can be shattered in a moment of discord, in a moment of irritation, in a moment of deception.

All of a sudden, when you pull that thread, you feel it's not taut anymore. The thread has been severed. You can pull the whole thread in because it is no longer connected to anything, and you find that you are quite enmeshed in the carnal mind, the carnal logic and its consciousness. That's a danger sign and you must immediately say, *"In the name of the Christ, I invoke the thread of contact with the Great White Brotherhood. I demand that it come forth, that it be reestablished in the name of my Christ Self."*

You reinforce this thread of contact by reading the

masters' words, by living in their consciousness, by loving them. Love is the great reinforcer of this thread of life. And it is reinforced by the "construction of nobility of character in imitation of the Divine." Each time you show a sculpturing in your being of the noble qualities of the ascended masters, you reinforce that thread.

Love Friend and Foe Equally

Let all, then, learn the lesson of loving friend and foe equally. Sometimes friends are more dangerous than foes; for enemies are known to be enemies, but friends are known only as friends yet their thoughts may reek with poison. Often, unknown to themselves, threads of selfishness motivate individuals to seek unwarranted and unrighteous control of other lives.

Jesus said that we should love our enemies and do good to them that despitefully use us.[3]

When you think of the friend and the foe *within* oneself, you can see the dangers that Kuthumi is speaking of. You can feel that certain habit patterns, certain modes of consciousness are harmless—they are kind of your friends, they make up your human personality, the way you do things— even though these ways are imperfect and compromising God. These things with which we are in sympathy in our own human consciousness are more dangerous than something that we know is absolutely incorrect, like a smoking habit or a drinking habit or some problem of that nature. We know that thing isn't right. We know it is our enemy. We know we are going to conquer it, and if we are smart, we know we are going to conquer it *now*.

But there are some habit patterns and some ways that

we tolerate, that we feel we can live with. Well, you have to get uncomfortable living with these so-called friends. Like the friends of Job,[4] they go along and they reinforce the patterns of your human consciousness. They are *within* and they are *without* and they do you no good.

Forces in the Subconscious

There are forces within ourselves that orbit our ego like satellites we have created—just like creating a satellite and putting it into orbit in space. There are forces that have gained a gigantic proportion within our subconscious, such as islands of greed or selfishness or narrow-mindedness or prejudice. These satellites revolve around the core of the ego and they begin to dominate us much in the way that worldly astrology can dominate the way we move and think and feel. In other words, they are like the sorcerer's apprentice.

The ego has created these defense mechanisms, and they have been so reinforced over the centuries that they have finally thrust out of the center of the ego and become momentums of energies in the plane of the electronic belt— and they are there as focuses of dark energy that control the mind. When you have a fit of depression or of weeping or of anger, you find that one of the satellites thrust forth from your own carnal mind into your electronic belt is coming into power. It is in focus or in alignment with other cycles of your karma.

It is probably being amplified by the worldly astrology of the macrocosm without, and is probably being played upon by the carnal mind of the mass consciousness that we call the antichrist or by Lucifer or one of the fallen ones.

So that seemingly innocent indulgence in patterns of self-ishness becomes amplified by coordinates of selfishness in other people, in the planet, in the solar system and beyond. Therefore that particular pattern becomes an open door. We magnetize to ourselves people who are also selfish. We don't know we are selfish. But we look at the people who are around us and we say, "Oh, they are so selfish. I've never seen anyone so selfish in my life. They are always thinking of themselves. They are never thinking of anyone else." Well, they are around us because the magnetism of our own satellites has attracted them.

By and by, if we get smart fast enough on the path of initiation, we come to realize that that which we see around us is that which we have attracted by the energies within. And we may see beauty and the glory of beautiful friendships and beautiful people around us. Look at yourself. Here you are at Summit University. There is definitely something in you that has attracted you to a place where there are people who are serving the light and loving the light, where there are ascended masters, where there is an established system for studying and putting God's law into practice.

So you can certainly know that you, out of your Christ consciousness, have also put into orbit in the heavens of your consciousness focuses of great light to attract to you great light and cosmic beings; hence you are on the Path. Knowing that you have the good momentum of your causal body is encouraging, because when you have all of that good momentum, why sustain the bad? As fast as you can get the bad carved away from the core of your being, that's how fast you will be free.

So when you observe energies around you that you do not approve of, you may wake up one day and say to yourself, "What am I doing in the middle of all this human nonsense?" And if you are honest, if you've overcome at least a portion of self-deception, you will say, "I am in the middle of this because I've created it, I've attracted it, I've called it forth. I am a co-creator with God, and I am going to undo it."

> *In the name of Jesus the Christ, I challenge the spirals of negativity manifesting in me as points or electrodes of magnetism, magnetizing the mass consciousness. I demand the shattering of that forcefield. I demand it be replaced by the Great Central Sun Magnet.**
>
> *I call to Hercules and Amazonia, beloved Mighty Arcturus and Victoria, beloved Alpha and Omega, to anchor within me that Great Central Sun Magnet to demagnetize from my subconscious all that is less than Christ-perfection and to magnetize the great cosmic con-sciousness of the mighty Elohim,† reinforcing in my chakras the God-qualities of light, love, victory, mas-tery, God-control, obedience to his law and the charity of the angels.*

These are illustrations of calls. It's not the specific call but the illustration that I want you to get, though you are welcome to use the specific call as well.

The Desire to Control Others

Kuthumi speaks of the "threads of selfishness" that "moti-vate individuals to seek unwarranted and unrighteous control of other lives." I feel that the desire to control others—and

---

*The Great Central Sun is the center, or hub, of all creation; the point of inte-gration of the Spirit-Matter cosmos. The Great Central Sun Magnet is the cen-ter of flaming love-purity within that hub.

†Elohim is a name of God in the Old Testament. In the order of spiritual hierar-chy, the Elohim and cosmic beings carry the greatest concentration, the highest vibration, of light that we can comprehend in our present state of evolution.

we face it on every continent in some way, through voodoo, black magic, witch doctors, and so on—is based on fear. It may manifest as pride, as ego, as all kinds of other things. But to me it goes back to the core of fear—fear that we have lost the real identity in God, fear that we have separated from God. In this fear, in order to recoup our lost estate, we have to control and dominate others. We've lost our own identity. We try to regain that identity by incorporating into ourselves the identity of others.

In psychology there is a term called *omnipotence,* where the individual feels omnipotent and that all people are instruments for the gratification of some need of his id or his ego. He may feel that other people do not have their own rights, their own freedoms, their own opportunity to find God; they are simply instruments of this person who has become omnipotent. It's a total perversion of the omnipotence of the I AM Presence.

In the level of the I AM Presence I can say, "I am you, you are me, we are one. You are instruments of my God Self fulfilling itself." I can say that without controlling or dominating you because I am saying it in the level of the I AM Presence. But there are many tyrants who have ridden the energies of the mass consciousness to become the heads of state, to rule vast empires in the level of feeling that the carnal mind itself is omnipotent and has the right to use humanity to achieve its ends.

Loving Our Enemies

As Kuthumi said, "Let all, then, learn the lesson of loving friend and foe equally." The reason we should love our enemies is because if we don't love them, we are bound to them. Hatred binds. Love frees. So loving them is a matter

of enlightened self-interest. If you are really enlightened in
the sense of the True Self, the God Self, you wouldn't dream
of hating anyone because it will hamper the service of the
God within you. You will be bound. And that hatred goes
all the way down in intensity to include mild dislike, irritation, and subtle, subconscious criticism of other people.

When you have that energy, it's a somewhat jagged
energy coming out of your chakras. You have a discordant
vibration, a discordant aura, and you are bound to everyone
else on the planet of that level of consciousness—not just
the person that you are hating, but everyone else like that
person—because the mass consciousness is one. So what
you really do is tie yourself to the whole mass consciousness, the whole of humanity.

The Dangers of Offering Advice

Now, this is a very interesting statement that Kuthumi
makes:

> When advice is sought, it can be offered with impunity.
> When advice is offered without being sought, frequently
> it becomes a karmic responsibility. When it is spurned,
> the invisible clash between minds creates karma for both
> parties. Unnecessary tension between individuals creates
> a sinking feeling in the belly because all discord sets up
> an interference to the pattern of light energy which flows
> through the solar plexus.

Often we tend to think that we know just exactly what
a person should do. We are certain from all of our training
and all of our vast experience that we can put ourselves in
his place and tell him what to do. We get so anxious about

this that we step in and offer advice when we haven't even been asked. The more you do this and the more you watch the consequences, the less likely you are to do it if you are smart, if you are learning from the interaction of energy, because you perceive in your soul that you make karma.

Now, people may respect you. I have found that people respect me as a messenger. And when they ask me advice in a human situation, I always tell them, "I cannot advise you, but I will call for the will of God in your life." Where I feel that they do need counseling, where they don't know which way to go, and where the masters are giving me a solution for them, I will always say, "I can't tell you what to do, but if I were you, I would do this."

I have found that I have a certain drive, a certain fiery disposition, a certain way of going through life and not allowing anything to stop me from reaching my goal. But I've met people who aren't that way, to my surprise. They will sit back and let life trample upon them. If I give them my solution, which is to drive through with fiery energy and to conquer, they are not capable of doing it. So I will tell them, and I'll make it very emphatic, "We are different people. If I were in your shoes, I would probably do something different than what you would do. If I were in your shoes I might do this."

That's the farthest I will go with advice. And I hope you don't go any farther and rush in and say, "You should do this and you should do that," because you just can't decide that for another person. (However, there are times when the masters, if it is called for, give an absolute directive, and in those cases I just translate it and give it to the person and tell them, "This is what the master says.")

People sometimes don't know enough to ask for advice.

So if you think someone is in need of help and that person is in a state of fretting, you may say to them, "Are you asking me for advice? If you are, I can offer a solution as to what I would do." But be sure you get their assent, "Yes, I am asking you. Please tell me what to do," because if you don't, that is where you cross the line and make karma.

People like their misery. That's something you have to learn about the human consciousness—it likes its misery. It likes to wallow in its misery. Misery is one of the crutches of the human ego. And people like to manipulate others by their misery, by their complaining about their plights, by their feeling sorry for themselves. By their drawing the sympathy of the community, they can have a whole town feeling sorry for them for a whole lifetime. These people really don't want to be healed. They really don't want to discover what is acting. And they highly resent anyone who comes in with the sword of discrimination and truth to expose what is acting.

I have learned the dangers of giving advice a very hard way in this life. I have had people give me advice which I followed implicitly because they were spiritual teachers—and it was definitely the wrong thing to do. But I surrendered my identity to those people, my decision-making faculties, my belief in my Christ Self, my ability to take a stand, to make a decision even if it would be wrong.

To make a decision is a good thing because you are exercising free will. If you make a wrong choice, at least you did it and you learned from your mistake. You can hold your head high and say, "Given the facts I knew at the time, I made this decision in total honor. It was a wrong decision. I learned a deep lesson from it. I'm not going to do it again, and I'm moving on."

If somebody else is always making up your mind for

you, you have given them power. It's just like cutting out a section of your brain and handing it to your mother, your father, your wife. If someone asks you, "What should I do now? What should I do next?" the kind of advice you give that sort of person is, "Make your own decision."

There is a most devoted student in the activity who for years and years has been begging Mark and me to tell her whether or not she should sell her properties and come to The Summit Lighthouse. She owns quite a number of properties. We have given her solutions. She has gone and done the opposite, come back, had problems, asked us again. About every two to three months we get a telephone call. "Shall I sell my property or shall I not sell my property?" The person is a beautiful soul, but she needs to exercise dominion in the flame of the Mother and the base-of-the-spine chakra.* There is so much effluvia of indecision that she cannot make a decision. It is best for her to make a decision—even a wrong decision—but do something.

So watch that tendency to give advice. Be very guarded and very careful. And watch taking advice from other people unless you are very sure. Exercise your free will. Start feeling your wings. Start feeling your muscles. Know who you are in your body and in your mind and what you can do with those vehicles. You have to make your own decisions in life. That is the only way you can attain self-mastery.

Tension and Anxiety

The removal of tension from one's consciousness is the first step toward wholesome integration with the Divine Presence. As the years pass, so do embodiments. Human

---

*Indecision is one of the misuses of the light on the six o'clock line of the cosmic clock, which is associated with the base-of-the-spine chakra. See p. 368.

affairs often become entangling, but the best way to dis-
entangle oneself and one's energies from karmic patterns
which return for redemption is to maintain a sense of unity
with the Creator and with all of his created sons.

Tension and *anxiety*. Note them well. These are enemies
of cosmic flow in your consciousness—anxiety and tension.
We are told that these two energies are killing our executives
in America. Hypertension is the number one cause of death,
of failure. Saint Germain says that anxiety and the anxiety
syndrome have to be removed in order for us to precipitate.

Anxiety is a problem that always occurs on the lines
of Virgo and Pisces.* When the moon and the sun are on
those lines, when you have planets in those signs and you
do not have the mastery of the flame of God-mastery and
God-justice, you will find the energies of anxiety and tension building. They come up through fear, through doubt,
through past records of failure and death, the records of
spirals going downward, disintegration spirals. They also
come through past experiences involving situations where
you were treated unjustly. If you keep holding on to that
record, it builds an anxiety that the same thing is going
to happen again in the future, and that anxiety becomes a
pulsating forcefield of gray substance that attracts the very
injustice that you fear will take place. As Job said, "The
thing I feared most is come upon me."[5]

It's often good to begin a decree session with giving the
decree "Strip Us of All Doubt and Fear." The white-fire ray
with a sheath of emerald green will come in to shatter tension and anxiety. It will even release the knots in the muscles
of your body that get tense just from the mass consciousness

_____
*See p. 368.

of fear. So I ask you to observe when there is a buildup of tension in your life. There are other ways to combat tension, of course—exercise and yoga, riding a bike, jogging and doing things like that, or listening to some good classical music. But for a real quick release from tension there's no better way than to give "Strip Us of All Doubt and Fear" and to see that substance peeling off of you.

I always see the action of the fearlessness flame as though you were a tree—"I see men as trees walking."[6] Imagine you are a tree and along comes this cosmic ray of the fearlessness flame, this white sheathed in green. As soon as it hits the bark of your consciousness it strips it right down; it peels off those pieces of bark. They come off just like you are pulling bark off a tree. It's as if you are stripping wood you are getting ready to use that still has bark on it. What happens is huge strips of these layers and layers of interaction with the mass mind are peeled off by that fearlessness flame.

Mankind are almost totally governed by fear, anxiety, doubt, tension. But they don't identify these momentums for what they are: the fear of a lost identity, fear of the separation from God that has occurred, and then the consequent doubt that he exists. And if we doubt that he exists, we doubt that we exist. We doubt the reality of God, so we doubt our own inner reality. And that subtle doubt brings insecurity and the inability to make a decision, because we are always in a state of doubting our ability since we doubt our reality.

Doubt and fear, indecision, anxiety, tension will stop all the flow of supply. They beget poverty. Wherever you find poverty—you go into a poverty-stricken section of your town, or you're working for the Peace Corps, or maybe you're working in a ghetto, or just working with underprivileged people—the poverty consciousness has to be challenged by the sword of the Divine Mother, by challenging the core of the momentums of doubt and fear. You will be amazed how the abundant life and the sense of the abundant life will simply flow into people's consciousness when you work diligently with them and for them challenging doubt and fear.

Doubt and fear also breed superstition. Superstition is one of the things that Saint Germain has spoken of. He said that if all of mankind's energies that were locked in matrices of superstition were released into constructive potential, it would solve the problems of the youth of the world.[7] We all have superstitions, but they get more and more rampant among the uneducated, the ignorant masses, and in the poverty-stricken areas of the world.

Unfortunately, education and the educational process reach a point of diminishing returns. A certain amount of education is good for us. We can understand our language; we can read and understand the masters' teachings and the depth of their thought. When we get overeducated, the carnal mind becomes omnipotent in the intellect. The intellect then considers that it can do all things itself because it knows all things and it is God. That's the elevation of the carnal mind into the point of the crown chakra—"The abomination of desolation standing in the holy place where it ought not."[8] That abomination of desolation is our own carnal mind standing in the place of the Christ consciousness—in the heart chakra, in the crown chakra, in all of the chakras—the holy place where it ought not.

Beware, then, of the educated carnal mind that has not the spirit of the Law. That is the type of educational program being forced upon our children in this age. It is being challenged in some parts, but we find that it is creeping in. And the intent of the fallen ones is to raise up a generation of highly technicalized or mechanized individuals who have a total reliance upon science, statistics or whatever field they are in and who feel that all the answers of life can be derived if the intellect will simply continue to pursue the conquest of space and time and matter. It's extremely dangerous.

As I was studying these *Pearls,* the master gave me those points that he said he wanted me to convey to you. That is the difference between coming to Summit University and simply reading the material. The master's mind is infinite. It has infinite spokes that radiate from the center. But a page is a flat page, our minds are finite, words are finite and paragraphs are finite. And even in a dictation it is not possible to release in the spoken Word all of the aspects of the master's consciousness of which the master is aware concerning a certain point. So our lectures take in other aspects of the unspoken or unwritten word in order to integrate your consciousness more with the teaching.

January 15, 1975

STRIP US OF ALL DOUBT AND FEAR

Beloved mighty victorious Presence of God, I AM in me, O thou beloved immortal victorious threefold flame of eternal Truth within my heart, Holy Christ Selves of all mankind, beloved Archangel Michael, beloved Ray-O-Light, beloved mighty Astrea, beloved Lanello, the entire Spirit of the Great White Brotherhood and the World Mother, elemental life—fire, air, water and earth! In the name of the Presence of God which I AM and through the magnetic power of the sacred fire vested in me, which I am consciously qualifying with the fearlessness flame, I decree:

Strip us of all doubt and fear,   (3x)
>   Beloved great I AM.
Strip us of all doubt and fear,   (3x)
>   Flood us with oceans of fearlessness flame.
Strip us of all doubt and fear,   (3x)
>   Remove each human cause and core.
Strip us of all doubt and fear,   (3x)
>   Give us faith never known before.
Strip us of all doubt and fear,   (3x)
>   Give violet-ray freedom to all today.
Strip us of all doubt and fear,   (3x)
>   In Victory's light sustain our might.
Strip us of all doubt and fear,   (3x)
>   By cosmic I AM fire, manifest thy desire.
Strip us of all doubt and fear,   (3x)
>   Command the earth now free.
Strip us of all doubt and fear,   (3x)
>   Ascend us all to thee.

And in full Faith I consciously accept this manifest, manifest, manifest! (3x) right here and now with full Power, eternally sustained, all-powerfully active, ever expanding, and world enfolding until all are wholly ascended in the Light and free! Beloved I AM! Beloved I AM! Beloved I AM!

CHAPTER FOUR

ANGER AND FORGIVENESS

In the name of the Christ, in the name of the Holy Spirit, I call for the light of ten thousand suns to pierce through the forcefield of the third-eye consciousness, the third eye and the throat, the throat and the heart chakra. I call for the release of energy into the flame. I call for the light of ten thousand suns to encircle the cause and core of all that is less than God's perfection.

Let the fires of freedom from the heart of Saint Germain consume the cause and core of all opposition to the victory of the soul. Let the light of freedom come forth and let the concentration of the violet flame within each heart be for the clearing of the chakras.

We thank thee and accept it done this hour in full power.

Commentary on Chapter 1, Part 4

Doctors who are enlightened will tell us that the cause of all problems in the physical body is the tie-up of energy which they call tension. The intense pain and disorders and diseases which follow result from the cutting off of the flow of light from the I AM Presence. Acupuncture, contact healing, zone therapy and foot reflexology are all designed to remove tension, which causes the tie-up of the organs, their functions, the muscles, and so forth.

This tie-up of energy is simply the physical outpicturing of tension in the etheric, mental and emotional bodies. In cases that don't give way in any other manner, the healing of the most chronic diseases can often be brought about through the removal of tension using the methods we have named and through decrees and meditation.

The balance of energy flow in the four lower bodies is a science that has not really been explored. People stop their examination at the physical plane. They do not take into consideration the flow of the 144 chakras—the 7 major, the 5 minor and the many other points for the release of energy. These are the same points that are used in acupuncture and contact healing. There is a vast area of healing that the ascended masters wish to open up and it simply demands the consecration of souls to this calling.

Be sure to keep this factor of tension in your notes on healing, and understand that decrees need to be given on the Virgo and Pisces energies for the stripping of the person of doubt and fear. Therefore, relaxation through recreation or *re-creation* needs to be pursued—not relaxation for the sake of pleasure or indulgence, but relaxation for the re-creation of the flow of energy within the four lower bodies. Re-creation is applying to the Source for resources, the resources of life.

The whole field of chiropractic was inspired by the ascended masters. The adjustment of muscles, tendons and bones is intended to release tension. When they are properly in place, energy flows. When they are out of place, they create a tie-up of energy. Whereas medical doctors will prescribe a pill to remove a pain or to remove some problem in the abdomen, a chiropractor will simply adjust the vertebrae.

Unfortunately, we need chiropractors because we don't perform the proper exercises ourselves to keep our bodies in shape. If we don't have the proper muscle tone, the bones don't stay in place. So yoga was designed for exercising the body, for the proper flow of energy and for keeping muscle tone. There are also sports that can bring about muscle tone, but the energy flow is definitely accomplished very well in yoga, particularly hatha yoga.

The masters caution against getting too caught up in yoga because we can become too centered in our physical bodies by that attention, just as we can become too centered in them by continually being involved in food and diet and all that goes along with it. Nevertheless, when we change our diet, when we begin a new way of eating, a new way of living, we have to give a great deal of attention to it for a certain time until it becomes automatic.

So regarding tension, realize that as you go along the path you will be learning all kinds of techniques, both from teachers and from your own experience, for the removal of tension. And tension is something that we will be combating for as long as we live in an imperfect world, because we are moving in the sea of the astral plane, the mass consciousness of mankind. That in itself, even if you had no other cause of tension, would produce it.

The tension of having to balance and handle the mass consciousness causes a certain flexing of the muscles of the psyche, just as you flex muscles to catch a ball or bat a ball or play tennis. There is a certain tension that is necessary in the physical body in order to meet the impact of the energy. There is also a flexing of the muscles of the mind and of the emotions in order to continually deal with the energy of the mass consciousness, which is actually foreign to the psyche.

I find myself almost continually ready for the next thrust or the next wave of energy from the dark ones, even as I am also prepared for the next wave of light from the forces of light. It makes you feel like a watchman on the wall twenty-four hours a day. And even if you are not this way in your outer consciousness, your body and your emotions are this way because they are being continually bombarded by rays—astral rays, psychic rays, mental rays, cosmic rays.

Our bodies are subject to all kinds of factors unknown to us, and the conditioning of the body field and the field of *all* four lower bodies to those factors creates tension. When you feel the weight of having to be one who stands to hold the balance for world energy, you long for that place where you can go, that retreat which you remember from having gone there at night while your body sleeps, that haven where there isn't this pressure.

It is actually this pressure that makes you feel the weight of the body. They say that gravity itself makes us feel weight. Well, it's more than gravity. It's karmic weight. It's the mass karma of the planet. It's the collective karma of the whole race. And because we are still part of the mass consciousness, we carry it collectively. So that is a weight, and it is a weight which we are so accustomed to that some of us don't even stop to think how life would be without all of these various tension-producing factors.

Quite a while ago, one of the masters gave a dictation regarding the weight of the physical body and our carrying this physical body around, telling us that we didn't realize what it would be to have a body of light and to feel the sense of weightlessness and mobility.[1] It was during that dictation that for the first time I really sensed what the weight of my body was. I hadn't yet come into alignment with the feeling of that weight, but once it was pointed out, I certainly felt it. And the older you get the heavier it seems, until you notice very elderly people having quite a bit of difficulty carrying the body around.

It is karmic weight, without question: karmic weight, the mass subconscious, the electronic field of the planet. We've come into all of this, we've learned to live in it, and so we are acclimatized. But make no mistake, it is tension-producing. When the masters tell us we don't even use one-tenth of our mental capacity, I would say that one of the reasons is the karmic weight, the weight on the mind and the emotions.

The violet flame gives us the joy and buoyancy of feeling weightless because it sweeps through and consumes a lot of this karmic weight. It builds up a forcefield like the forcefield of a retreat, so when we are in the violet flame we sense what it will be like when we are free of the factors of this earth.

"Let Not the Sun Go Down upon Your Wrath"

The fact that you have had problems with individuals does not mean that they should continue. Experience should teach the soul how to relax and find freedom from oppressive states of consciousness. Like a curtain that cloaks the sun, so a feeling of anger or resentment against anyone is most undesirable. Therefore the apostle said, "Let not the sun go down upon your wrath."[2]

When you go to sleep, which is the meaning of the sun going down, you are not in control of your astral body. If you go to sleep in anger or with a feeling of resentment, however subconscious, that feeling will move freely in your astral body. And the astral body moves freely on the astral plane, reinforcing and amalgamating with other momentums of hatred and perhaps causing very serious grief to other parts of life.

If you have resentment towards an individual and you see that individual in your mind's eye just before you fall asleep, you are practicing black magic. Your astral body will go forth to deliver the full weight and momentum of that energy to that one's doorstep. People who die in their sleep are often the victims of psychic murder caused by the hatred of other people.

Marilyn Monroe was the victim of the sex fantasies of millions of men. It was so great a weight upon her that night after night after night she could not sleep. She resorted to two things: being massaged and taking sleeping pills. No one really knows what caused her death. But whatever she died from, she was suffering from the mass projections of energy due to her posters and pictures and images in the movies, and the projection of sexual energy was so intense it could have literally taken her out of embodiment.

When individuals become public figures, when they are at the fore of the consciousness of mankind, they are the target of mass energies, and according to their ability to garner soul energy and the light of the Presence, so are they able to withstand it. Some of them cannot, and so they resort to various things. Drinking and heavy eating are used as ways of balancing the weight of the world. People eat a lot, drink a lot of alcohol, smoke, take drugs—which all tend to numb the system to being sensitive to these psychic projections and astral energies.

Some people have so much of this energy swirling around them that in order to get out from under it, they insulate the sensitivities of the soul with heavy food. That heavy food puts weight on them, and the blubber itself becomes an insulation. These people are dull, insensate. They are not sensitive to the masters, but they are surviving in the world where the energies are so heavy that they indulge in these things as a defense mechanism of the ego.

Sex also becomes a means of releasing tension and of creating a forcefield conducive to relaxation, to overcoming projections, and so forth. *All* of the mad cycles of the race, of human living, are really other ways of tackling the problems of tension and of mass karma and the mass consciousness.

When you are on the spiritual path and you give up those things, your diet becomes lighter so your sensitivities return to you. And you are not only sensitive to light and the masters, you are also sensitive to the mass consciousness. If you don't have your balance and your sanity, you begin to think that these projections are your own mind and that you are going insane. Many of the insane are those who have not been able to solve this problem of tension. Nervous breakdown after nervous breakdown may finally result in a split personality and other disorders. If people had accepted the ascended masters' teachings long ago, we would not have all these problems.

Alcoholism is at a very high incidence in the United States and in other countries of the world. It is one more way of escaping the tension and the confrontation with karma that one has to face when one is sober. You can go on and on and on and see how people attempt to circumvent energy.

When you go to sleep, then, and you do not have your accounts settled with your fellow man—when you have failed to extend forgiveness, when you are annoyed about what your boss did to you that day—you can be sure that you are karmically accountable for all that happens during sleep, for everything that passes through your four lower bodies. If what passes through you is not of the light and you are not in conscious control, entities, fallen ones, and momentums of the mass consciousness will multiply whatever it is. And because you had a hand in that energy going forth, you are accountable for perhaps a mass murder, mayhem, war breaking out, or whatever it might be.

As if that is not enough responsibility, Gautama Buddha or one of the Buddhas who was training disciples made the same point. He put each of them in a cell to meditate alone for several days. And they all went in to meditate with sincerity, with the determination to meditate in the highest way they knew. When they came out, he very angrily accused each one of having caused a plague in this country, a famine in another country, an earthquake here, and so on. And they were all astounded.

He explained to them that the subconscious patterns of their motivations had not been adjusted or cleared, and therefore those factors were amplified by the light they drew forth in meditation—the light amplified the darkness that was in them. This corresponds to Jesus' statement, "If the light that is in thee be darkness, how great is that darkness!"[3] So their darkness was multiplied by the light in their meditation and projected onto the field of the planet, therefore they had a karmic accountability.

That is a bit too much for us to swallow at this moment, to think that perhaps in meditation, because of our impurity, we could be projecting impurity upon the planet. But at least we can be responsible for our thoughts and feelings before we retire. At least we can be responsible for daily giving the violet flame and the decrees to Astrea necessary to constantly keep clearing the momentums of the subconscious that are up for transmutation, so that to the best of our knowledge and ability we aren't putting energies into the world that are going to be used, misused and multiplied by the mass mind.

So when you go to bed at night, you must have made peace, at least in your heart if you cannot contact the people and settle it with them in person. In your heart there must be God-control and the flow of love. If you have become angry during the day, it is necessary to call upon the law of forgiveness, to ask that that energy be transmuted and the record sealed, to see that no other part of life can be harmed by it. You have to go to bed with a clean slate—feeling you have done your all, you have done your best, you haven't left anything undone in terms of frequency or vibration—and you look forward to the next day for the settling of other accounts.

There is a recording angel who writes down everything that happens during the day. The last thing before you go to sleep, the recording angel has to decide what is going to be made permanent and what is going to be made semi-permanent. If you call for the violet flame and the law of forgiveness, you can have erased from your etheric body—before they become a permanent record—the situations of conflict and of discordant reactions to other parts of life.

If you don't settle the account, the record becomes deeper. It's almost like the pen of the angel can penetrate certain thousandths of an inch into the paper, and if the account is unsettled, the mark is deeper. But if it is settled and the flame has been passed through it, it would only become a permanent record if you went back and continually did the same thing over and over again.

If you keep on repeating the same mistake and continually asking for forgiveness, after a while the Great Law says, "We have to withdraw forgiveness and make you accountable for all of your misdeeds along these lines because it has not been shown that you have made use of the mercy of the Law and of the flame of forgiveness." At that point, what is almost like a watermark becomes deeply written as a record, and then of course, it's much more difficult to remove. This is a very real thing that happens.

It is important, then, that you do not let the sun go down upon your wrath, that you understand the full implication of that statement, and that you do not allow yourself to be fooled—because the remainder of your days on this planet, whether it is one year or fifty years, should be preparatory to your ascension.

None of us know how long we will be here. Just because we are young does not mean we are going to be here forever.

As you know, circumstances, accidents, karma, cataclysm, illness have always brought untimely transitions in the past and they will in the future. So our days are numbered and we must make every day count. Settling your accounts each day is one way you can eliminate making additional karma.

Righteous Anger

There is such a thing as righteous anger, but this involves principle not person. When principles are violated because of the misleading activities of the dark spirits, one's feeling of anger—like unto that of the Master Jesus when he drove the moneychangers out of the temple[4]—should be against the spirits that defraud men of the wholeness of their seamless garment of light* and not against the innocent victims of the plight.

Many times you will find yourself in an argument with someone you love—a dearest friend, a member of your family—and somehow you can't get off the track of this argument. It's going around and around and it's like a wire band. You get into it and you start talking faster, your voices start getting raised, and usually it leads to a very unpleasant experience. When it is all over, you wish it hadn't happened.

Well, it doesn't need to happen if people will understand that we don't fight each other. We fight the common enemy: the carnal mind, the fallen ones, the discarnates, the demons that move on the astral plane and try to trip you up so you enter into an argument and they can puncture your aura and steal your light.

---

*Through the right use of God's energies, man daily weaves his seamless garment of light, a garment which envelops the etheric body and is the vehicle for the soul's return home to God. This garment of light is also known as the deathless solar body.

You find that when you're engaged in this argument you are not being yourself, the friend is not being himself, and the whole thing is quite ridiculous. That is because it is manufactured and contrived by the fallen ones, by the demons and their projection of ideas, feelings of resentment, feelings of anger that are amplified by you. Until you become astute, you do not realize that these thoughts are not your thoughts, these feelings are not your feelings. They are manufactured, contrived and projected at you.

Righteous anger is something very different. It is not really anger. It is a welling up of energy and a determination and a thrust of that energy to reverse the momentum of the dark force, to challenge the accuser of the brethren, to challenge the challenger of your peace and your harmony, to defend the individual with whom you are having the argument, to defend his Christ consciousness against the intrusion and the intruder.

It is so easy to get annoyed, for instance, at children or at people who are around us for something they are doing. It is so easy to fall into the trap of thinking they are behaving the way they are because it is them that is acting.

The Screwtape Letters, by C. S. Lewis, is an important addition to this course in psychology. It is C. S. Lewis's version of how the hierarchy of fallen angels works—their plots and their deliberations—to move against the consciousness and the daily activities of those who are trying to live the life of a true Christian. The fallen angels are determined to postpone the individual's pursuit of the light.

This is an aspect of psychology that you must be aware of because it is something that controls almost 100 percent of the psyches of the population. It is energy, influence, consciousness beyond one's forcefield. It is these spirits who defraud men of the wholeness of their seamless garment of light. Our energy should be thrust in that direction, and not toward the innocent victims. Perhaps they are not altogether innocent. Perhaps they have a little bit of substance in their electronic belt that is argumentative or fearful or greedy or hateful and they attract this energy. Nevertheless, in the total picture of being aware of all the forces involved, most people are quite innocent. They cannot see; they do not know. They are ignorant. They are naive.

God as a Personality

When men wear the garb of greed or egoism, when they cloak themselves in the raiment of senseless idiosyncrasies, when they shape their lives by whimsy rather than by cosmic law, when they imagine God to be wholly impersonal having no personal interest in themselves, they close the door to joy and reality.

When you look at what Kuthumi is listing here, you see what takes from us our joy and our reality: greed; egoism; senseless idiosyncrasies (not being able to surrender, but always having it my way or your way and then it's an argument); moving by whimsy (the blowing of the winds of the human consciousness); and thinking that God is wholly impersonal.

When God becomes an impersonal law or an impersonal vapor, a vapory spirit that permeates everywhere, there is no image that we can tether to that makes us feel that he really cares, that he is in contact with us personally. No matter how much we say to ourselves that we believe and we know that God cares for us, there is still the plane of consciousness where we have a certain cynicism and the

scientific approach that tells us that God is not personal.
Now, if God is not personal, there can't be ascended masters
or angels or elementals, and it wipes us out too because we
are God in manifestation. We are God personified. So it is
really a philosophy of nihilism.

I have a little girl in the second grade. Last night she
told me that they had a substitute teacher at school, and the
substitute teacher was reading them a story about witches.
Included in the story about witches there was mention of
angels, and the teacher said, "I don't believe in angels. Angels
aren't real." So my little girl spoke up and said, "I believe in
angels." Then the teacher said that the story was a lie and
there were no angels.

So my little girl said, "Well, I believe that you are lying
when you say that there aren't any angels." And the teacher
had some response to that. My little girl made one more
statement to the effect that she knew that angels existed.
Then she said, "Let's discontinue the conversation so we
don't get into an argument." And the teacher said, "Okay."

You never know what rubs off on children. But it was
a very good challenge of the lie. My little girl really wasn't
upset with the teacher. She felt it necessary to state the truth
in the classroom. She wasn't afraid to do so. She wasn't
afraid because the teacher was an adult and she was a child.
And then she knew that the situation shouldn't get out of
hand and the discussion should be discontinued.

However, I was thinking to myself this morning that
I've heard my children come home at other times saying
that teachers have stated that there aren't any angels. This
is an interference with religious freedom. Both the Old and
the New Testaments of the Bible are filled with accounts of
angels, and to me, to deny an angel is just as great a sin as to

deny the prophets or Jesus Christ or Mary or any of the biblical accounts. And I thought to myself, "You know, I could start quite an uproar in the school by calling up and saying, 'I object to the teachers telling my children that there aren't any angels.'" As a matter of fact, I don't really need to do this because my children seem to be handling it very well on their own. But you wonder at what point you should begin to protest.

Of course, the woman didn't bother to say that she didn't believe in witches, you see, because everybody is supposed to know that witches aren't real. But the children don't know that. So she told them that the angels were just fairy tales.

That's why we need our own Montessori school. It's not the specific thing the teacher said. I resent the fact that anybody should encroach upon this hallowed circle of consciousness that I as a parent have the right to pass on to my child, that you as a parent have the right to pass on to your children, that there should be an invasion of that area which is sacrosanct. And when I say I resent that, it's righteous anger.

One step further down the line, when you have state control of religion, you ultimately have the replacing of religion by the state itself. You get a figurehead; you get the big pictures of Karl Marx, Lenin, Stalin, or whomever, and they become the saviour of the people. The state promises the people everything they need, a substitute for salvation, a substitute for ritual. The mystical experiences of the church are replaced by the parades and the slogans and the fervor of political meetings and gatherings. Pretty soon this destroys the metaphysical aspect of the individual and destroys the individual in the process.

That is what Jung gets into in *The Undiscovered Self*. He's talking about the modern state replacing the religion that is an archetype in the soul. One of his differences with Freud is he says that every man has a propensity within himself to reach for the *meta*-physical, for what is beyond the physical, and that part of the subconscious need of the psyche is to have something that is beyond the tangible.

When the state comes in and destroys this, it splits the personality. Aside from assuming the role of religion for the individual, the state has deprived the individual of this very necessary component of consciousness and has substituted for it the very dark energies of the carnal mind (which Jung calls the shadow) and the madness and mania of the mob.

The spirits that defraud men of wholeness are the same spirits that tear down the image of the personal God. Wherever the individual is under attack, God is under attack. Wherever your identity—your unique identity—is attacked, your own I AM Presence is being denied, as well as your opportunity to become one with that Presence.

When you become a statistic, you are no longer an individual. A statistic is not real. A statistic is a norm of a million people. But you can't find an individual who is a norm of everything. A statistic is never fulfilled in an identity. But science has replaced the individual with statistics and says, "According to statistics your behavior pattern should be thus and such." So you get analyzed clinically on the basis of being a statistic instead of being an individual.

Freud retained a personal concern for his patients. But those who followed him became more Freudian than Freud and became so stiff that they completely disregarded the individual and they psychoanalyzed a statistic. This is the big problem with psychology today.

Every single individual is a new psychology, a new psyche, a new set of karmas, and the lines of statistics can only go so far. If you allow them to go too far, you destroy the individual. When you destroy the individual you destroy God—remember that. God can only be realized through the individual. You are the personification of the God flame. You are the individualization of the God flame. The attempt to make you just one of the masses is the way—the very subtle way—that the Luciferians are destroying God on the planet.

Our fight is a fight for individualism, but not an individualism that is rebellion against the law of God. Lucifer fought for individualism, but he went too far. He saw himself as the individual independent of God, challenging God, thinking that he could do it better than God. Our purpose of individualization is integration with the God flame, *realizing* God. So even individualism has been misused.

> In this series we come to flood the soul, the mind, the consciousness, and the being of man with an awareness that will shatter the chains that have created conditions of unhappiness and strain. We wish to restore the boundaries of the temple of God, to reassert the dominion of the individual over his own life, to help him in his search for reality, and to assure him of our living presence in the universe as his brother and his teacher. As we represent God, so may he.

Now you understand that last statement a little better: As the ascended masters are the fullness of the God flame incarnate, so they desire that you should be also. And when they say "so may he," they are uttering a prayer to Almighty

God because they see what is coming upon the race. They see what is coming upon mankind.

> To one who is learning to understand himself, the world is a stella nova [a new star]. Each day is a freshening dawn. The weary soul sheds its false sense of frustration and at last opens its eyes to behold reality. From the beginning through the ages of instruction, God has sought the gradual and permanent elevation of all of his children into that wholesome vision of the whole divine man—the Real Self.
> Be at peace in God.
> Lovingly, I AM,
> *Kuthumi*

There is no peace outside of God. There is no peace in being your not-self, because in doing that you are being the not-God, you are denying God, who is the reality of your person. God wants to elevate you to your Real Self. That is the desire of God. And knowing that God so desires, the masters have come forth to give this instruction.

Questions and Answers

Do you have any questions on what has been covered in this course thus far?

Student: Concerning the personal God, do you consider this to be the Mother?

ECP: We call the Mother the personal personality of God, but God is also personified as Father, as Son and as Holy Spirit. And different aspects of the personality merge with aspects of the impersonality.

The most personal aspect of our being is Mother. You'll

notice in the study of psychology, that is the first image you have. The first awareness you have of something apart from yourself is mother, and that image is retained forevermore as the most vivid element of God. And when you realize the fullness of that, you will be the most personal personality of God to all parts of life.

The sons and daughters of God are impersonal personalities; the Holy Spirit is the personal impersonality. And God as Father, even though he is considered the impersonal impersonality, is still a personality, even while being impersonal.

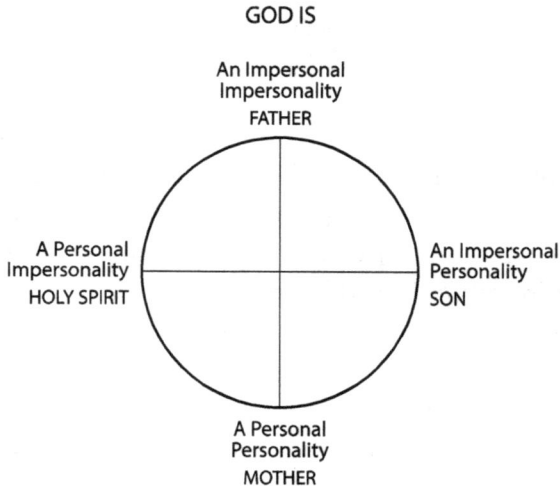

GOD IS

An Impersonal
Impersonality
FATHER

A Personal   An Impersonal
Impersonality   Personality
HOLY SPIRIT   SON

A Personal
Personality
MOTHER

The four personalities of God

God as Father is a little bit remote, a little bit up the mountain from us. He personifies the Law, and the Law is impersonal, yet we can identify with the Father figure. But he is always just a little bit removed, one step, from the Mother. And that is the way it's supposed to be because that's the law of forcefields. By being a little bit less personal, he can be a little bit more strict, more disciplined. He can enforce the Law, and we need that—we need that Father figure.

Student: When you are invoking light through decrees and your consciousness is not cleared of anger or resentment or ill feelings, are you going to magnetize these?

ECP: Yes. It's not good to start yelling decrees when you are angry. If you feel yourself caught in a riptide of anger, you don't start shouting decrees. A riptide is a mass floating grid of energy that moves in the sky of the astral, and it will tie into a vortex of your own irritation and suddenly you're blowing up with anger.

Instead you say, *"In the name of the Christ, I call to the Elohim to seize this energy."* You do some deep breathing, you sit quietly, you keep silent. You get out of the way of the people you're shouting at or having a confrontation with. You go to a quiet room. You let yourself calm down and you start speaking very slowly and deliberately, because speaking slowly will control the anger, and you say, *"I AM a being of violet fire, I AM the purity God desires."*

Of course, you have to *want* to be that being. You have to have enough control of yourself to know that you want to overcome this momentum. You see the violet flame passing through you. Through your deep breathing or doing Djwal Kul's breathing exercises,[5] you feel yourself beginning to reestablish the norms. Your adrenals calm down, your blood pressure calms down, your heart calms down—all these things that are affected by this riptide. And you let the violet flame start flowing slowly.

Then when you feel in control, you say:

> *In the name of the Christ, I call on the law of for-*
> *giveness for the disruption of the flow of my harmony.*
> *Let it be reestablished. I call to the great Elohim to seize*
> *that energy so that it cannot affect any other part of life.*
> *I call to the angelic hosts to take up that substance, encir-*
> *cle it, purify it with its cause and core. In the name of the*
> *Christ, I challenge all entities, discarnates, fallen ones, the*
> *consciousness behind this riptide, this anger momentum.*
> *I call to the hosts of light to bind them and remove them*
> *from the forcefield of the earth, from the forcefield of my*
> *consciousness and from all who are endangered thereby.*

And when you have your peace restored you really start giving decrees; you give your Astreas and your violet flame.

One can decree with fanaticism, and I have seen it. And it is a death knell to the culture of the ascended masters. The fanatical frenzy of religious zeal, right-wing hatred, left-wing hatred, decreeing to get even with someone, decreeing because one is invoking the energy of the gods down upon one's enemies—all of this is very bad.

It's bad for your karma; it's bad for the energy of the planet; it's bad for the image of the ascended masters' teachings. It's an energy that is catching and that people will pick up, and pretty soon you could find yourself in the middle of a movement of some kind of mass hysteria.

So you must be careful. For instance, you can get very determined in your reversing the tide,* but don't get emotional. Remember, it is God that is reversing the tide, not you getting emotional giving the decree for reversing the tide.

---

* "Reverse the Tide" is a decree invoking the heavenly hosts to turn back forces of darkness that are negative or dangerous to life, either on a personal or planetary scale. See decree 7.05 in *Prayers, Meditations and Dynamic Decrees for Personal and World Transformation.*

The spoken Word is a science, and it takes years to really learn all the uses of energy and power through the chakras.

Student: We talked about sympathy and I'm just wondering if when somebody confronts you and says your friend, somebody you are close to, is doing such and such...

ECP: What do you mean by such and such? Something bad?

Student: Something that's negative, a bad spiral. And in a sense it's true. If you defend him, would it be sympathy with that negative spiral?

ECP: Well, you don't defend the person's actions, you defend their right to be an overcomer; you defend their right to be the Christ. If you know that the person is trying but has fallen in a weak moment, you can say, "I know this person. I know he's making progress on the spiritual path. This happens to be a weakness that he has. I certainly am not defending his weakness or his actions, but I do believe that he deserves the opportunity to be an overcomer." And you might say, "I've called this to his attention," or "I intend to call it to his attention."

But the thing you have to say to the person who reports it to you is, "Won't you pray with me for his soul?" If you say that to someone they may realize that this is obviously what they should be doing. And you can set an example by stopping right there and saying, **"In the name of the Christ, I pray for the soul of so-and-so and for his overcoming victory in this area,"** and perhaps the person will join in.

Then there is the situation where people say, "Well, I stopped going to church twenty years ago because of all the hypocrites in the church, all the people there who weren't really practicing their Christianity." That itself is idolatry.*

---

*In a broad sense, idolatry is investing one's faith in any outer manifestation instead of the spirit of God.

As Jesus said, "What is that to thee? Follow thou me."[6] You're not going to church to be with or without hypocrites. You're going to church to worship the flame. Your eyes are supposed to be closed. You're not supposed to be watching who is there and what they do during the week. Nevertheless, that is what many, many people say.

Of course, when the minister misbehaves, it gives additional fuel to the fire, and it becomes a losing proposition to be part of a group of people who are all living contrary to what they are preaching. But we cannot kick over the traces just because people are not living up to the teaching. We have to realize that the teaching is more than one bad example or one person's failure.

When we make imperfections and bad examples and misdemeanors so important, we are engaging in idolatry. We are taking an opportunity to condemn something outside of ourselves because, really, we condemn our own frailties and shortcomings. We seize upon the opportunity of someone's misbehavior to say "What a terrible thing," and it releases us from that self-condemnation which we can no longer bear and for which we have to find an object.

This has been a problem, especially in the ascended master activities—the condemning of individuals and constantly saying, "Well, if a person isn't living up to the teaching, the teaching must be wrong." So don't take yourself too seriously. Don't take your failures too seriously. Take them seriously enough to correct them, but not so seriously that you destroy the opportunity for evolution. It's at the point of getting too serious over people's shortcomings and frailties that you lose perspective and you find that all the while you were an idolater.

The problem is we can always make allowances for our

own shortcomings, our own frailties and weaknesses. We can understand why we don't do this thing we're supposed to do. That's the way we are. We've been that way a long time, and we make those allowances.

But someone else comes along and they are perfect in that area and they look and they see that thing in us and, oh, it's a terrible thing. Well, they have another fault. Of course, what the person who comes along doesn't realize is that probably on another layer of the electronic belt in a past embodiment he had that identical weakness—because if it wasn't in him, he really wouldn't be seeing it in us; he really wouldn't be bothered by it.

There are certain densities or problems that people have that I only see when I'm in the masters' consciousness of correcting it, or when I'm in the Christ consciousness. As a person I never see it. I'm not bothered by it. It doesn't disturb me because I have nothing in me to expose it or attract it unless I'm in the role of the teacher.

I find that the masters continually use me to get to areas of people's consciousness that I don't even know are there. Sometimes I make what I think is a very innocent remark or an innocent request of a person to do something and they just fall completely apart and go through rebellion and tears and all kinds of problems, and I can't understand what's the matter. When this happens I realize that the simple little statement I made hit that hornet's nest or that pocket of consciousness that the master wanted them to be exposed to and to overcome. And I always say, "Well, if I'd known it would have caused this problem, I never would have said it." But it's lucky that I didn't know it because I would have been betraying what the master was trying to accomplish.

Sometimes you are used as a catalyst for people's coming

to grips with themselves. Sometimes you do this innocently, sometimes in the role of the teacher, and sometimes you are definitely in that situation because something inside of yourself is drawing it to the surface in you and in them and creating the confrontation, which is more like a karmic situation.

January 16, 1975

I AM THE VIOLET FLAME

In the name of the beloved mighty victorious Presence of God, I AM in me, and my very own beloved Holy Christ Self, I call to beloved Alpha and Omega in the heart of God in our Great Central Sun, beloved Saint Germain, beloved Portia, beloved Archangel Zadkiel, beloved Holy Amethyst, beloved Mighty Arcturus and Victoria, beloved great Karmic Board, beloved Lanello, the entire Spirit of the Great White Brotherhood and the World Mother, elemental life—fire, air, water, and earth!

To expand the Violet Flame within my heart, purify my four lower bodies, transmute all misqualified energy I have ever imposed upon life, and blaze mercy's healing ray throughout the earth, the elementals, and all mankind and answer this my call infinitely, presently, and forever:

> I AM the Violet Flame
>   In action in me now
> I AM the Violet Flame
>   To Light alone I bow
> I AM the Violet Flame
>   In mighty Cosmic Power
> I AM the Light of God
>   Shining every hour
> I AM the Violet Flame
>   Blazing like a sun
> I AM God's sacred power
>   Freeing every one

And in full Faith I consciously accept this manifest, manifest, manifest! (3x) right here and now with full Power, eternally sustained, all-powerfully active, ever expanding, and world enfolding until all are wholly ascended in the Light and free! Beloved I AM! Beloved I AM! Beloved I AM!

CHAPTER FIVE

THE FIRE OF COSMIC PURPOSE

Commentary on Chapter 2, Part 1

To Those Who Have Surveyed the Summits of the World:
The happiness that one feels when the flow of one's energy is toward the straightforward purpose is an expression of universal harmony. As men seek to understand their own being, they must see that God has implanted his purpose within them as within nature. Each seed bears after its kind, each creature expresses according to its own inherent pattern. As man is a free agent, he should also hold understanding of the meaning of freedom in his exercise of free will.

Let us meditate for a moment on this concept of purpose being implanted within you. You can see this in animals as instinct. They have the instinct to do what their group soul has been doing for as long as they have existed. And we have a certain instinct to fulfill, a certain inner matrix, and that is the purpose planted within.

I was recently asked to explain evolution versus man being created outright in the image and likeness of God and how to explain the fact that scientists have proven the links between stages of animal life showing this evolution. Of course, the masters teach that God's energy is used in the creation of animal life, imperfect as it may be, and that there is evolution because God's energy is always evolving toward the purpose of perfection.

The purpose that is implanted within life is the goal of perfection itself. And even when energy is locked in a limited matrix of an animal form, it tends to evolve to a higher form, reaching for the image of the Christ, which is found only in man.

When you see how powerful this purpose is in nature, enabling flowers to germinate and push right through the soil and the rocks and the roots of trees; when you realize what a tremendous impact of energy is required for a child to be born—how hard even the male sperm itself works and fights to get to the egg, which is the focal point of the universal egg of the Divine Mother, how there is this pushing within primal life to realize a goal of perfection and wholeness; when you realize that every atom of energy that is within us is impressed with purpose, you get the sense of the whole lifewave of creation moving back to the central source. And in the process of moving back there is this integration, this evolution and the energy of God is continually transcending itself. The law of transcendence comes out of the sealing of the purpose in life.

When you realize that this purpose is sealed within you, you realize that to unlock that seal, to break that seal, means ultimately that this purpose is going to fulfill itself within you. Have you ever heard the hymn, "God is working his purpose out as year succeeds to year"?[1] God *is* working his purpose out, and that purpose is a molecule of fire in you that drives you to the fulfillment of your sacred labor and ultimately to your soul's reunion with God.

This purpose is implemented through free will. Man as a

free will agent can put the brake on this cosmic purpose, can bring it to a screeching halt. He can burn those brakes until they fire and smoke, and by the perverseness of a free will dedicated to the self and selfishness, he can completely turn that purpose around. So as soon as Lanto tells us about the locking of purpose, he tells us about free will.

Free will can be, then, your foot on the accelerator, accelerating cosmic purpose, accelerating divine energy, giving more gas to it, giving more energy, more fuel to this molecule of purpose. That's what you do when you decree, when you make invocations, when you get more of the sacred fire in your being. And even before you learn to make an invocation, doing your darnedest to fulfill the highest that you know how to fulfill is accelerating cosmic purpose. Going against everything that is holy, everything that is righteous, everything that is the Law—*that* is putting the brake on.

Free will determines what happens to that seed of purpose. And of course, the seed (which Morya equates to the soul identity[2]) can be finally destroyed by putting the brake on so hard that there is no essence, no life energy given to the seed to grow. So you can run the gamut of this tremendous range of choices: idling (just like you idle a car, idling the motor of life and not really getting anywhere, not going up or down the stream), putting the brake on, or really accelerating at top speed. All that is in your hands.

That is what gives variety, diversity, individuality. That is what makes up your personal identity, your own astrology, your own psychology—the amount of energy you apply and what type of energy you put on the accelerator, whether it's the first ray or the second, third, fourth, fifth, sixth or seventh. The type of energy that you are applying to the opening of that purpose will determine how that purpose unfolds.

Karma and Free Will

Each man's culture is dominated by the patterns that lie deep within his subconscious being. Frequently men say that they do not understand themselves. They do not know why they act as they do. It is not possible for them to open the doorway of consciousness, to roam the corridors of memory and see each habit in its development, and then to weed out each undesirable thought. There is a better way, and that way is the saturation of the consciousness with the flame of cosmic worth.

The way in which we use free will, then, even unbeknownst to us, will be determined by the patterns of the subconscious formulated in this and other lives merging together. If I had to choose between karma, heredity and the environment, I would not choose the environment or heredity; but I would say that the main factor in determining why people act as they do is karmic patterns. But life doesn't begin and end with karma, because the first definition of karma is energy in action.

Karma *is* energy in action. We are making karma every moment, and we are either governing the flow of energy within us according to the Law or we are not. Let's say you are a child back in embodiment with your karma, which means the sum total of how you have governed energy flow in your past lives. But from the moment you are born, your parents are governing the energy flow. They are creating conditions around you that are going to mold your outer personality in this life. Your outer personality is almost like the soil in which the seed of the soul is buried, and the soul has to push through that soil to come to the sunlight of its own I AM Presence.

There is a determination of purpose anchored within the soul that is going to push through the soil, the rocks, the obstacles and reach for reunion with the light. So to a certain extent, regardless of what you have gone through in your childhood, the fire of purpose anchored within you is greater than the sum of the parts of all that has been brought to bear upon your personality. And your soul, if given the freedom to act upon its free will, is going to overcome environment, heredity and karma, all of these, to fulfill that inner destiny.

If you want to visualize where that destiny is anchored, you can visualize it in a mother-of-pearl sphere that is anchored in the seat-of-the-soul chakra, the point where your soul is anchored. Have you seen the jewelry that was popular for a time, a mustard seed sealed in a little plastic ball? Well, you can see the plastic ball as your soul and the fire of cosmic purpose—the purpose of your life—being that seed in the center of your soul. It's a good matrix for you to visualize. It's very vivid.

Then you can see the entire electronic belt as the soil, the earth, the dense substance into which that seed is planted. And in order for the soul and that seed to be nourished and to grow, the nutrients must flow through the soil, which means that an alchemy has to take place. The chemicals of light, of energy needed for the growth of the seed must come from the flame of God being passed through the electronic belt, just as water flows through soil.

It is the combination of the water, the soil, the air and the sun that brings forth in the plant whatever that plant is going to be. That is alchemy. It is the transformation of energy. So in order for the energies of your electronic belt to be useful to you, they have to go through the alchemy of contact with the sacred fire, with the flow of your love, with your invocations, with your service. By all of these ingredients, those energies are transformed back into their original light, and that is the light that the soul has to have to ascend. This is a very important parallel.

Did you ever look at how a plant grows? The typical example is the lotus in the mud. But think of corn or potatoes or carrots or beans or berries. Look at the tree or the plant, look at the fruit of nature, look at the soil, and think, "How can all these vitamins and minerals, how can this substance and this matrix come out of this handful of earth?" It is the alchemy of the purpose within the seed itself, the blueprint of life that God impresses there, that draws together all the energies of creation to bring forth year after year the same design. The same is true within you.

In Psalm 1 we hear the psalmist talking about the blessedness of man. "Blessed is the man that walketh not in the counsel of the ungodly.... He shall be like a tree planted by the rivers of water, that bringeth forth his fruit in his season."[3] You are like a tree, a special tree of God with a special fruit. It's the fruit of your soul's striving. But it's that special imprint of purpose that is in the soul, *cosmic* purpose. It's as if you were an avocado tree or an orange tree or an apple tree—you are going to continually bring forth throughout cosmos the special fruit of your tree, and it can never be changed or altered. It is the unique pattern that you have, just as unique as the patterns in nature.

When you realize this, you realize you really do have something very special of cosmic purpose on one of the rays that is your gift, your snowflake, your design and you continually put it forth into the cosmos. And it is the balance that is needed from your lifestream combined with the contributions of all other lifestreams that makes up the glorious mandala of the Cosmic Egg.*

Why am I telling you this? Because I want you to understand the biology of the soul, the law of producing after one's kind. This law is sealed. And unless it is tampered with by black magic or witchcraft, the release of that energy can only result in producing after the cosmic purpose that is within you.

The seat-of-the-soul chakra, the anchoring point of the flame of freedom,† is very important in our study of psychology because that is where the patterns of the cells of life are anchored. And much of the witchcraft and black magic of the fallen ones is directed against the souls of mankind and the soul chakra because there is the essence of life, there is your ability to procreate, there is the energy of the seed and the egg that carries the imprint of your Christ-identity, your cosmic purpose. So the soul chakra needs to be cleared and kept free and kept protected so that your soul, in the fullest potential of its God-identity, can bring forth after its kind.

The Purification of Consciousness

The masters don't want us to roam the corridors of memory—the lower etheric body, the electronic belt—and go through the caverns of consciousness identifying all of the past. We can wander through the grasses of the jungle and see the beasts through the trees and realize that each one of these things is a facet of carnality, of animal magnetism that we have been involved in. But there is a better way. And that is the "saturation of consciousness with the flame of cosmic worth." We must keep that concept to the fore.

---

*The Cosmic Egg is the spiritual-material universe, including a seemingly endless chain of galaxies, star systems, and worlds known and unknown.
†The seat-of-the-soul chakra is the chakra of the seventh ray, the violet ray, of freedom, alchemy, forgiveness and transmutation.

The old statement "Our God is a consuming fire"[4] is a source of great comfort to those who understand it, for the divine image is truly ablaze with benign activity. The pulsations, or risings, of the sacred fire, in all of their naturalness, convey the essence of the higher consciousness. These [not only pacify and] deactivate all malintent that may be locked within the subconscious world of the individual, [but] they [also] create and re-create in his total consciousness the most outstanding designs[5] reflecting cosmic law. Such patterns enable the individual who accepts them and uses the higher consciousness they convey to be completely free and yet to remain under the dominion of his Divine Self.

Therefore, when you invoke the sacred fire on any aspect of the seven rays, you can know that that energy is conveying the essence of your own higher consciousness, which is your own Christ Self, your own higher mental body. When we think about energy flowing or about electricity, we often leave out the most important ingredient or aspect of energy, which is intelligence.

We don't think of electrons as being intelligent. We don't think of energy that is lighting our lights as being intelligent. But if you realize that intelligence is an attribute of God, hence an attribute of his energy, you will understand that that energy is programmed with intelligence to fulfill cosmic patterns in all life. Energy is programmed to fulfill the blueprint of every seed, of all things that are living, and especially of the seed of your own soul.

"The pulsations ... of the sacred fire ... deactivate all malintent." Now, this is a great boon and a great gift. In pockets and in sockets of the subconscious there are sometimes tremendous concentrations of hatred. And hatred itself is a malignancy of the astral body long before it ever appears in the physical—and this is true of fear or resentment or revenge. The fact that these can be deactivated, that the sting of energy can be taken from them by the sacred fire so that energy—if any of it has to pass through your consciousness when going into the flame—will not have the virulence that it had when it was originally misqualified. This is important, and it is the gift of the Holy Spirit in the fire itself.

On top of this, these pulsations of sacred fire create in your total consciousness "outstanding designs reflecting cosmic law"—not just any old designs, but *outstanding* designs—making you an individual par excellence, making your individuality so rare, so precious, as to be loved and admired and adored by all other parts of life.

The Flame of Cosmic Worth

Sometimes we look at people and we realize that they have a very low self-image. Sometimes you find this in children. They don't have a sense of worth. Lanto says to invoke the flame of cosmic worth.

Cosmic worth is an accentuation of the flame of the will of God, the wisdom of God and the love of God. It is a balancing action of the flow of the fires of the threefold flame.

You have to have a sense of individual worth. That sense of individual worth is rooted in the Christ, and it replaces the conceit and the deceit of the ego, the false pride, the false humility, the inflated and deflated ego, *all* sides of the ego.

The sense that you have worth, that you are worth something to God, is irreplaceable. It is something that goads you on to the fulfillment of your sacred labor. And the more you develop that labor, the more you are educated and refined and centered in the talent God has given you, the more you realize that you have this worth, the more you become irreplaceable in the cosmic scheme.

Of course, the masters say that no one is indispensable, because they will not attribute or give power to the human consciousness. But I can tell you that the God consciousness is indispensable, your God consciousness is indispensable. You should write that down: "My God consciousness is indispensable to the creation." And you can really say, **"My God consciousness is indispensable to the Creator and creation."**

That is very important, because there comes the test along the Path—and it may come well along the Path— to decide that you are not worth too much and there isn't really much point in your existence. What does it really matter if you decree today? Or what does it really matter if you go back to school and perfect your talent? What difference does it make if you don't do it—someone else will. Of course, that is the deadly lie of the carnal mind that does not want you to fulfill your own Christ-potential. And you have to reject it with that same statement, **"My God consciousness is indispensable to the Creator and creation."**

You are indispensable—and this is your sacred worth, which comes to you with the flame of cosmic worth. The flame of cosmic worth is a flow of sacred fire which when invoked comes forth as a threefold flame. But it comes forth in different measure to each one who invokes it because it will provide you with the exact ingredients of the blue, the yellow and the pink that are required to bring out your individuality.

The flame of cosmic worth brings out the worth of the individual. So if you are excelling in love, as you invoke the flame of cosmic worth, it will manifest as the wisdom of love and the will of love to give you the balance and the matrix for that love. You can see the lines of force of the cosmic threefold flame of the Cosmic Christ coalescing in you to bring you into balance, because only when you are in balance in the threefold flame do you realize the fullness of your cosmic potential in Christ. You really aren't the fullness of your Christed being until you have that threefold flame balanced.

"The divine image is ablaze with benign activity." The divine image is the image of God in which you were made. And God said, "Let us make man in our image and likeness," and so man was created. "Male and female created he them."[6] When you have the divine image, it is the magnet of God's consciousness that polarizes and restores your soul and your being to the original blueprint.

> *In the name of the Christ, in the name of the I AM Presence, we invoke the divine image for each one. We call forth the divine image from the heart of Almighty God, from the heart of the glorious I AM Presence and causal body of each one, which is the unique individuality of the Godhead.*
>
> *I call forth the divine image from the heart of Alpha and Omega. I call it forth for every Keeper of the Flame* and every son and daughter of God upon this planet. Blaze forth the divine image out of which all were made, male and female! So let the flow of the masculine and feminine ray of the twin flames of each one be now*

---

*A member of the Keepers of the Flame Fraternity, founded by the ascended master Saint Germain to uphold freedom and the sacredness of life and to extend that flame to others who do not know that they have a divine spark within.

impressed in the planes of Matter in the heart chakra.
Blaze forth the divine image and let it be the fiery core
of the Central Sun Magnet to magnetize each one to the
fulfillment of that sacred image.

In God we trust. Gloria in excelsis deo. In the name*
of the Father, the Mother, the Son and the Holy Spirit,
we accept the anchoring of the divine image for the ful-
fillment of the plan, the plan divine, and the spirit of
cosmic victory in each one, in each one who has passed
through Summit University and all who are striving for
the goal of oneness in the ascension in the light.

Remaking the Self in the Divine Image

The goal of the fallen ones, of the synthetic society,
of the mechanization concept, is to separate you from the
divine image. It's a blueprint that is intricate. It's just like a
section in the DNA chain, but it's the RNA molecule. It is
very intricate, it is a forcefield, it is your pattern.

What you are manifesting now is the best that your
Christ Self and your body elemental could put together
according to that blueprint, given your karma, given that
which has stood between your soul and your I AM Presence.
Your face, your body temple, your talents, all that you are,
is the best that God could coalesce in form given all circumstances, parents, and of course environmental and heredi-
tary factors, which are themselves a result to a large extent
of your own karma.

So you look at yourself and say, "Here I am, this is me,
this is what I am. I'm going to trace what I see back to the
Source to see what I ought to be." And you will find as the
flame passes through you that your face, your body, all of

---
*Glory to God in the highest.

your being, is refined by the flame. And year in, year out you find yourself looking more and more like the Real Image.

Physical characteristics do not pass away so easily. But you find that the light shining through your flesh, through your eyes, through your soul, through your heart, has a tremendous transforming power so that even if the features themselves are not drastically altered, the aura itself is so altered that it impresses upon you the appearance of the new man or new woman being born within you.

It's interesting how you can read people's faces and determine what moods they are in. I have noticed when people have self-pity or self-condemnation that there is a flow of energy to various centers and organs that momentarily will make part of their face or part of their body actually change its form to fulfill certain energy levels where they have decided that they are going to have a niche for a while. You will find people's noses will get thicker when they're feeling sorry for themselves or when they're angry. Or their eyes or their heads or whatever it might be will change, even their posture. People do change momentarily as their auras change, and there is a much greater effect on the physical body than we would consider at first.

"The divine image is ablaze with benign activity." As this divine image lowers into your forcefield, you can see it coming down as a grid that is truly on fire with the fire of your Presence. The Real Image, or the divine image, is the link to Reality.

Each time we come into incarnation, Mother Mary takes the energies of life, of our good karma, the best that we have to offer, and forms the best heart that can be formed, and then forms all the rest. But by our use of free will, we have altered the blueprint. The divine image is intended to be impressed upon the soul and outpictured through the soul. It is impressed there, but by free will it gets altered or stretched in various directions and distorted. These distortions then come out in the four lower bodies.

We begin the remaking of our total being by exalting the Real Image within our soul—infiring that image, protecting the image, calling forth the divine blueprint and knowing that it has the power of cosmic purpose. It is the seed of cosmic purpose in you. And all energy revolving around the soul must be drawn in and must coalesce around the best matrix that you can anchor there.

We all want the best for our offspring, and we all want our offspring to be the best. If we have even a smidgen of selflessness, we would like our offspring to exceed us. We don't feel the jealousy or the possessiveness that our sons or our daughters can't exceed our own measure, because we understand evolution. Innately, inherently in our being, we want our offspring to be better, to have more, and to have more opportunities than we had.

Then how does it happen that some people who really seem to have everything in terms of talent, intelligence and ability have offspring that are the opposite, are fairly worthless, and some of the most humble people have the most brilliant offspring? Here's the key. What you pass on to your children is not necessarily what you are manifesting right now, because that is your karma. The key is how clear is the focus of your seat-of-the-soul chakra and how clear is your soul, because it is your soul that is going to magnetize the souls to whom you give birth. And it is the purity of the soul chakra that determines the purity of the seed and the egg in man and woman physically.

You may not have an education or background or

wealth or means, but you may have tremendous devotion and tremendous fire for the purification of your soul. If you are of childbearing age, you will find that by that devotion you can attract to yourself extremely high souls because of the purity of that chakra. And you can give birth to children who far exceed your wildest imaginations for your own individual attainment.

This is something to think about, because even with all the intellect and all the accomplishment you may have, if you can't pass them on through the soul chakra, you can't pass them on to your children. And if your entire soul chakra is blocked with rebellion, stubbornness, human will, it distorts the Christic pattern and you may have very average children.

I went to grade school with a boy who was very intelligent and went to military school. He now has four sons, and three of them are mentally retarded. One explanation for this is the improper diet of the mother, improper vitamins and minerals. But on a karmic level there was a serious block to the seat-of-the-soul chakra and its flow of energy. There was a perversion of its light, a perverting of the flame of freedom into patterns of rebellion to the extent that his soul or his wife's soul or these two souls in conjunction were not able to attract souls who could bring forth the light of the intelligence of the mind of God.*

I want you to understand that this is an important key. It is one of the great mysteries of life given in the temple of the God and Goddess Meru and taught to parents who

---

*In this paragraph the messenger is giving an explanation of the karma of these specific parents and their children. In other situations there may be different factors involved. For example, sometimes very advanced souls volunteer to incarnate in bodies that are severely handicapped as a means to bear a portion of planetary karma.

want to sponsor lifewaves: the clearing of the imperfect patterns of your own soul is the necessary preparation for bearing children. As Archangel Raphael escorts parents-to-be through the halls of his retreat over Fátima, Portugal, he teaches them that gazing upon the images of perfect forms, like the art of Michelangelo, will impress upon your soul the original archetypal patterns of your own root race, the Christ consciousness of your root race.

A root race is a lifewave. It is a group of souls who come forth on one of the seven rays at a certain point in cosmic history to fulfill a certain destiny. The first three root races on earth came forth and outpictured three golden ages of perfection. They never departed from perfection. They never engaged in imperfection. They learned their lessons of free will and of mastery of energy on the blackboard. They were shown the energy veil. They were shown the consequences of the misuse of free will. They learned their lessons well in the retreats of the Brotherhood. And when they were embodied, they never responded to the temptation to taste of the fruits of the energy veil.

So they remained the holy innocents and they ascended in very short order. They say fourteen thousand years was all that was required for the fulfillment of the individual divine plan and the ascension. The members of the first three root races are all cosmic beings now, and Saint Germain has told us that we can call to their causal bodies to help us. The descent came in the fourth root race with the fall of the Luciferians.

The bringing forth of the perfect patterns of the causal body can be accomplished if one will return to the holy innocence of the soul, which the soul knew before its descent into matter. You may be part of the fourth, fifth or sixth root race, or a root race that has come forth on another planet in another system of worlds. Or you may be of an order of angelic beings who took embodiment to help those of the root races who fell. There are many possibilities for your origin in the planes of matter beyond this earth, beyond the root races that came to this earth.

The Christic pattern of a root race is the archetypal pattern of the Christ, of which the masters say there are 144,000 types. Within the root race there is an archetype of the Christ consciousness that is the purpose or the design implanted in the seed. And the seed brings forth after its kind.

When Mother Mary was assigned to bring forth Jesus the Christ, she was bringing forth the pattern of the Christ for the sixth root race. Jesus focused that pattern in the masculine, Mary in the feminine. That pattern was set. And all members of the sixth root race then had the clear example of the path of attainment and of what one who has self-mastery in the sixth ray is like in terms of the Christ consciousness.

Each root race has its Christic pattern fulfilling a certain aspect of the seven rays. And you, by your invocation to your Real Image, will draw forth that Christic pattern of your root race. And that pattern, anchored within your soul, is the magnet that will draw to you the Christed ones.

Freedom within God

The patterns that come forth from the Real Image enable you to be totally free. You understand that although there is a pattern, you are completely free to move like the electron in a random flow through it. But you never go beyond the bounds of the archetypal forcefield because in your freedom you are under the dominion of the Divine Self. The boundaries of man's habitation, which are spoken of in the Bible,[7] are the boundaries of the archetypal pattern of the Christ. So when we accept freedom as it is truly intended to be, we find that we are free to live and move and have our being in God. This is an enormous freedom. This freedom extends physically far beyond this earth, beyond this system of worlds. But there is the boundary of the archetypal pattern. This little electron of selfhood, moving around, will reach the bounds and bounce back so that in all of its

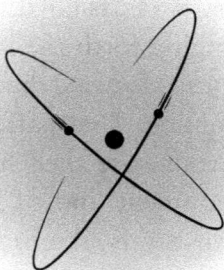

Electrons "orbit" around the nucleus of an atom in a manner that is seemingly random and impossible to predict for any individual electron, yet which follows well-defined laws.

movement, it is simply fulfilling the cycles of this archetypal pattern.

Although the movement seems random, it is responding to a cosmic design so intricate that the observer cannot detect what that design is because the movement of the electron appears so random. But if we had a computer where we could enter every movement of this electron, perhaps after thousands of years we would be able to detect a return to a certain pattern. Thus far scientists haven't determined the pattern. And you yourself, as you see the motions of your life, don't always see the pattern. But the more you understand about your cosmic astrology and your cosmic clock, the more you do put things into patterns and the more you see that there are patterns. And these patterns have been repeating themselves over the centuries.

The concept of freedom within God definitely contains within it restraint and constraint: You are restrained by God and by the Law, and by free will you constrain yourself to move within these patterns. You confine yourself to these patterns, yet you feel totally free within them. You are happy and joyous within these patterns.

That is the sense of freedom that you need to launch the Aquarian age. And make no mistake, *you* are launching the Aquarian age. Whatever your root race, wherever you come from, when you go out into the world, you are an electrode of Saint Germain to outpicture that age.*

So you have to know what freedom is. You cannot be fooled by the cycles of rebellion. You cannot be fooled by mankind's cycles of selfishness, defending a freedom that is beyond the flame of freedom, defending a position that is license, that is rebellion against the law and order of your own consciousness.

You have to be true freedom. You have to be independent individuals. You have to fulfill your individuality. But it must be within the circle of your own God-awareness. Any time you go outside of that circle, you don't exist. When you are outside the circle of your pattern, you are in a land of nonexistence. You are a non-entity. Why? It's very scientific:

---

*The ascended master Saint Germain, together with his twin flame, the ascended lady master Portia, is Hierarch of the Aquarian Age. He is the great sponsor of Freedom's flame, and Portia is the sponsor of the flame of Justice and Opportuniy.

If you are not where you are actually conforming to the matrix of the geometry of God, you are not sustained by God, because only the design of God sustains your motion. And his design is the energy for cosmic purpose.

When you go outside of his design, you are operating on borrowed energy and borrowed time, and that energy and that time are going to run out. When they run out, if you are still outside this archetypal pattern, you are going to cease to be. So *you have to be sure* that you are inside the archetypal pattern at the conclusion of the cycles of your incarnation.

Souls May Be Lost

We have had a report from one of our students that Mother Mary has appeared in Mexico, north of Mexico City. It has been exciting to hear his account, because so much of what was reportedly said there is in keeping with ascended master law.* She was very stern and exact in her directions.

The message spoke of these being the last days and of her concern about the enormous weight of karma that is about to descend on humanity unless they respond to the light. She also made the statement that it is difficult for her to hold up the arm of her Son. The interpretation of this is that the arm of the Law is in Jesus Christ, in the Son, the Logos—the Logos being the Law of the Word. When his arm goes down, it signifies the descent of karma. The Mother, who is the intercessor for her children, for the children of God, holds up that arm. In other words, she is holding back

---

*While the messenger is not endorsing the authenticity of this apparition, she is pointing out the parallels between what was reportedly said and the ascended masters' teachings.

the karma by holding up the arm of her Son. So Mother Mary is saying she can't hold up that arm much longer and that people must give the rosary daily and they must pray to Archangel Michael. She says the times are very bad, and there will be many souls who will be lost.

The fact that souls can be lost is the point I want to make. If the electrons of humanity are outside the pattern of their identity when that karmic hammer falls, that is the point when they are lost. When they are no longer tethered to God or to the fulfillment of his plan and his will, then when the karma falls and judgment comes, they are found in the not-self, in the not-universe. They do not exist in God. That which does not exist in God does not exist, because God is the only existence. So if they are not inside the matrix of God, where are they? They are nowhere. They don't exist.

According to this report Mother Mary is talking about the terrible things happening upon the earth today and the fact that many souls are being lost as the result of a liberal and progressive trend in the Catholic Church, of a theology that is not the theology of Jesus. She is deeply concerned. So we too should be concerned. We should realize that God has bestowed free will because the soul demanded free will, but the use of that free will can backfire, and by free will souls can be lost.

There are psychic organizations that claim to have received messages from the masters who will say that the second death[8] has been abolished. This is one of the false doctrines of the false hierarchy. They teach that by some miracle God overstepped his own Law—which he never does—and abolished the second death.

If the second death is abolished, it means that all the

rebellious ones, the fallen ones, and those who are completely outside of God can never cease to be. So God would be burdened with this creation he has made that has chosen to go against him yet cannot be destroyed.

The second death is an act of mercy. It means that at the end of opportunity for incarnations in Matter, at the total end of cycles, if your soul has not brought itself into alignment with the Spirit of God, with your own I AM Presence, at that point the soul is canceled out. It ceases to be. Your Christ Self merges with the universal Christ. Your I AM Presence merges with God. But your individuality is canceled out; it is no more. That is the second death. There is nothing left. It's an act of mercy because the soul is made of God's energy. God's energy is imprisoned in your soul until you liberate that energy.

God is not going to forever be crucified by mankind's rebellion. God demands liberation. If you don't join him in the will to be liberated, then at the conclusion of your cycles of opportunity, he cancels out the matrix of your soul and releases the energy, because God *is* that energy and God wills to be free. The matrix is broken, the clay vessel is shattered so the energy can return to the source. The energy out of which your soul was created is then repolarized and used as a part of the vast reservoir of energy in the Great Central Sun.

So beware of the false doctrine that the second death has been abolished. Do you know why it is given? It's very subtle. If you can convince people that there is no second death, why should they repent? It means they have eternity to go on experimenting with free will, to go on rebelling against God. It gives a carte blanche to the fallen ones and the Luciferians. As the serpent said to Eve, "You shall not surely die."[9] It's a little euphoria that the fallen ones, the

Luciferians, have tried to put over on the ones they are trying to get into their camp: "It doesn't matter what you do
because you'll just go on reincarnating and reincarnating
and reincarnating."

And it's not true. Otherwise why would it be written
in the Book of Revelation that the devil knoweth that his
time is short.[10] The time that is short is that allotment, that
opportunity, that cycle for him to repent. If by the end of
that cycle he has not repented, he will pass through the second death, as so many of the false hierarchy have already
done. So you can see the subtlety of one false teaching and
how it can alter the course of your attitude in life. But *you*
won't believe it because you understand the logic of the carnal mind in telling this lie.

Passing the Flame through One's Consciousness

This so-called overshadowing of the human consciousness by the Divine, when it is accompanied by the correct
use of the flames of God, will magnetize the sense of reality
that in the innocence of childhood was realized by many
men embodied on earth today. The passing of the flames
through one's consciousness above and below, that is, in the
conscious and subconscious minds, is a ritual that has been
practiced for centuries by devotees of the mind of God.

"Above" signifies the conscious mind; "below," the subconscious. "Above and below" also means in your upper
chakras and your lower chakras—those above the heart and
those below the heart. The chakras that are at the point of
the heart and above focus the energies of the plane of Spirit,
the masculine polarity. The chakras below the heart focus
the energies of the plane of Matter, the feminine polarity.

You have to sense yourself as porous to imagine a flame passing through you—almost have the sense of the different planes, of the flame being a spiritual fire that is penetrating a material grid, which you are.

Pause for a moment and visualize yourself as being porous. Visualize a cross section of a part of your being and see the atoms and molecules in your mind's eye and the pattern of the atom, which has so much open space in it. If you meditate upon that pattern, you can easily see how there is plenty of room for the flame to pass through.

The more you meditate on this pattern of the molecule or the atom, the more you can gain the mastery of time and space. That meditation is how the ascended masters, when they are yet unascended, learn how to pass through walls. Because in seeing it, you see that you yourself and the walls are both composed of these atoms. You just have to get yourself aligned so that your electrons don't bump into the electrons of the wall and you pass through the open spaces.

In the name of the Christ, in the name of Saint Germain, in the name of Almighty God, I invoke the roaring violet flame to pass through the four lower bodies, the soul, the soul blueprint, the seed of the soul, the seed of cosmic purpose. And I call for the liberation of the energies of God locked in subconscious matrices. Blaze forth the light! Burn through! Blaze the roaring violet flame! Blaze the roaring violet flame! Blaze the roaring violet flame!

In the name of the Christ, in the name of the Holy Spirit, in the name of Almighty God, I call for the light to descend now. I call for the flame of cosmic worth and the cosmic honor flame. Blaze through! Burn through each chakra! Blaze through the heart, the throat, the solar plexus, the third eye, the seat of the soul, the crown and the base of the spine! Blaze through! Burn through! Blaze the light of cosmic worth! Blaze the light of the violet flame and let God's will be done!

The light of God never fails! The light of God never fails! The light of God never fails, and the beloved mighty I AM Presence is that Light!

In the name of the Christ, I call directly to the heart of the Maha Chohan to seal each one in the Real Image. Seal the boundaries of each one's habitation. Seal the soul within the light of God according to the free will of each soul. Let it be done in answer to our call according to the will of God. So let that point of light, that grid and force-field now be the guardian action of the sacred fire of the tree of life and the real-eye image of each soul blueprint for the fulfillment of the law of cycles, for the fulfillment of the energy of each one.

In the name of the Father, the Mother, the Son and the Holy Spirit, I accept the fulfillment of the will of God. I accept the fulfillment of the wisdom of God. I accept the fulfillment of the love of God. Now let it be established on earth as it is in heaven. Now let the souls of these thy children return to the heart of the flame. Now let them be free from all impositions of the carnal mind. Roll back all satanic influence in the name of Jesus the Christ!

I challenge all that would stand between each one and the Real Image and the I AM Presence. Blaze forth the light! In the name of the living Christ, I challenge all opposition to the soul. Blaze forth the light! Blaze forth the light! Blaze forth the light and let God's will be done.

It is done, O God. We thank thee for answering our every call.

When you think about this ritual of the passing of the flame through consciousness, above and below, having been practiced for centuries, you wonder how it is that we just happened to find out about it. When I say "just found out," it can't be more than a few decades, if that, that we have known about passing the flames. When you think that every devotee—everyone who really surrenders enough of the self to come into alignment with the inner flame—has had the visitation of an angel or a master or someone who has apprised him of this ritual, we say to ourselves, "Where have we been?" We must not have surrendered enough quickly enough.

But remember, you could only have gotten the knowledge of the flame by that surrender. Therefore, you must confirm and affirm your own sense of cosmic worth, that deep within your being there is that surrender, there is that worth that has made you worthy to receive this teaching.

Then you start thinking of mankind who do not have the teaching. There are probably a million souls out there whose separation from the understanding of the flame passing through might be one little grain of karma that is left, one little tiny grain, because there are an awful lot of good people and devoted people in the world. And something, almost like a cataract on the eye, some little grain of substance is preventing them from clicking in to the awareness of the passing of the flame. Have you ever thought about the fact that, if they were educated according to this teaching, they themselves would rise up and cut out that mote in their eye?

Our Mission to Convey the Teaching

Therefore, the conveying of the teaching, the conveying of the understanding of the Law is your mission, our mission, because you never know when you might contact someone who by just a little understanding sees the whole thing and says, "That's it!" And you become the instrument bringing the cup of the elixir that can mean the difference in an individual's ascension in this embodiment. Aside from the joy of just experiencing that, think of the good karma you make for yourself by having initiated the spiral of a God-free being who is going to be a cosmic master someday. That's quite a few ramifications.

But what's so exciting about the ascended masters' teachings is that there are so many people who just need a little bit, a little nudge, a little rearrangement of the logic of the mind, and all of a sudden they are going to contact the inner guru and the passing of the flame and have the vision of the violet fire.

So nothing is more important than your studying the Law and the Word of God. Nothing can take its place, because it is your refined instrument that enables you to pass the teaching on to souls whom you meet. And every soul is different. It's like you are being the good physician of souls. Every soul has a different problem, a different malfunction, a different disease, and you have to know the specific formula of the Law that is going to reach that person, that is going to remove the obstruction to the flow in the chakras.

You'll learn by experience. There will be some trial and error. But the more you rely on the Holy Spirit when you go forth, the more you will find that you will say exactly the right words that are needed and no more. You can kill your patient with an overdose. Many a zealous apprentice of the Master Alchemist has done this. Truth is very, very powerful. It's the most potent medicine and a little goes a long, long way.

A simple statement of the Law is the alchemy to transform a life, to unlock that energy. And you can destroy the effectiveness of the medicine by giving an overdose. You cancel it out. You get the system so full of the medicine that the individual can't operate on his own steam to make it back to wholeness.

The medicine of truth is designed to be something that gets the organs of consciousness working again so the individual himself can, by his free will, be restored to the original blueprint. The problem we have in modern medicine today is that all the drugs and chemicals will perform the work in place of the body, so the body stops manufacturing its own enzymes and vitamins or the processes of the glands no longer function because this is accomplished artificially through drugs or stimulants or whatever it is.

The teaching of the Law cannot be a prop that replaces the flow of individuality—the flow of the flame that contains within itself this whole cosmic purpose. So you want to give enough truth to set in motion the inner law of a man's being, but not so much that it replaces the working out of its own destiny itself.

I once got all excited about juices—raw juices and all types of juices. I bought a juicer and I was trying out every juice in the book. I was probably consuming gallons of liquid a day. Then someone a little further along on the path of health politely told me that I was drowning myself in all this juice. And it really was true. There is only so much that the body or the consciousness can take.

Overcoming Undesirable Qualities

We trust that you will understand that each *Pearl* in our series is intended as a specific for one of the forms of the universal disease of unhappiness. For through creating in consciousness a correct understanding of the self and then outlining methods of overcoming the undesirable qualities that have been inextricably conjoined with the self, the symptoms of unhappiness can be alleviated.

This illustrates that the masters use the same method we just discussed. They like to use a specific. In looking at you as an individual, they will assess what is the key element in your consciousness that prevents you from uniting with your God Self. When you have applied to be a chela and the master looks at you, he will define what that element is. He will define priorities. He will define what is most calculated, most likely to destroy the soul itself if it is not arrested.

Then he puts you in situations in the world designed to shatter this aspect, designed to make you see through it and beyond it and to overcome it. And if you happen to be on the Path and consciously studying the writings of the masters, you will find in their writings a specific that is intended to shatter whatever portion of selfhood you have retained that is preventing you from merging with God's consciousness.

It is well to make the call to your Guru, to your Master, for the specific that is required for the one problem that is greatest in your life. So with your kind permission and according to your free will, I will make that invocation.

In the name of the Christ Self and according to the free will of each one, I call forth from the heart of the

*beloved master Hilarion, the specific for the problem
of each chela, that problem which presents itself as the
greatest hindrance, the greatest shadow, hiding the sun of
being.*

*I call forth the specific light, the specific teaching, the
specific essence of the sacred fire to be manifest consciously
and unconsciously. Blaze through the world of each one!
Anchor it now in the mental body, the emotional, the etheric and the physical bodies. So let that be brought to the
fore and to the attention of each chela in the twenty-four
hours ensuing from this hour. Let it come forth as inspiration from within, as teaching from without, as the light of
the I AM Presence, as the cleansing process and the power
of the secret rays and the violet flame.*

*So let it be done. So it is done. And we thank thee,
Almighty God.*

Holy Innocence

We plead, then, for a return to that state of holy innocence which has no need to defend itself against a host of
enemies. It is not that we would deactivate those defenses
that are necessary to the maintenance of one's spiritual life
or the protection of one's family. But we ask you to set
them aside temporarily during your periods of study in
order that your consciousness may enter once again into
the happy state it once knew before its nature was warped
by the opinions and verdicts of men that are based on a
hard view of the world and its people.

"Holy innocence." When I say that, does a ripple of
feeling go through you of a yearning to be in that state and
yet a feeling of being unworthy to be in that state, almost

as if we can't possibly get back there? That's how we feel in the world.

May we conclude this discussion with our decree 40.05, "Decree for Purity." May we stand in honor of the great master Serapis Bey, who restores us to our original purity, and in honor of beloved Hilarion, who presents us with the truth that sets us free.

> *Beloved Hilarion, by the action of Truth, we call for the saturation of each one's aura in the flame of living Truth, that in that flame and by the ray of that flame we might trace that ray back to the Source, the white-fire core of the holy innocence of the soul that we all once knew, that we all can have again because I AM. The I AM in me and in every one is worthy to receive the Christ and the purity of the flame.*
>
> *So let it be done in this hour of the consecration of these souls to the sacred fire.*

DECREE FOR PURITY

In the name of the beloved mighty victorious Presence of God, I AM in me, my very own beloved Holy Christ Self, Holy Christ Selves of all mankind, beloved Goddess of Purity, beloved Jesus the Christ, the beloved Elohim of Purity, beloved Lanello, the entire Spirit of the Great White Brotherhood and the World Mother, elemental life—fire, air, water, and earth! I decree:

> Open the door to Purity!
> Open the door to Purity!
> Let the breezes blow and trumpet Purity
> Over the sea and over the land;

Let men understand
The voice of Cosmic Christ command.

I come to open wide the way
That men without fear may ever say:
I AM the Purity of God
I AM the Purity of Love
I AM the Purity of Joy
I AM the Purity of Grace
I AM the Purity of Hope
I AM the Purity of Faith

And all that God can make of Joy
and Grace combined.

LORD, I AM worthy of thy Purity. I would have thy Purity surge through me in a great cosmic burst to remove from the screen of my mind, my thoughts, and my feelings every appearance of human vibratory action and all that is impure in substance, thought, or feeling.

Replace all that right now with the fullness of the Mind of Christ and the Mind of God, the manifest Power of the Resurrection Spirit and the Ascension Flame, that I may enter into the Holy of Holies of my being and find the power of transmutation taking place to free me forever from all discord that has ever manifested in my world.

I AM Purity in action here, I AM God's Purity established forever, and the stream of Light from the very heart of God that embodies all of his Purity is flowing through me and establishing round about me the power of invincible Cosmic Purity which can never be requalified by the human.

Here I AM, take me, O God of Purity. Assimilate me

and use me in the matrices of release for the mankind of earth. Let me not only invoke Purity for myself, but also let me invoke Purity for every part of Life. Let me not only invoke Purity for my family, but also for all the family of God neath the canopy of heaven.

I thank Thee and I accept this manifest right here and now with full Power as the Purity and authority of thy words spoken through me to produce the instantaneous manifestation of thy Cosmic Purity in my four lower bodies, intensifying hourly and accelerating those bodies until they attain the frequency of the Ascension Flame.

In the name of the Father, of the Mother, of the Son and of the Holy Spirit, it is finished. It is sealed in light. It is sealed in oneness. It is sealed in the Father-Mother God. So is the soul made whole.

January 20, 1975

CHAPTER SIX

THE DISCIPLINE OF THE FOUR LOWER BODIES

In the name of the Father, and of the Mother, of the Son and of the Holy Spirit, we call forth the light to burst forth in each heart as the diamond-shining mind of God. We call for the electrode of the jewel of Gautama Buddha to increase now and intensify in the brain of each one. Let the mind of God be in us. Let the mind of Christ be in us, beloved Jesus, beloved Kuthumi. Seal us now and let thy will be fulfilled as Above, so below. We thank thee and accept it done this hour in full power.

Commentary on Chapter 2, Part 2

The more you move on the path of wholeness or holiness, the more you become sensitive, not only to your body, but also to the body of God. Although I am functioning most of the time in the etheric plane, beyond the forcefield of the physical and free of the confinement of my body, I still find that the more light I have and the more I become aware of my body as the body of God, the more I become sensitive to its functions.

The concept of you being a body of light with a great deal of space in it is important. Then there is the concept of realizing that the higher you go in Spirit, the greater the mastery you have of matter. Now, the dark force would have it the other way—that the more spiritual you become, the less practical you are in matter. So the perversion of this level of attainment is seen in both Eastern and Western religions.

In India it is considered beneath the rank of a spiritual man to enter into politics or to work in the government because that is a much lower caste and shows a much greater density and a lack of overcoming personal pride and ambition. The ascended masters don't see it that way at all. The higher you go in spiritual attainment, the more you are concerned with your fellow man and the more you desire to serve.

In the West it is thought that a main characteristic of the Christian path is to embrace the poverty consciousness: the more spiritual you are, the less of this world's goods you should possess. Saint Germain did not follow this. When he was the Wonderman of Europe, he received a dispensation from the Karmic Board[1] to come as an ascended master and to appear in a physical body. And what did he do? He showed himself dressed in all of his velvets and his jewels, dispensing amethysts and all kinds of jewels, perfecting diamonds, and so forth.[2] The real point is *nonattachment*.

I want to tie this in with what we learn in psychology: how so many of our moods and so many aspects of our personality are based on our physical functions; how people (our parents, our teachers or we ourselves) have responded to them; and how, according to Freud, our own interplay with our desires and wants focalized in our physical body seems to have the power to determine our very fate on the planet.

When you move into the level of spiritual attainment, it goes the other way around. Your soul becomes the dominating force. Your soul uses the four vehicles, your four lower bodies, and it decides when and how these vehicles are going to be used. To be a well-balanced master, an unascended master—which you should strive to become; every one of you should determine to walk this earth as an unascended master—you need to have the correct integration with your physical body, to be in a place where it does not dominate you with any of its desires, any of its wants. Likewise your dominion must extend to the emotions, to the mind and to the memory.

The memory of the cells is to a great extent the programming of the cells. Your cells are programmed by your actions. As actions become habit, ritual and rote, the cells are programmed. The cells are like tiny computers; whatever you feed into them is what they are going to be. If you feed children candy, the cells are going to reach a point where they have a saturation of sugar. Then, when the sugar is metabolized, the cell is going to crave sugar again because it is programmed to have that sugar, and so you build a desire for candy. This programming takes place through the poling of the etheric and emotional bodies.

That which is done physically is in response to an idea or an image. For example, usually before you eat a piece of candy you have an image of it. You see that piece of chocolate, you have a craving for it, you decide you are going to eat it, and then you have to go and find it physically.

All cycles proceed through the four lower bodies according to God's energy moving around the clock. When the concept is formed, the mental idea moves into the emotional body and is clothed with desire. You have the image, you have the desire, and then you have to have the physical fulfillment, or you are going to experience frustration.

If you can't find that piece of chocolate, the local store doesn't have it, and you can't bring your body into contact with that chocolate, it remains an unfulfilled desire—it is hanging right at the point of precipitation. Say you have enough control of yourself to think, "Oh well, there is none in stock, so I'll go on my way." You forget about it, but you haven't transmuted it. That desire is still there. Sooner or later it is going to be fulfilled.

The desire pattern that you have built reflects into the etheric. Each time you have such a desire or a thought, it has its counterpart in the etheric body. Every cell in your being has a counterpart at the etheric level—you have etheric cells,

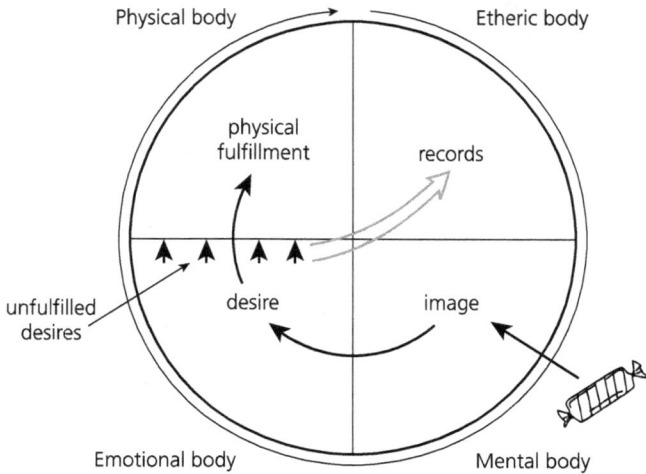

Seeing something creates a mental image, which is then clothed with desire in the emotional body. If the desire is not fulfilled physically, it remains in the emotional body. Since the emotional body and the etheric body are in polarity, this unfulfilled desire pattern then reflects into the etheric.

etheric organs, etheric everything—and this registers in the aura so that you can read someone's health matrix by their aura. If this desire is unfulfilled again and again, but it is no longer at the surface of your consciousness, it falls back into the etheric plane or the subconscious as an unfulfilled desire.

There are all kinds of things in this world that we desire and that we don't fulfill because we have self-control. But there are records of those desires and they persist. What I am getting at in this concept of polarity of the physical-mental and emotional-etheric is that there is an interplay of energy between these bodies, and you can use this awareness to program yourself to be what you want to be.

Programming the Four Lower Bodies

As we learn in psychology, we are being programmed from the moment we are born by how our parents treat us, how they respond to our needs, how hard we have to work to get what we want, whether or not we are continually condemned or continually protected. All of this is a certain programming, but it is a programming of the four lower bodies. Let's say, symbolically, the soul is somewhere in the center of the four lower bodies, so to a certain extent the surface of the soul is going to be influenced by this new programming.

But when you take on a new body, the conception occurs on the three o'clock line. You bring with you your old etheric body, which is the body that remains intact between embodiments. There is a certain veil drawn over the previous mental and emotional bodies. Depending on the attainment of the soul, these may be retained, but generally there is a definite decay rate in those bodies and they are formed anew in the next embodiment based on the patterns in the etheric body. The period of nine months gestation is three months in each quadrant for the anchoring of these patterns in the mental body and the emotional body and into the physical form. Then birth occurs at the twelve o'clock line and you start plotting your cycles.

So even before you are born, you are already programmed. You have programmed yourself for many incarnations. And all of this programming of every cell and every pattern of your being is in the etheric body. The programming is so intense that the very features of your face, the size of your legs, your thighs, how your toes are formed, your elbows and everything else is in that etheric body. That is how you can have almost the same face today that you had

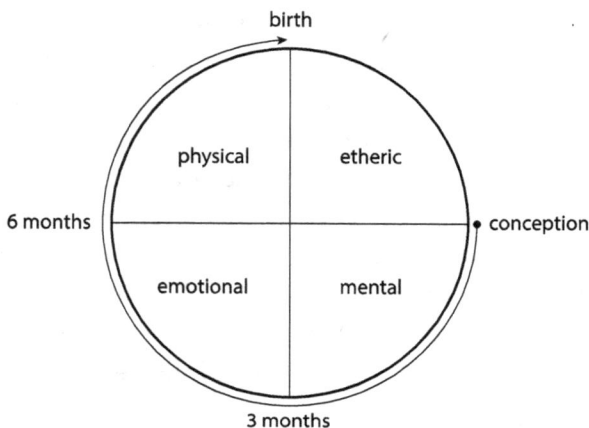

birth

physical   etheric

6 months ——————————————•— conception

emotional   mental

3 months

The conception of a soul in a new embodiment takes place on the 3 o'clock line, since the etheric body carries over intact from one lifetime to the next. The new mental, emotional and physical bodies are formed following the patterns stored in the etheric body. This process takes nine months, one month for each line of the clock from the 3 o'clock to the 12 o'clock, three months for each of the remaining four lower bodies.

ten thousand years ago in a previous incarnation. That is how you can pick yourself out in the encyclopedia, because there you are; there is your electronic pattern in your electronic belt and in your etheric body.

We have to understand this programming. The programming of the soul came in every incarnation all the way back to the first one, and even before that in the formation of the layers of the causal body when the soul was journeying around the I AM Presence gathering skeins of light for its identity and for its thrust into Matter.[3] So we can hardly be confined to a psychology which starts analyzing us at birth. Obviously this is just a pinprick of our existence.

It is good to bear this in mind; it is very important to know what we know. I'm thrilled and excited about the concepts that are being brought forth, and especially for the incoming avatars and children who must be trained and must not be overindulged by us because the latest layer of programming on the soul is going to have a key influence.

In any case, when you look at life from the standpoint of wanting to be an initiate of the sacred fire and a chela of the ascended masters, it's an entirely different viewpoint than wanting to be a well-adjusted ego in a human body, balancing all of the human wants and desire patterns and being successful and well adapted in this plane. Fulfilling a certain amount of that is necessary. The misfits and those who have psychological imbalances who come to the feet of the masters have very little to offer. They have to be remade and reborn and adjust themselves in this world before they can really be responsible chelas on the Path.

The ideal in this world is to meet the needs of the four lower bodies just to the point where they have enough energy to sustain their function with a sense of abundance, but not a sense of lavishness or luxury, and to understand that the principal thing is the projecting forth of soul consciousness and soul awareness. In order to do this, a certain amount of discipline is necessary to keep the four lower bodies in line.

So the more you give in to the demands of your four lower bodies, the more they will demand. Your four lower bodies are your four children. How you treat those four lower bodies, whether you spoil them, whether you are strict with them, will determine how free your soul is to move.

I happen to have four children. And I am very aware of the fact that the first child I had was the outpicturing of Mark's and my etheric consciousness; the second, our mental; the third, our emotional; the fourth, our physical. I can see this so clearly. Your children will be exactly what you allow your four lower bodies to be. If you limit your four lower bodies and their expression of the Christ, you will probably limit and frustrate your children. If from early life you have learned to discipline your consciousness, that discipline will carry over. And when a soul is in your womb, this incoming child will have impressed upon its soul the momentums of your own four lower bodies as well as the momentums of your causal body.

The four lower bodies are receptacles for the influences and the vibrations of your causal body. So the more you can make your four lower bodies fitting chalices for your I AM Presence, your causal body and your Christ Self, the more you can be an unascended master walking the earth.

Uses and Misuses of the Etheric Body

Let me give you examples of how you indulge the four lower bodies. The memory body is indulged by continually revolving past records of the human scene. I was noticing, as I was giving the rosary this morning, that various records of things that happened yesterday or the day before, problems with people, were coming in front of my mind. I had the choice to indulge myself in thinking about these things or to strictly shut them out and visualize Mother Mary, rivet my attention on my vision of her, listen to the Bible verses, and say the Hail Mary with devotion and love.

If I chose to allow myself to indulge in this thought gazing and this revolving, there would be no flow of light. The radiation would be cut off because I would be attuning to my own etheric body, not to Mother Mary. The projections were on the line of Pisces-Virgo substance—fear, sense of injustice, doubt, idling, anxiety. "What's going to happen with this situation? What's going to happen with this lawsuit? What is going to happen with that thing?"

And I said to myself, "I am not going to indulge my

etheric body. I am not going to give power to these things. This is my time with Mother Mary and I am going to have my communion with her from my soul, my chakras, my heart flame. And everything else is going to be shut out." So I made my attunement, held my visualization, beheld the Blessed Virgin before me, gave the rosary, and shut out all the rest. While I was giving it, of course, showers and showers of light and energy and a complete flow of the Macrocosm-microcosm was established. That happens over a figure-eight pattern.

By giving the rosary with absolute attention on your I AM Presence and on Mother Mary, all of her energy can then cycle into the chalice of your being because you have a cup, you have a matrix that can magnetize it and receive it.

Things equal to the same thing are equal to each other. If you are seeing Mother Mary in all of your four lower bodies, she then will fill the whole of your four lower bodies with herself, and you actually become Mother Mary. You are Mother Mary for as long as your attention is on her and nowhere else—a figure eight, as Above so below. Mother Mary's energy descends, cycles through your four lower bodies, and ascends back to her. She receives it, it is transmuted, and it goes into your causal body. The Blessed Mother then uses your energy for blessing all life.

This is the flow that should be taking place while you are decreeing. You are building a giant forcefield of energy below that keeps on building until you have a veritable causal body anchored through your chakras, and the ascended masters receive your energies on high. So you are actually ascending. You are ascending to the plane of the ascended masters and they are descending to the plane of mankind. The meeting ground is your Christ consciousness, and that is where heaven and earth meet—at the point of contact with the Christ mind, which is the nexus of the figure eight.

So revolving past records is an example of indulgence of the etheric body. It is a choice—to indulge or not to indulge. This is your choice. Often it comes when you go to sleep at night and you are really supposed to be rising into your higher etheric body because your soul is departing from your lower bodies. Or it may come when you are returning to your body when you first wake up in the morning.

Constantly going over these records becomes a habit pattern in the etheric body, and you go over and over and over the records. This revolving flows back and forth with the emotions. It is in constant polarity with the emotions. So the desire body, with its anxiety, excitement and nervousness, keeps feeding the records, making them more intense, getting you all excited about these records. Then it goes into lower and lower mental images where you imagine somebody is persecuting you or this terrible person is doing this thing to you. It can get lower and lower in the mental plane and finally it cycles into the physical with disturbances in the physical body, such as being all tightened up and anxious, or having headaches, or nervous tension, or what have you.

There are people who come to me with problems who can never get off this track of revolving in the etheric body. When things come before you, they have to be put into the flame. If they come before you sixteen times, you have an etheric body problem. You've got to master that problem because it is going to affect all of your cycles. You cannot let the subconscious, the records of the past, the electronic belt dominate your vision. If you are doing so, you have a spoiled brat of an etheric body and it is your own fault for not taking dominion.

When people get into old age, this becomes a major problem because they are cycling back to their records. They are preparing to go on and it's like a second childhood. In early infancy, from birth to age three, you are in your etheric cycle, in your etheric body. You can return to that in old age because in old age your Christ Self attempts to accelerate the transmutation of the records in your electronic belt and your subconscious.

So old people sit around, talk about the good old days and what they did when they were in their twenties. They have a decay rate in the mental, emotional and physical bodies, and they can no longer experience the vitality they had when they were young. They live in their etheric body; they live through their records. And they live through watching other people do the things that they used to do. They get extremely sentimental because their etheric body poles with their emotional body; they cry when they hear the good old songs, and so on.

These people are going to be doing the same thing when they are out of the body on the astral plane. That constant revolving of the etheric cycles is what is known as purgatory or hell because that is all you do when you are there. You go into the astral plane and you relive a thousand times a thousand times all of the happenings of your life—especially the terrible things you did, because the demons torment you by amplifying and energizing your records and playing them before you and making you see yourself as this terrible person who fifty years ago, when you were sixteen, did this awful thing that has been bothering you ever since.

That is where the whole concept of hellfire, damnation and eternal punishment comes from. Can you imagine a sacred fire that took eternity to burn you? If the sacred fire is the sacred fire and you are going into this hell that is supposedly composed of fire, you should be dissolved in a second if God is the God that I think he is. God is not going to take eternity to burn up this form. The physical form can be burned within an hour or two.

The whole concept of burning eternally in hell is manufactured by the dark force. They get a hold on your soul, your astral body, your mental body. They get you out of your physical body on the astral plane, and they keep on having you revolve and revolve and revolve. And you never get out of the astral plane. It seems to you as though you are there an eternity before your next incarnation. And that is your karma for self-indulgence, indulging that etheric body.

The first lesson we have to learn on the Path is that the force, the fallen ones, the entities, will look into our etheric bodies, study our records systematically, make a graph of our past karma and our past incarnations. Then at the right cycles of the cosmic clock, according to the moon and the sun, they play before us the records of the two o'clock line, the three, the four, the five—the whole electronic belt.

This will come as a parade at certain times of day, many times in the morning, many times at night, and various other cycles. It parades before you, and pretty soon your consciousness becomes a grid and forcefield of the tromping and the galloping of the beasts of the astral plane. Every day they make their regular gallop across your consciousness. Every day you sit there aghast looking at all these things and thinking about all these terrible things that either happened or are going to happen to you—right at the same time you are mouthing the decrees.

You are sitting there decreeing, but you are looking at this whole scene. You wonder why you don't feel any radiation, so you do more and more decrees. You might spend hours decreeing, but you never really plug in because you aren't holding the immaculate concept; you're not really riveting your gaze on the masters, the Christ consciousness. And so the flow of the figure-eight is not taking place. You must not let the ascended masters' teachings descend into being rote where you sit and decree with your mouth but your mind is in the sewer.

Visualization and Thoughtforms

The discipline of your four children is the whole thing. Once you discipline the revolving in the memory body, you are going to shut that off. Then you are going to use your mind, your mental thoughts to formulate the image of the Christ. The masters help us do this with thoughtforms. It's important to have a thoughtform that you see. You put this in your mental body, it's anchored there and it becomes an image that you think of, that you gaze upon. If you find it difficult to visualize during a decree session, you should collect thoughtforms in your decree book. When you are going to give decrees to Archangel Michael, have a thoughtform on the opposite page.

I hear from people that when they close their eyes and give some decrees, they can't remember what that thoughtform looked like. People tell me all the time, "If I am supposed to be visualizing, I should be able to look at something, close my eyes and see it, but I can't." I have a letter on my desk to that effect: "What should I do? I can't visualize."

Lots of people can't visualize. Don't worry about it. Put effective aids for visualization in your decree book. Decree so many repetitions, and if you have lost the matrix of it, open your eyes, look at it, decree while you are looking at it.

Reinforce images in your mental body, reinforce the matrices of perfect patterns—pictures of the masters, perfect geometric thoughtforms, a rose, pictures you cut out of a magazine of irises in the springtime, or orchids, or any of these lovely thoughtforms. They are matrices of perfection; they hold light. When you gaze upon them, you are at the level of the high etheric plane or ascended master octave because that is the matrix.

Your mental body has to be filled with perfect images. Likewise the imperfect images have to be flushed out. Where do the imperfect images lodge? Where do they come from? They come from your intestines. That is why Jesus fasted forty days and forty nights. The incrustations in the walls of the intestines are where the records of the astral body and the mental body are anchored in the physical. That is why when you start to fast and you start flushing them out, you have headaches, you get real thick in your head, you can't think. You take an enema and all of a sudden your head is clear—you can't imagine how clear you are or why—because your intestines were holding the patterns of imperfect images.

Desire and Devotion

Every once in a while I will go to a movie because Mark tells me to. It will show me something about what is going on in the world that I am supposed to know about. For the first time in about six months I went to a movie, *The Odessa File*, which is about the secret police, the SS and the Nazis who were in the Second World War. There was a great deal of violence in that movie. And I noticed how, even though I did not look at the violence, the records of the experience with that movie stayed in my consciousness for maybe three days after I saw it, despite the mastery I have.

It is so important to not allow your desire momentum or your mental body to be spoiled to the extent that it constantly needs the stimulation of loud music, violent movies, something always blaring at you. This is the insecurity of our modern society; people leave the radio going night and day. They constantly have to have some level of noise stimulating their emotions. It is just like eating sugar to have this bad music going all the time. If you constantly have to look at television or have the radio on and are unable to be quiet, that is the spoiling of your mental and emotional bodies.

The emotional body can become programmed to needing violence or some kind of drama or some kind of soap opera experience—this melodrama of getting into the sympathies of the human consciousness. Periodically and regularly your emotional body will make a demand for this kind of an experience. So you have to discipline it. You have to say to yourself, "I have a vehicle and this vehicle is intended to be a chalice for the feelings of God. I am going to fill it with the feelings of God. I am going to flush out all this blaring of the astral plane, and I am going to discipline that emotional body so it becomes God's energy in *motion* (emotion)." The emotional body is where you have flow. The enormous flow of the waterfall of God's consciousness flowing through you comes through the perfected chalice of the emotions.

My experience of the figure eight is multiplied a thousand times by the image of Mother Mary that I have placed on the right side of my internal cosmic clock as a mental memory. It's an etheric memory because memory is etched in fire. In my mind, I see this very vivid image of Mother Mary.

So it is both etheric and mental. It's hard to separate a memory from a thought sometimes; they are separate but they are one. It's the fire that gets clothed upon with the air.*

So I have a memory somewhere in my being of seeing Mother Mary. I call forth this memory and I make it very concrete by making it a mental image. I put it before me, I give my Hail Mary and I visualize Mother Mary before me. As I visualize her, it's a matrix which she can actually come through, step through and appear to me. Her electronic presence will be drawn to that image that I have thrust into the etheric-mental plane.

When I am sitting there and I put the full weight of my desire body behind it, here is what happens. The desire becomes the devotion to Mother Mary, the feeling of love for her. The feeling of love for her cycles into the etheric body and recalls memories of experiences with her on inner levels, because the etheric-emotional energies pole and are always cycling back and forth. It is an oscillating pattern, back and forth with the speed of light. I am sitting there in this ecstasy, this joy of communion with Mother Mary—all of my energies in motion, all of my desire body caught up in the love of the Divine Mother.

This becomes a tremendous gigantic sweeping action because the desire body has the most energy and the greatest ability to have more energy. So the more love I feel for Mother Mary, the more the flow from Mother Mary is activated and intensified, and it becomes a cycle that never ends. The flow begets flow until my desire body becomes so large and filled with Mother Mary that the entire earth and all of its evolutions are contained within it. You can become as large as the planet in an instant, and it is based on your devotion.

*See p. 366.

Now, if I didn't have any devotion, praying would just be a mental-etheric cycling—da-da-da-da-da-da-da. That's about how the rosary sounds when you hear it on the radio in the morning from the Catholic Church as I heard it when I was growing up. There is just the sound of counting the beads and rattling off the prayers. And what is happening is the people are thinking about their work, they are thinking about other things. They are not entering into the feeling. So the whole matrix stops at the mental plane, and there is just a trickle going around on the figure eight.

The way we are going to make that mental thought and that etheric memory very tangible in this world is to clothe it with feeling, the feeling of God. When it is truly clothed with feeling, it is ready to burst and ultimately it becomes physical.

It's because people have prayed to Mother Mary for centuries—and many of them with devotion—that she has been the one who has appeared. Her image has been seen by the physical eye because enough feeling energy has been given by mankind to precipitate that image, and this is because the rosary as a form of prayer has been given by millions through the centuries.

Mother Mary's recent appearances are a part of what the masters have said: that she would be appearing in the West; that she would be the ascended master who would step through the veil and pave the way for the other ascended masters to step through the veil. This is possible because of the tremendous devotion of the people.

Discipline in the Mental Body

The spoiling of your mental body occurs when you use it to continually study and acquire mental concepts, mental thoughts—in other words, being the perpetual student, the person who is continually stimulated mentally by the knowledge of this world. These people are constantly reading and accumulating mental knowledge. Yet Paul has said that the wisdom of this world is foolishness with God.[4]

What is the mental body for? The mental body is for the mind that was in Christ Jesus to express.[5] It is the chalice for the mind of God. The greatest masters who have ever lived have always had an instantaneous knowledge about anything in the universe that they wanted to know through the mind of God that was in Christ Jesus.

That is not saying that you should not be educated or educate your children. A certain amount of education is necessary, whether you decide to complete high school and get a degree in some kind of trade or a business skill, or whether you want to go on to college. It is necessary to be educated to function in this world.

How you are educated and how you allow your mental body to function is what is important. You have to develop a sense of listening. It is a state of listening grace wherein you expect the mind of God to mesh with your own and to teach you, acknowledging God as your teacher and expecting to be God-taught.

When I was in college, I had the experience of the professor speaking before me and God speaking within me on the identical subject. I would keep two columns in my notebook: what the professor was saying, and how God was interpreting it to me.

The professor would ask a question and I would have already received the answer from God before the rest of the class even heard or could grapple with the question. I would raise my hand and give the answer. It would be like a perfect dictation. And the faculty and students (these were adults in college when I was taking courses in religions with Protestant ministers) would be astounded at the clarity, the perfection of the wording and how the subject was thoroughly covered. There would be a stillness in the room as everyone would contemplate the answer. I was offered an opportunity to work under this professor to get my doctorate, and I was still an undergraduate student.

In any case, this experience can be yours, but you have to attune for it, you have to prepare for it, you have to make it your goal. The way to make it your goal is to maintain the state of listening grace. It is the discipline of the mind where the mind does not get all caught up in following the patterns of the intellect, but you realize that the patterns of the intellect and the teachings of this world are just so many tracks, like the mazes in books of puzzles.

There are many tracks in the mental body. What you have to do is make the track like an airstrip for the airplane of your mind. You follow this track as long as you need to follow it in order to get a momentum. And suddenly you've been on that track long enough and you are airborne; you are into the plane of the mind of God. You have enough information, enough understanding of a certain subject or something you are into, and you click into the mind of God. All of a sudden that which was linear becomes spherical and you have an awareness of all sides of this question rather than just the linear understanding of which the lower mental body is capable. That is all it can do on its own.

You have to be constantly ready to go up in that plane. And of course, going up like a rocket, you are actually breaking with the gravitational pull of the lower mental body, which is really the forcefield of the carnal mind. You see people in this world whose mental bodies are spoiled brats. As Paul said, "Ever learning but never coming to the knowledge of the truth."[6] They are always learning because that is where their energy is.

As a cross section of society, the people who have spoiled mental bodies have to get out of the mental body sometime. And they pole with the physical body. You will find that the average intellectual is quite sensual because his intellectual pursuits will flip over into physical indulgences. Therefore, it's always the intellectual crowd that has the rationalization for free love, self-indulgence and the gratification of all phases of the senses.

Lucifer is the intellectual par excellence on the three o'clock line, if you want to even use that word for him. He is the ace in the hole for the perversion of the Christ mind. His intellectualism has fostered total self-indulgence in the physical plane, total selfishness on the ten o'clock line. The philosophy of the Luciferians is quite complex, and all of it is used for the justification, the rationalization of complete and total indulgence in the physical.

Indulgence in the physical completely and totally spends the energy of the Christ and the energies of the chakras so that there is nothing left. You will find that the intellectual who has a spoiled brat for a mental body usually has a spoiled brat physical body. The intellectuals are the ones who are in charge of our educational systems today because they are the ones who are the most highly developed mentally. They are the ones who are fostering sex education in the first grade, the second grade, and free love and experimentation, and so forth.

What's happening is they have so much energy tied up in the mental body that they look down upon anyone who has feelings or desires because that is beneath them. You can't be emotional or have feelings if you are a hard-headed intellectual. But that energy has to go somewhere because it goes round and round and round in the mental body and becomes a frustration. So the energy sort of skips through the desire body and is not indulged in. It then lands in the physical.

One really devastating thing you always notice about intellectuals is that they have such corny intellectual jokes. And they will sit and titter over these little jokes that they make with each other. I am talking about people who are the presidents of corporations and banks, and people in high echelons of society. They will get in their board meetings or in their caucuses and someone will make this little remark and they will all go "Hee, hee, hee, hee," and laugh together.

Believe me, I have been around these people. And it's a substitute for the real feeling of God, for the real joy, the real expertise and the humor of God which comes through the violet-flame angels. These jokes are usually nasty and filthy. They are so limited and are almost always based on the lower mental body that has never, not once in its existence, ever come out from the maze of the intellect, soared into the consciousness of God and received one idea from God himself.

Can you imagine people in this world today who have not had the joy of being visited by the angel of the Lord mentally and received a beautiful thoughtform, an idea that came straight from God? If I couldn't hear the mind of God speaking to me, existence would be just completely devastating and purposeless.

Yet there are people who go lifetime after lifetime tying

up all their energy in the mental body and the physical, and they never ever have a thought from the mind of God. They are perverts. They have psychological problems. They have abnormal psychology, yet they dominate the planet. In Theosophy, the masters K.H. and M.* made the statement that there is nothing more dangerous than the highly educated carnal mind—the highly trained, highly skilled carnal mind where the mental body is trained to the exclusion of the Christ.

Indulging the Emotional Body

Next you come to the spoiling of the emotions. And the emotions are definitely tied up with the etheric body and etheric memory, with weeping and getting excited, re-experiencing what's been experienced before, and becoming emotional about every passing scene.

It is all right to have feelings, zeal, fervor and the intensity of the light within you. I played El Morya's dictation from the recent conference for an intellectual, and it just about wiped him out. He was freaked out for at least three days. He couldn't believe that someone who was an ascended being could pack that much feeling, fervor and zeal into a dictation.

Morya was really excited about his lost chelas in that dictation, and this intellectual that I played it for happens to be one of his lost chelas. Now, he had asked to hear a dictation. I didn't force it on him. But it so panicked him that he had to find a comparison for it. And all he could think of was mob psychology in the concept of Hitler controlling the people with emotions.

Now, there aren't any generalizations, and I am not

*Kuthumi and El Morya

trying to put everybody into a sack of statistics. I am just trying to show you earmarks so you can have a basis on which to study people and to know what's functioning.

People have a dominant body that they center in, and whatever body they center in is going to have a polarity. If it is the emotional, they are going to pole with their etheric. If it is the etheric, they are going to pole with the emotional. If they are centered in the mental, you watch out for the physical—physical violence as well as physical indulgences. If they are very physical, they may or may not get to the point of the mental. There are people who are so physical that the energy never gets up to activate the chakras of the brain, and they are the lowest order of evolution.

The spoiled emotional body is the body that is pulled by every little story, every little problem, every little piece of gossip, everything that anybody in the neighborhood is going through. They get all wrapped up in it, and they can't hold the matrix of perfection that comes from the memory of God. And without being able to hold that immaculate concept, they are just always in a sea—a cork bobbing on the sea—and they can never hold onto anything because they are just so involved in emotions.

The Alchemy of Healing

I am going to give you another example of what happens when you meditate on a matrix. I woke up one morning while I was traveling and I had a headache—a very violent headache. I wasn't about to indulge this headache. I had a lot of joy in my heart and a lot of love for God. I started thinking about Serapis Bey and the great opportunity that he was giving to mankind, and the joy of his retreat, and the joy of being a candidate for the ascension, and how wonderful it was that so many people were becoming candidates. I was really working up a tremendous joy by this memory of Serapis Bey.

So here was the interplay. My etheric body, my soul, had just come back from the inner planes. I was integrating with my form, more at the level of the etheric and the emotional first before I was really into the physical. I was very joyous and I was seeing Serapis in his retreat. I was seeing the action of the flame and the initiates there and it made me so happy.

Then all of a sudden I would remember that I had a headache, and there would be this pain, this sharp pain going through my head. Then I would start thinking about the headache and the headache would get worse. Then I would think back and flash back to the image of Serapis in his retreat. I found that as long as I had my attention riveted on Serapis Bey, I had no headache. As soon as I would let go and think about the headache, I would have the headache.

It was just like Peter walking on the water with Jesus.[7] As soon as he took his attention off the Christ—as soon as he lost confidence in the mastery of Christ—he began to sink. Jesus reached for his hand and reestablished the flow of energy between them. Saint Germain explains this in his alchemy course.

I had the identical experience. As soon as I took my attention off Serapis, I was aware of the pain. Well, it really got exciting because I could see this was definitely a laboratory experiment that I was experiencing so I could tell you and everyone else. And I came to the conclusion of how powerful the immaculate concept is. I am certain I could have been thinking of any master, any retreat or my Christ Self, but it was the combination of pure feelings and pure memory cycling through me as I lay in my physical body—and right then it was the energy of Serapis, the energy of the ascension flame.

It took a while for the work to be completed, for that energy to be sufficient to clear my physical body of whatever the toxins were that perhaps had accumulated in my head, or to clear whatever the attack was by astral entities. Probably as I was passing through the octaves and coming back to earth, I had an encounter on the astral plane with certain hordes of darkness who were still projecting energy at the focal point of my mind. By fixing my attention on Serapis and the flame, I stayed long enough in the etheric so that when I started functioning through my mental body and my physical, the headache was gone. This experience shows you that it does take time and space for healing.

I remember learning of that when I read the books of Saint Germain, the three in the series by Godfré Ray King—*Unveiled Mysteries, The Magic Presence* and *The I AM Discourses*—which I recommend for your reading.[8] There was a healing that took place in France where Saint Germain put his hands on a girl who was ill. He had to put his hands on this girl for a period of five minutes.[9] In reading this, I was extremely impressed by the fact that an ascended master, in order to heal an unascended being, had to take time, had to leave his hands on this person for this period of time, because the way I imagined it, any ascended master could heal anybody of anything instantaneously.

We have this image because of the Bible accounts where Jesus healed people instantaneously. Well, that's what it appeared to be in terms of healings by Jesus, but we don't know what preparation went into his healings. We have no right to judge how he healed. He never told us how he

healed. The fact that the miracle happened when he pro-
nounced the words doesn't mean that he wasn't moving into
action for hours before it happened.

The alchemy of healing is the concept of energy flow
through the four lower bodies going around the clock, the
flow "As above, so below" going over a figure-eight pattern.
In that experience, Saint Germain was anchoring the energy
of his causal body in the girl's form. As that energy cycled
through her four lower bodies, it flushed out and transmuted impurities and imperfections.

Encrustations of thousands of years need to be flushed
out gradually. If the master infuses the light all at once to
dissolve the darkness, he could destroy the four lower bodies by short-circuiting them, by overloading the circuit, just
like when you touch an electrical charge of so many volts.
The body can't take it all at once. There is the time-space
factor where the holding of the hands above the chakras
or on the body in physical contact is necessary for healing.
It's necessary to establish the flow and to increase that flow
until a balance is brought about.

The Physical Body

A spoiled physical body comes about by lack of regularity of meals. You see children who eat all day long. They
never have a meal. Their parents aren't organized enough to
set the table. The children go to the refrigerator and they eat
a peanut butter sandwich. An hour later they make themselves a chocolate drink. Next thing they are munching on
pretzels, then it's peanuts, then it's hot dogs. Lunch time
comes and they eat half a hamburger. It goes on all day long.

I know this because I babysat in homes where this went
on all the time, much to my dismay. I couldn't believe that

this was a pattern, but it is a pattern in many people's homes. And what happens is there is never the balance of the body being filled and then the assimilation, the digestion, the passing through, and then the starting all over again. The body never experiences the yin and the yang of being filled and then being emptied, and being completely empty in order to be the magnet to be filled.

This occurs where the parents, or you as the parent of your physical body, continually give in to all indulgences. Every time your physical body has a want, you give in to it. It gets restless, so you leave what you are doing and you go outside to play or do something. There is no control, no making that body do what you want it to do.

I have had various periods in my life where I decided that this body was my instrument. It was going to do what I wanted it to do and not what it wanted to do. One of those experiences was the year in which I was working night and day on *Climb the Highest Mountain*. To finish that volume took fourteen to sixteen hours a day for twelve months. During that period of time I sat in the tower at the Retreat of the Resurrection Spiral* and worked. All my meals were brought to me. I came out a few times a day, and I set up a program where for a half hour in the late afternoon I would jog around the property. And that was that—summer, winter or whatever it was—because that book had to get out.

I can tell you that the craving of my physical body to either go out in the sun or have exercise or do something different reached tremendous proportions. It was a real temptation. But I cracked the whip and I said, "Body, you are going to be my slave, you are going to work for me. You are going to do what I tell you to do and nothing else." I would

*The headquarters of The Summit Lighthouse at that time, in Colorado Springs.

talk to it and discipline it like a child, just as you give your child a scolding. By the time I got through bawling it out, I even believed it, and then I would be good for another ten hours or whatever it was. It was a very interesting thing.

During that period I also gave birth to my fourth child. I was aware of nourishing the child, and everything else involved in the pregnancy. But I found in that birth that during the twenty-four hours of the delivery—where I used the methods of natural childbirth for the first time—I had absolute control of my physical body, which I had not had in my three previous deliveries.

To me it was a major victory of total, absolute control, of releasing that baby when I was ready to release that baby, and that baby and the muscles and organs of my body not taking me over, but me directing them from the level of the Christ. I said to myself after that twenty-four hours of difficult labor and yet being in total God-control, if one can do this, if one can prove that one can master one's physical form, one can do anything.

You can master any of your bodies if you can master the physical, because the physical is the densest body and the physical atoms respond the least quickly. For example, you can change your mind in a second. But try changing the length of your big toe or your finger—you'll probably wait for another incarnation before the matrix is shattered and becomes changed. So if you can master your physical body, make it do what you want it to do when you want it to do it, you really have a sense of mastery, a sense of walking the earth with your head held high knowing "I am not dominated by these four lower bodies."

You ought to try it just through fasting or try regulating

your intake of food if you feel that you constantly eat too much, then you get drowsy after you eat or you get a stomachache. Sometimes you can feel like the wolf who ate the sheep and the mother sheep came home and found the wolf snoozing under the tree. He was so full of the sheep that he hadn't even left the scene of his crime. So the mama sheep cuts his tummy open and all the sheep come out. Then she fills his tummy with rocks and sews him back up again. When the wolf wakes up he can't move, he is just too heavy.

If you ever feel like that wolf after you get through eating and you have eaten too much, you definitely have a spoiled physical body. And your mental body is probably spoiled along with it because it is the mind that really controls what the physical body is doing.

With all indulgences of the five senses, indulgences of the lower chakras, it is not a question of desire or need or frustration. It is a question of how much you are going to let your four lower bodies get away with. How much energy are you going to give them that is going to detract from your mission, from your soul, from your Christ consciousness? That's a very different situation than looking at it from the standpoint of Freud or the Luciferians, of satiation of every want, every need, every desire.

When you are a chela on the Path, you are looking to see to it that your four lower bodies get exactly what they need and no more—the minimum. But as soon as it goes below the minimum need, you definitely start having psychological problems.

Balance in Life

The new ego that is born, that comes into the world—the new identity—has to be integrated in the four lower bodies.

It can't be pushed or rushed; it has to have its natural cycles of unfoldment. There are certain things that have to be fulfilled in a life. If you allow these things to be fulfilled, you are giving your four lower bodies exactly what they need. But don't overindulge.

Take, for instance, the tendency or the desire to procreate. Childbearing is very important in a woman, the need to fulfill the feminine ray by giving birth to a child. Yet certain religions have said that it is wrong to have sex and therefore it is wrong to have children. They have tried to cut this desire completely off.

The key is balance and the middle way. That is what is taught in the path of Hinduism. There is a time of life to be physical, then there is a time of life for the emotions, for the mind and a time for the etheric. People start life in the physical, then go through the feelings and through mental development. Old age is the etheric cycle when you go into the plane of Spirit, the contemplative life. So there is a time to be a householder, a time to bring forth children. There is a time to go to college, a time for mental development. And then there is a time to withdraw for contemplation.

It's necessary to pursue balance, to let our children and the children that we call our four lower bodies have contact with this plane of Matter to the extent that certain basic needs and drives are fulfilled—because having tasted these things, we can then give them up. Having not tasted them, there is always the wonder, "What was it like? What would it have been?"

I am not advocating experiments in all forms of sex or sexual perversion in order to find out what it's like. But for example, when we are raising children, we should not think that we are going to bring them up to be little saints or little angels by not allowing them to ride their bikes, or by having a fit when they get in a fight with someone at school, and by trying to make them live some kind of existence in a vacuum or an incubator where they don't come to grips with the world and with life and experience some of the world's knocks on their own.

This approach can lead to problems later in life. For example, psychologists have said that where there is an inability to read, where people have reading problems in the fifth or sixth grade or even later in high school, these individuals have skipped a stage, and this has resulted in imbalances in the brain and a lack of development.

They work on such things with prison inmates. I saw a program about this where people were working with inmates who had a very low self-image—they never got out of the seventh or eighth grade, their IQ is low, they can't read, they're not adjusted in society—so they took the way of breaking the law and being a criminal, partly to get attention, partly because of this very low self-image. They put these inmates on the floor and made them crawl so many hours a day because crawling is a stage whereby you balance both sides of the brain for mental development, and it is a balancing of all your four lower bodies.

People of lower income and lower mentality will often force their children to walk before they are ready to walk so they can say, "My baby walked at nine months" or "My baby walked at eight months." The whole point is that the child needs to crawl because it's a stage of development. If the child is forced to the next stage before it has gotten through that stage, there is going to be a reverberation later.

If you force your child to do something that he is not ready for, or you force yourself in later life to do things that aren't natural to you, you are going to warp the soul and the soul's expression through the four lower bodies because the four lower bodies will be warped. A warped lower body is like a pane of glass that has irregularities in it, so when you look outside the trees look funny, or other things look funny, because the glass isn't properly made. It is a major distortion on the scene of life.

The idea is to find a norm and a balance where all four lower bodies are developed. Maria Montessori has a program for this from the day of birth on. Mother Mary has a program of meditations from conception on.[10] Let those four lower bodies be formed, let them go through a natural existence, but let them be disciplined by the parent. Let the parent instill self-discipline in the child—not self-condemnation, not limitation of creativity, but a discipline that keeps the bodies happy because they are not overindulged.

An overindulged body is not a happy body. It tries to make itself happy by craving more indulgence, more of the same, but it never gets happy. It is only when it is disciplined, when somebody can say "no" to it, when it is brought in line, that there is an exhilarating feeling because the body is satisfied; it has its quotient of energy and the consciousness returns to the center of the Christ and the soul. That's when you really feel happy. A spoiled child is not a happy child. An indulged child is not a happy child. And you are not happy when you are indulging your four lower bodies. You are out of attunement.

Education and the Mind of God

Now I will take any questions.

Student: [Comment about Carl Rogers.]

ECP: This student is saying that Carl Rogers performed

tests showing that those who can render the greatest psychological assistance are not those who have a lot of education, like six years of training, but it is actually those coming straight out of high school because they still have the ability to relate to others.

As a matter of fact, the masters saw to it that Mark Prophet never went to college because they didn't want him overtrained in the plane of the mental body, because it seems like the more training you have, the more tight matrices you have that don't allow for you to take off into the plane of the mind of God.

The thing I noticed about Mark was how uninhibited he was. For instance, I might get an idea, but I might not carry out that idea because it is socially unacceptable or because I have had training in some course that tells me it is not a right idea. If Mark got an idea he was going to leap six feet into the air and shout "Hurray!" he would do it on the platform or wherever. And it would shatter a mental matrix of people in the audience. It would release the energy for the flow of God through him, and it would put people so off guard and so out of their mental body that whatever he said, whatever followed, they could immediately take in because they were not centered in that intellect that would prevent them from taking it in.

I found that in Mark's poetry or in his dictations or in many things that came through him, they would be so contrary to the logic of the carnal mind that anybody who had any development of the carnal mind would have rejected them at face value. That's what I mean by uninhibited. He was uninhibited and untampered with, so his pure genius could contact the genius of God and he could bring forth the tremendous dispensations that we have in the knowledge and the teachings of The Summit Lighthouse.

The masters saw to it that I completed college because they knew what my role would be here and that this university would have to have the respect of the academicians of the world. So somebody had to have a degree, and that was me.

Mark was very, very highly educated in his previous embodiment as Longfellow. He studied in Europe, studied in New England, knew many languages and was a scholar all of his life. It wasn't a requirement for him to go through that again in this particular embodiment.

He lived almost exclusively in his etheric body, with very good coordination and contact with his other three bodies, but he operated from the plane of total and pure inspiration. That was backed by the training from the previous life so that he would use all kinds of words perfectly, words that perhaps I had not heard before. I would dutifully look them up in the dictionary and find out that they contained the exact matrix or meaning that was being conveyed by the vibration that came through the spoken Word.

So it's interesting how when we really have a purified etheric body, we can not only have the inspiration of the masters and our causal body, but we can also have access to all the good momentums of our other three lower bodies from other existences. I really feel that if there is one body you want to be unspoiled and cleared and purified, it is your etheric body, because immediately your mental, emotional and physical bodies will begin to follow. When the etheric cells are divested of their habit patterns and their matrices of indulgence, they begin to put out a matrix of discipline that is picked up by the others.

Conversely, you've got to start unwinding those habit

patterns with the physical—those cells programmed to eat meat, programmed to get that charge of nicotine or alcohol. They are programmed, and unprogramming them starts with physical discipline. You give your physical body a lecture. You tell it it's about time it stopped taking in this substance and you are not going to have it any longer. You have to speak with absolute determination. You speak to that body and you say, "Look, this is the way it is. Now you are going to eat what I tell you to eat and you are not going to eat anything else, and this is what you are going to do."

You get into the consciousness of your Christ mind and into your soul and you discipline that body. And that body comes right into line; you can feel it getting frightened and doing what you tell it to do. Then it gets very happy and pleased because it feels secure that finally it's not being left to flip-flop on its own, but there is a matrix of alignment that is being placed upon it.

With that rejection of overindulgence, whatever it may be, you are starting to correct the patterns in the etheric body. You are having to overcome a tremendous desire momentum because all of this has registered in your emotional body. That's the biggest thing to overcome because the desire body carries such a tremendous flow of cosmic energy.

The idea is replacement. Don't shoot your human—don't shoot it dead. If you do that, you will not have a matrix to evolve through. Be sensible. Give these bodies the minimum of what they need and then let them evolve out of the indulgence gradually. You have to have compassion for the situation of the four lower bodies and their indoctrination. And let's face it, your four lower bodies are children that already have an edge on you because they already have a certain number of years of development. You can train a two-year-old, but to train a twenty-two-year-old is a different thing—you have to discipline him in a way that's effective.

If you give the bodies the minimum but don't overindulge them, you have a much greater sense of freedom. You cannot continually have this sense of guilt that every time you do something wrong you are shot down and you can't get up and you can't overcome. You have to have a sense of freedom in your overcoming. Certain habit patterns can be broken on a dime, especially when you feel the Holy Spirit—all of a sudden it's over with and never again do you partake of it. Other things are very entrenched and based on imbalances in the system, and when dealing with those you have to have compassion with yourself and definitely give yourself time to overcome.

So you have to gauge the discipline. You can't be burdened with such a superego of your parents that you discipline yourself to the point of destroying the matrix the ascended masters need, destroying their ability to work through you as a chela. You can make yourself absolutely miserable by denying everything in your four lower bodies until you just can't find yourself in your body anymore because you are saying that the bodies are evil and Matter is evil, and you are trying to live an other-worldly existence.

In fact, as I said earlier, the higher you get spiritually, the more you will be absolutely on that line of practicality in the physical plane and the more you will experience yourself in your physical body. But your physical body is going to be something very new and transcendent because everything is going through this purification, and you will become aware of yourself as being like Jesus in the illustration of him as a cosmic being.

Disciplining the Etheric Body

Student: Do we have to discipline the record body, the etheric? Or can that be done through clearing it with decrees?

ECP: You have to consciously will, determine and

exercise discipline. The decrees can only fulfill a matrix that you set with your mind. That's why I was talking earlier about people decreeing but thinking about the past. They are not clearing that past because they are not replacing it with a pure matrix and they are not disciplining themselves to stop thinking about it. You can't just sit there and only decree. You have to say, "Okay, I am not going to revolve those records anymore. It is over and done with. I've called on the law of forgiveness. I've forgiven myself, I've forgiven the other person and I am not going to look at that image one more time."

If a record comes up, immediately you erect the picture of a flame, the picture of Mother Mary. If you can't see it in your mind, if your mind isn't that strong yet, get out a picture and say, "I am going to look at that picture and I am not going to see that event, that record. *In the name of the Christ, let that experience be put into the flame.*"

That's when you start bringing that etheric body in tow and into alignment. You are holding that horse by the reins and he is not running away with you.

Student: I meant clearing past lives.

ECP: From past lives, when it is not a record going in front of you, but it's just an accumulation? That goes by transmutation and by your decrees. But it is tremendously enhanced by a pure thoughtform. If you are decreeing and you are blank or you are looking around the room or at the chair in front of you, you are not creating a chalice that can hold a cosmic matrix.

But if you are decreeing and you are seeing the eyes of the master before you or you are looking at a picture, that becomes a chalice. That itself becomes a record in your memory body, a thoughtform in your mental body. And into that chalice, into that matrix, the violet fire pours, the sacred fire pours. It scrubs and it cleans other records of your life that you aren't even aware of.

A thoughtform is a magnet, just like the Great Central Sun Magnet. A pure thoughtform of a master magnetizes a tremendous quantity of energy from the cosmos down into your four lower bodies. So you can get a lot more cleaned up a lot more rapidly if you use thoughtforms when you decree.

Student: When we are decreeing and past things come up, can we overcome that by just thinking of the flame and forgetting about those things? Is that pushing them back?

ECP: When you are decreeing and these old records come up, you say, *"In the name of the Christ, let it go into the flame. In the name of the Christ, put it into the flame, beloved I AM Presence, beloved Saint Germain."*

You will find that when these records come up, you will feel the pull of your emotions, you will feel the record, you will feel the mind, you may feel the physical involvement. You may be in the middle of a decree session to Astrea. What you do is intensify that session. You give it more power, more throat chakra. You give more love to the Elohim, and right while you are saying the words, you are mentally saying, *"Astrea, take this from me. I surrender it into the flame."*

Sometimes you will decree more quickly, and the more quickly you decree, the more you will feel the light flowing around you. It may take you three or four or ten Astreas and all of a sudden there is this tremendous pull—similar to the way a wave feels when it pulls your body—and then it quickly snaps and falls from you. You are no longer aware of the record. And you feel like the battle is over, that the forces of light and the forces of darkness have fought and the forces of light have won because you kept on decreeing, because you kept on and you plowed through; you held the matrix and made the call.

You don't suppress the record, but you rivet your attention on God and you say, *"God, you take this!"* After all, you can't really consume it. The flame can. God can. The thing *you* can do is keep your attention on God so that it can happen, because if your attention isn't there the flow isn't going to be there.

I can remember that when I didn't understand this science I might give a series of decrees and all of a sudden become very tired and sleepy and say, "Oh well, I won't give as many today," and I'd give the sealing of the decree and that would be the end of it. What I didn't realize then was that the fatigue and sleepiness was a sign that I was coming into contact with very dense astral energy in my own electronic belt or in the planet. The flame hadn't been worked up enough to really cut through that substance, so it was causing a sleep ray and a sleep energy to come over me. And I gave up before the decree actually got through this clump of substance that was up for transmutation.

So when you sit down and you say, "Now I am going to give fourteen Astreas," don't get up until you have given fourteen. If you say, "I am going to give three," give three. But whatever you decide to do, see it through to the end because that decision is immediately put into the computer of your Christ Self, and your Christ Self determines what energy can be transmuted in that session and it will start coming up for transmutation. If you stop decreeing, that substance will just be hanging there in your four lower bodies and then you are going to have a problem.

Control and Repression

Student: Can you say anything about the difference between control and repression?

ECP: Repression, repressing feelings, is a stopping of flow. When you suppress something, you stop the flow; you are stopping a cycle.

Let's say you have a cell in your etheric body that has a momentum on a certain cycle of sexual indulgence that you recognize now, at your point on the Path, is too great an indulgence. Say you want to cut this cycle in half. It comes up again. It is used to flowing that way, you see. You establish a flow, you establish a matrix in your four lower bodies and then they expect to run that way because our bodies are creatures of habit and we program them. So you programmed yourself to this certain amount of indulgence which you now want to transcend, and you want to cut in half.

Well, the energy comes cycling around and it's ready for physical manifestation. Right there is where you have to say, *"In the name of the Christ, I call for the arresting of the spiral of this momentum."*

The Great Divine Director taught us this key—the arresting of the spiral—because energy is a spiral, and once that spiral starts it is going to finish. Once a spiral is released, it can't do anything but keep going.

The repression or the frustrating of this energy is pushing it back from the physical, pushing it back from your desires, pushing it back from your mind and finally pushing it back into the etheric body, and it gets suppressed down into the subconscious. It hasn't been overcome. You just stood there and gritted your teeth and didn't do anything about the transmutation of it or the arresting of the spiral.

So that's a complete stoppage of the flow of your being and you are extremely uncomfortable.

The difference between God-control and repression is that to have God-control you have to have joy because joy is the key that unlocks the flow of energy. It's like a bubbling brook. So you have to have joy, and your joy is in the Lord, and your joy is in Mother Mary and the masters.

You visualize the masters. You commend your being to them, "Into Thy hands I commend my being."[11] You joyously offer this energy into the flame. You invoke God-control. You invoke the violet fire through the cause, effect, record and memory: the etheric record, the mental thought-form, the desire body and the physical matrices. You do your invocation to the resurrection flame.* You call for the energy to be raised. You joyously submit yourself unto the Christ, and you ask the ascended masters to step in, take this energy and use it for the glory of God.

When you maintain joy, you give your decrees and you have the sense of this bubbling flow. You know that you have transmutation, you know that you have won a cycle. So the way to know the difference in whether or not you have God-control or repression is the amount of joy you can release in the situation.

The idea of getting over our aversions is something that Ramakrishna taught. The moment you have a record come up of some past experience that you don't like you say, "Oh, that's bad." You feel ashamed, you repress it because you don't want to see it, you don't want to look at it, you don't want to be identified with it. It's in your past and you

*A simple invocation for the resurrection flame is Jesus' mantra "I AM the resurrection and the life." Additional decrees to the resurrection flame may be found in *Prayers, Meditations and Dynamic Decrees for Personal and World Transformation.*

want to get rid of it. So immediately you push it down; it's almost a reflex action. That is repression.

Don't be afraid to look at it; just don't look at it all day. You have seen it. So what? So that thing happened. You forgive yourself. You call on the law of forgiveness and you call to the masters to put it into the flame. You aren't flip about it. You are sincerely sorry, and you really aren't going to do this thing again. But don't get all emotionally involved with it again.

If you are not sorry and you are not penitent, you are more than likely going to give in to it. You can't use the violet flame and the law of forgiveness on these things and then go out and keep repeating them. That is the problem with people who are confessing regularly on Friday or Saturday and then going out and doing the same things all over again during the week. That has been a way of life for certain people for thousands of years. If you do that, the violet flame will not work for you anymore; your Presence won't release it. But if you are sincerely sorry and you have forsaken the old ways, you don't have to feel bad about being joyous. You don't have to feel bad about forgiving yourself.

January 30, 1975

DECREE TO BELOVED MIGHTY ASTREA

In the name of the beloved mighty victorious Presence of God, I AM in me, mighty I AM Presence and Holy Christ Self of ___(insert names of individuals for whom you are making calls)___ , by and through the magnetic power of the sacred fire vested in the threefold flame burning within my heart, I call to beloved Mighty Astrea, the entire Spirit of the Great White Brotherhood and the World Mother, to lock your cosmic circles and swords of blue flame in, through, and around:

Insert 1: [my four lower bodies, my electronic belt, my heart chakra and all of my chakras, my entire consciousness, being, and world.]

Cut me loose and set me free (3x) from all that is less than God's perfection and my own divine plan fulfilled.

1. O beloved Astrea, may God-purity
    Manifest here for all to see,
    God's divine will shining through
    Circle and sword of brightest blue.

First chorus
    Come now answer this my call
    Lock thy circle round us all.
    Circle and sword of brightest blue,
    Blaze now, raise now, shine right through!

2. Cutting life free from patterns unwise,
    Burdens fall off while souls arise
    Into thine arms of infinite love,
    Merciful shining from heaven above.

3. Circle and sword of Astrea now shine,
    Blazing blue-white my being refine,
    Stripping away all doubt and fear,
    Faith and good-will patterns appear.

Second chorus
    Come now answer this my call,
    Lock thy circle round us all.
    Circle and sword of brightest blue,
    Raise our youth now, blaze right through!

Third chorus
    Come now answer this my call,
    Lock thy circle round us all.
    Circle and sword of brightest blue,
    Raise mankind now, shine right through!

And in full Faith I consciously accept this manifest,
manifest, manifest! (3x) right here and now with full Power,
eternally sustained, all-powerfully active, ever expanding,
and world enfolding until all are wholly ascended in the
Light and free!
    Beloved I AM! Beloved I AM! Beloved I AM!

Give the entire decree once through, using the first chorus after each verse. Then
give the verses again, using the second chorus after each one. Next give the verses
followed by the third chorus. Conclude with the closing "And in full Faith..."

CHAPTER SEVEN

MASTERING THE FLOW OF ENERGY

Commentary on Chapter 2, Part 3

We are picking up our reading of Lanto's dictation where we left off.

> Ask yourselves why men have developed this hard view of the world and its people.

When people don't have a tube of light to protect themselves against the onslaughts of the world, they build a wall of pride and they surround themselves with this wall, which is the combination of all their defense mechanisms.*

> Our answer in part would be, What they have received many of them have also given out. Yet not all. Those who have given harshness to the world and then have received it as recompense are often the first to chafe at the bit of their own energy as it returns for redemption.

When we see the plight of people and realize they are receiving hardness from a part of life, we tend to enter into sympathy, feeling sorry for them because they are on the

*For further teaching on the wall of pride that is the perversion of the tube of light, see Mark L. Prophet and Elizabeth Clare Prophet, *The Path of the Higher Self* (volume 1 of the Climb the Highest Mountain series), pp. 287–89.

raw end of things. In doing so, at that moment we are reinforcing the negative energy of hardness. Instead, at that moment we have to toe the mark, toe the line of compassion, of becoming one with the Christ within, and reinforce the Christ so that they can overcome and get through those conditions which place them on the receiving end of what they have sent out previously.

We must especially take care not to become sympathetic with the Luciferians whose time has come, who are receiving the recompense of what they have given out. The key weapon of the Luciferians is sympathy. They make you feel sorry for them, and in feeling sorry for them you give energy to those conditions of human imperfection.

> They want to be free from responsibility. They want to feel that they have the privilege of damaging other parts of life and of expressing an immense dislike of the very life principles—such as the quality of mercy—which in moments of stress they expect to assuage their own existence. What they think to accomplish by stressing their own importance through destroying the self-respect of others remains a mystery to many.

The desire to be free from responsibility is part of the energy of rebellion. We can feel it when the moon is in Scorpio on the ten o'clock line, drawing and magnetizing the negative four o'clock substance.

Some people want to be free to damage or to put down other parts of life. They have absolutely nothing to do with mercy. It's like the game that children play with the little hammer and pieces of wood that they poke through a base. They hammer them all through and then they have to turn it over and hammer them back through the other way. When one or two of those pieces are down then the children are up. Their egos are up when they can hammer someone else's pieces down, and it is directly proportionate.

Wanting freedom from responsibility for the consequences of action is rebellion against the law of karma. We speak about the misuse of the four o'clock line as "disobedience, stubbornness and defiance of the law."* Defiance of the law. When you consider what law they are defying, it is the law of karma. Rebellion is fundamentally the rejection of personal responsibility for personal actions.

How the Force Tries to Direct Energy at Us

By contrast, the great teachers who have walked the earth have again and again showed men how to live. Their instructions have been simple. They have taught men not to hate but to love. These admonishments were for the most part accepted by those who heard them; yet when the first tests came, it was as though they had never been schooled in the righteousness of God. Struck with self-righteous indignation at the ignorant acts of untutored souls, they hurled wounding arrows from the bow of emotion and then stepped gingerly over the bodies of those whom they felled.

Love is not just a feeling that we have for people because they evoke a response of love. We should learn to define love as a frequency, and we can determine the vibration of this frequency that is sent forth from the heart.

Getting back to those energies that are projected when we give the rosary or when we give our decrees: We see how

*See p. 368.

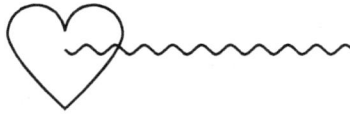

We can learn to define love as a frequency
that we send forth from the heart.

the etheric cycles parade before us, how the force tries to direct energy at the four lower bodies, all kinds of arrows and forcefields that are like a cherry bomb. Those energies move into our forcefield and explode as pockets of hatred, pockets of resentment, pockets of contempt for other parts of life. They come into the forcefields of our karma, our electronic belt and they try to collide with the point where the moon or the sun is.

We have a square today of the sun in Aquarius and the moon in Scorpio, and that is a tremendous forcefield of opportunity for divine love and the creativity of love. Aquarius is the genius of invention, science, discovery; Scorpio energy is creative energy. You combine these in pure love, and you get a tremendous release from your causal body of a potential to realize your divine plan.

Astrologers say that anywhere there is a square in your chart—in other words, where there is a ninety-degree angle between two planets—you will have difficulty there. Well, the masters have told me that wherever there's a square there's a cross, four ninety-degree angles. So wherever there is a square in your chart, there is the meeting of the lines of Alpha and Omega. And wherever those lines meet, you have an explosion of the Christ consciousness.

When you have a natal chart that has squares in it, you really have a lifetime of initiation, and you pass through those initiations by the crucifixion. Every square is an

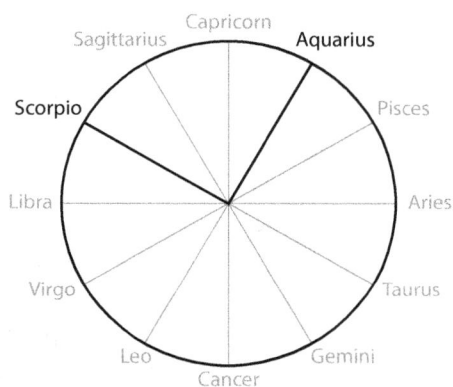

Scorpio-Aquarius square

opportunity to crucify the lower self so that the Greater Self can burst forth.

Let's say there is all this love energy waiting to be delivered from your causal body over the flow of the figure eight. You're feeling tremendous love coming forth from your heart and you feel it as a vibration. It's definitely an energy forcefield that you can detect, and you can read its vibration as love.

Along comes a pocket of world energy or a mass entity or what we call a riptide of energy, which can be a gigantic pocket of astral darkness amalgamating as hatred. Obviously it's coming up for transmutation. It moves in on your aura and suddenly it tries to tie you into an etheric record of something terrible that happened to you so that you will have resentment or hatred or whatever it is.

If during this moment of a very high peak of attunement and radiation with Mother Mary or the masters you allow yourself to become engaged in revolving of resentment patterns, you will be opening the door of your consciousness and suddenly this riptide will be engaged in your own energy. If you're open to it and it enters your world, it puts you into a vortex almost as if you were a pair of jeans in the washing machine. All of a sudden you're tumbling with this energy because the riptide is so heavy.

You find yourself completely taken up in this energy and it becomes so intense that you have to get rid of it. So you press it through your chakras and you direct it at the object of your resentment, the image or the individual. Or maybe you hate the Russians or you hate the Chinese or you hate the left wing. There are all kinds of momentums of hatred that can incite you to suddenly release this energy and think how righteous is your hatred and how righteous is your anger because it's for a good cause. All of this may happen while you are in the middle of your prayers and invocations.

This may not happen to you, but I can guarantee that it happens to people who don't understand what they are doing. When they are in prayer or they are in church, they get extremely excited and emotional about causes and things they are thinking about—all those terrible people out there who hate Jesus. They have no power to detect the difference between this energy and the very smooth, even line of love energy that is not engaged in human consciousness.

When this riptide comes into their electronic belts they are suddenly releasing jagged patterns of hatred, a tremendous amount of sympathy and emotionalism, and the whole experience becomes totally emotional as an interplay of

**The heart releasing jagged patterns of hatred
instead of the even line of love.**

energies in the electronic belt. This is how hatred and hurling "wounding arrows from the bow of emotion" happens.

You can feel these islands and this energy trying to come into you to overtake you. This is where the discipline of the third-eye chakra comes in. This is why Cyclopea is on the ten o'clock line.* There is so much power of love in Scorpio. But in order to have the full ability to use that love you have to have some mastery of the third eye, because it requires that in the face of all the misuses of love, you keep your attention riveted on the immaculate concept of the situation, on the master that you are visualizing, on whatever you're doing. You have to keep your consciousness high.

If you do this—you keep your attention and your vision locked on Mother Mary, on the vision of perfection—what happens when this energy comes? You have love going out from you. And the love not only goes out in a straight line, but it also begins to create a whirling forcefield around the heart that is very much like your causal body.

Remember you have a threefold flame. And because you have a threefold flame, you have a focal point to magnetize the energy of your causal body, of your I AM Presence, because the center of the causal body *is* the threefold flame. So you have God incarnate in the center of your heart, and by your love you can attract this vortex of light. The more you're concentrated, the more you are visualizing that love, the more this vortex of light begins to turn—until you have a huge, fiery vortex of sacred-fire white light in your heart.

Then along comes a mass of hatred. What happens? The light in your heart is whirling energy and the mass is sucked

---

*Cyclopea is the cosmic being charted on the ten o'clock line of the cosmic clock. The third-eye chakra corresponds to the four-ten axis of the clock. See p. 368.

in by this vortex. The vortex moves and transmutation takes place—without you ever experiencing one erg of that hatred or that substance, without you outpicturing it, without you requalifying it with your own electronic belt. It is sucked into the vortex of light and transmuted. And when it is transmuted, you have that much more energy that is a blazing sun, because everything that gets transmuted is yours. You have claimed it; it's like staking out a claim.

I was talking to one of my children the other day about squatter's rights. You move in and squat on this energy; you transmute it and it's yours. It is going to ascend into your causal body, into your cosmic bank account. But it's also going to remain as the weaving of your seamless garment and as your momentum of light here below in your aura, in your four lower bodies.

So here is the choice, and it is written in the Bible: "Be not overcome of evil [the energy *veil*], but overcome the evil with good."[1] That is the formula. It has taken us two thousand years to figure it out scientifically, but that is what it means. Don't be overcome by a mass of negative energy; have the fire of your heart so powerful that when that energy comes it is whirled into the vortex of the living God.

Setting God Free

That is the challenge of a lifetime. And this challenge is so joyous. You develop compassion for life and compassion for God himself because this mass of energy, this mass of hatred that has been fed by everybody's hatreds—for example, by all the right- and left-wingers hating each other and by all the wars that have ever been fought—is full of atoms of God's energy. That's all it is.

At the center of each of those atoms there is a white-fire

core; there is the white light that is God. God is imprisoned in that hatred. You are going to set him free. Electrons are whirling around the center of each atom. They've elected to do God's will. But man has imprisoned them in a matrix of dark hatred and then rejected his responsibility for so doing. So when you see the dark clouds of adversity coming toward you, remember that it is really God coming and saying, "Set me free!"

God is really subject to you because this is the octave where man is given the opportunity to take dominion over

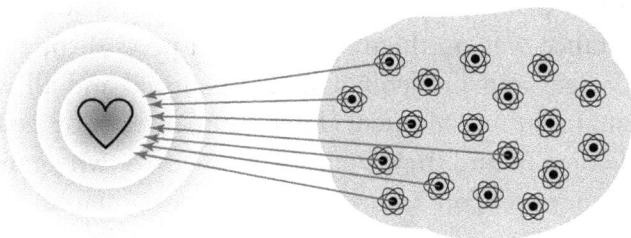

Mass forcefields of negative energy are made up of atoms and electrons of God's light imprisoned in matrices of darkness. These atoms and electrons are freed when they are drawn into the whirling vortex of light around the heart.

the earth.[2] All of the energy in the plane of Matter is subject to man's free will. God is crucified in this globule of hatred. God is crucified in this cross of Matter, and only you can set him free because you are God. It takes God to set God free. The light in your heart is God. Therefore, by that light in your heart you call these electrons home. You are calling God home into your heart. This is *true* responsibility. This is overcoming that crust of hardness. All these electrons can't wait to get home, and everything that imprisons them is broken by that whirling vortex of sacred fire.

That energy can be extremely heavy, extremely vicious.

You have to be on guard. You have to give your calls to Archangel Michael and Mighty Astrea. You have to really set your forcefield. But when you are on a high plane of attunement and engaged in an intensity of invocation, you can feel masses of energy passing through your heart chakra, passing through the flame and being set free.

That is what happened yesterday in answer to your calls—enormous quantities of mass effluvia were drawn into the flame. The people who were in the sanctuary all afternoon said that they experienced this in waves. They would feel completely bowed down as a tremendous wave of substance was on them. They would press through with their decrees and suddenly it would be lifted and all would be light and peace. Moments later another wave of darkness would come in and they would feel bowed down again—as though they were on a ship that was rocking in a hurricane.

When you understand what is happening spiritually, you are not surprised by this experience. You recognize these are momentums of human consciousness that have to pass into the flame because the planet is being overpowered by them and nobody is taking the responsibility for freeing God from being crucified. Nobody is standing up and saying, *"God, you are free! I command you free! I command your energy free!"*

You don't have to be afraid or concerned when this happens. It's a natural thing that when so few among mankind understand this Law, when those few start decreeing, that energy, that God that is absolutely sealed in these vortices of hatred, desires to be free and is going to rush into the fiery core that you create. So the more you decree the more opportunity you have for transmutation. It's a great privilege, because you are becoming God and you are becoming

God very rapidly, because all that is transmuted through you then bears the mark of your identity.

That is how you have the tremendous opportunity of attaining cosmic consciousness in this age—because we live on a planet that has such an abundance of misqualified energy, and you attain cosmic consciousness by being the sieve or the vortex through which this energy passes. Every erg that is transmuted adds to the measure of your God Self–awareness because it *is* God, and it adds to your dominion and your mastery. The fact that you can stand and keep on standing and reprove and rebuke this darkness and claim the light as your own is what self-mastery is all about.

Attitude Is All-Important

Such reactions are unnecessary in the life of the man of God. He can walk the earth and maintain not only a graceful dignity and God-control, but also the correct attitude toward every part of life.

Attitude is all-important, for it is like a screen through which the ingredients of life are pressed. What comes out as the individual's life is molded by his attitude.

Your energy is your life. So what comes through the screen, the screening process of the heart, is your life. And your attitude is all-important. Attitude is like the refinement of one's third-eye vision. You can have an attitude, a kind of boredom, a kind of "Oh well, let's get this over with" sort of feeling when you sit down to decree. And it will color the energy of your decrees. It's a half-hearted sense of "I'm being bound to this ritual and I have to do this. The Law says I have to do it." That kind of tone puts a damper on the spirals of life. Actually that tone, if you are really sensitive, is like a corkscrew grinding into your solar plexus and into your soul.

There are many types of attitudes that come out in the voice. People use the power of the voice as an irritant to control one another, to convey disdain or pride or belittlement, belittling you or downing you just by a tone of voice. Take for instance, "What are you doing here?" "What are *you* doing here?" It's the intonation used that either uplifts people's energies in their chakras to the joy of the Lord or depresses them and drives that energy down.

To be a messenger I was required to take quite intensive training in the use of the throat chakra and not abusing the throat chakra so that the instrument would not be perverted. I was shown how in the particular area where I grew up, which was on the East Coast, there are peculiarities of speech habits. People speak to one another and they get in the habit of a certain irritating twang or a certain downing of other people. And I found that I was using my throat chakra at a level of discord that I didn't even realize, just by not saying things in an uplifting or positive manner, or by sighing, or this or that. So for quite a long period of time I was made to continually listen to myself speaking and to gauge the decibels of that energy and how it influenced life.

By and by you develop an absolute God-control of the use of your throat chakra. You realize how damaging the misuse of that throat chakra can be, just by a little turn of the voice, especially with the amount of energy that we invoke.

You can do this to your children. "So-and-so, what are you doing?" And the child immediately gets this punch of energy because the parent is irritated or the parent is fatigued or the parent is impatient. You can convey enormous impatience. People do this to their dogs. They direct all of their frustrations and energies at their animals through the throat chakra.

That is jagged energy, and it is definitely preventing you from achieving full mastery of the spoken Word and the mastery of water, because the throat chakra is the polarity of the solar plexus. It's also the mastery of air and of the release of the thoughts of the mind because the throat chakra is on the five-eleven axis. So let's watch the way we use our throat chakra, the way we speak, and whether or not we are conveying feelings of depression or belittlement.

I have come to the place where I have almost decreed a certain shield in front of my solar plexus and my chakras just to protect myself and screen out the way people misuse their voices when they speak. It becomes a cross for me to deal with that energy, and I go through the day expecting a certain amount of it because I know that, since I uphold the throat chakra, a certain amount of that energy seeking redemption is going to come at me.

Yesterday I had someone come to me and apologize for the way they had spoken to me earlier. I said I didn't have any knowledge whatsoever that they had not spoken to me properly, that I couldn't even remember. The individual assured me that he had spoken improperly to me. I thought to myself, "I wonder why that didn't register, since I am so sensitive." And I realized the reason was that I so anticipate a certain amount of this that I have a shield that almost automatically deflects it, otherwise I couldn't survive.

You have to keep your shield and your armor, but never an encrustation of hardness of heart, never a defense mechanism. Having a shield is just fine. Archangel Michael never

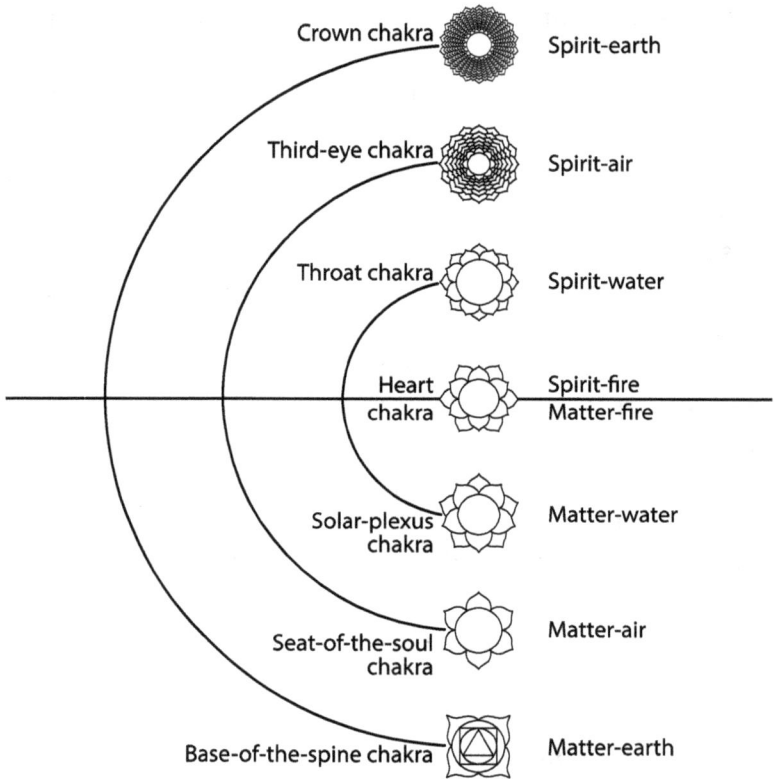

Crown chakra		Spirit-earth
Third-eye chakra		Spirit-air
Throat chakra		Spirit-water
Heart chakra		Spirit-fire / Matter-fire
Solar-plexus chakra		Matter-water
Seat-of-the-soul chakra		Matter-air
Base-of-the-spine chakra		Matter-earth

The chakras above and below the heart are in polarity. The throat chakra (immediately above the heart) is in polarity with the solar plexus (the chakra immediately below the heart), and these correspond to the water element. Similarly, the third eye is in polarity with the seat of the soul, the air element, and the crown chakra is in polarity with the base of the spine, the earth element. The heart chakra is the fire element.

goes forth into battle without his armor. But don't let your armor become the crust of the human consciousness.

The "hurling of wounding arrows" is going on continually, so your "attitude is all-important." Your attitude is expressed by the joy in your heart and how you speak to one another. And be careful about the sigh. Sometimes you can heave a heavy sigh before you start talking to someone.

You think "This poor person just doesn't understand. He's too stupid to understand what I'm trying to say," so you say (sigh), "Well, I'll explain it one more time." By the time you've said that, the poor person is so on the defensive about himself being unclear and unable to deal with what you're saying that he's in the position of being subservient to this very powerful person you have made yourself seem. A sigh like that is an attitude, and that's the kind of thing that sullies your aura and stands between you and sainthood.

So think about it. Think about the joy and the beauty of loving life free in all ways, in all of your chakras. "Attitude is ... like a screen through which the ingredients of life are pressed." Imagine that you put a little screen, a little circle that is a grid, on the front of all of your chakras. It's your attitude—the attitude of your heart, the attitude of your mind, the pride of the intellect, and so forth. It's over each chakra; and you press out the energy of the chakra through the screen and that determines what your aura will be, what your life will be.

The Tares and the Wheat

Therefore it is utterly important that every follower of truth understand the folly of patterning his life after human conduct. Instead he should recognize the peace that passeth understanding[3] which comes when he kisses the hands and feet of the law of God as his saviour. For the law leads men to life eternal. The law frees the consciousness from the dregs of darkness that have taken hold of it.

We dare not eliminate the tares without realizing that if we do so prematurely, we may also uproot the benign and helpful aspects of human nature.[4] The safest way is the way of using the flames of God, but the knowledge of just what the flames are is seldom realized by men; and when we speak of them they are often puzzled.[5] Let us say again, then, that there is a natural order and universe and there is a spiritual order and universe. The glory of the terrestrial is one, and the glory of the celestial is another.[6] The flames of God are of the spiritual order; and these, by the grace of God, penetrate the natural order with the transforming power of the Holy Spirit.[7]

It is important to keep in mind this simple diagram that we are using concerning the flow of energy from the causal body to the four lower bodies of man. When we are talking about the natural order and the spiritual order and the celestial body and the terrestrial body, we are talking about the spiral of consciousness that forms a figure-eight pattern. Within the circle of life that we call the self, there is a figure-eight flow between the causal body in the upper half and the four lower bodies in the lower half, with the Christ Self being in the center.

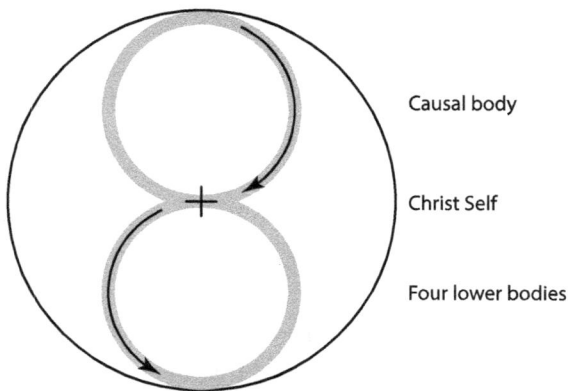

Within the circle of life that is the self, the flow of energy from the causal body to the lower self follows the pattern of a figure eight with the Christ being at the point of the nexus.

The tares and the wheat are sown among each other in the lower half of the figure eight. If you ever garden, you see how the roots of the tares, being quite gross, will intermingle with the delicate roots of flowers and plants, and if you pull them apart you can destroy the delicate plant. Sometimes students ask, "Is there any way I can get rid of my karma all at once? Is there any way I can transmute extra energy all at once?" The *only* way to get rid of the tares is not by God's intercession because you say, "God, get rid of my tares," but it is by *the penetration of the flame.*

The flame comes from the heart of the I AM Presence; it

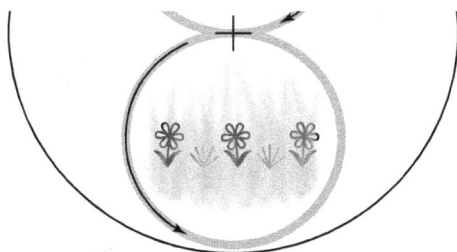

The tares and the wheat grow side by side in the consciousness of man. The flame descending from the I AM Presence and causal body over the figure eight penetrates the four lower bodies and removes the tares without damaging the wheat.

cycles into manifestation within you, and it starts penetrating through the tares and the wheat. It has the action of dissolving the tares, separating out the tares without disrupting the wheat. That happens by using the flames of God, knowing what the flames are.

Here is the whole thing about psychology. We take ourselves apart like a Swiss watch; we take all the parts apart and lay them on the table before us. We find out that our mother did this to us and our father did that to us and we had this traumatic experience and that traumatic experience.

All these things are supposed to be the components of our human identity. We have them all apart in front of ourselves and we look at them and we say, "How can we ever put this self back together again with all these problems?"

The masters have said that the power to analyze is the power to destroy. They didn't say the power to psychoanalyze. I'm just talking about basic analysis. Whenever you can break something down into components, you have in your hand the ability to destroy it, because you don't have to put it back together again. And sometimes taking it apart makes it impossible to put it back together again, as when you tear the petals off a rose.

So we are on a fine line here. It's important to understand our psychology, but once we've understood it, it is important to almost close the book. The lie has been exposed, we understand the formation and the influences of the human personality—but we close it up again. We close the electronic belt. We go into the Christ consciousness, the center of the figure eight. We invoke the flame and let the flame do the penetration, let the flame do the dissolving of the tares.

The flame *is* God. The flame knows how to do what has to be done. It knows exactly what should be transmuted first in order to leave us in a state of balance and equilibrium. The flame is the Holy Spirit; it is the grand healer of the totality of man. So we invoke the flame, we name the conditions we are aware of that must be consumed, but we let God decide how and when, in what measure, in what portion. This is the only way that the tares can be uprooted before the harvest. Otherwise the fire would destroy the total personality, good and bad.

That's what the spiritual order is for. The flames of God are of the spiritual order, the top part of the figure eight.

And these, by the grace of God, penetrate the natural order with the transforming power of the Holy Spirit. What more can we ask?

Spirit and Matter

The experiences of the devotee who loves the truth enough to search it out will help him to understand that the qualities of God are inherent within the spiritual order and that although these qualities penetrate the material order, they are not native to it.* It is in the correct understanding of Matter in its relationship to Spirit, therefore, that men become enlightened.†

Matter is always the passive receiver of the energies of Spirit. When we say these energies are not native to Matter, we really mean they are not native to the planes of misqualification in Matter. They are native to the Divine Mother. But they are native to the Divine Mother because the Divine Mother is the receiver of the energies of the Father.

To understand oneself as a spiritual-material being is to apprehend one's relationship to others. To understand the need to purify one's consciousness insofar as it has taken on a limited, self-centered view of existence is to apprehend one's relationship to Life as a whole.

The reception of the consciousness of God as though one's physical form, one's mind, and one's consciousness

---

*When this *Pearl of Wisdom* was published in the book *Understanding Yourself*, this was revised by the messenger, under the master's direction, to read, "...they do not originate in it."
†The enlightened understanding of the relationship between Matter and Spirit may be found in *The Path of the Higher Self* (vol. 1 of the Climb the Highest Mountain series), pp. 319–33 and 409–11.

were wholly permeated by the fire [energy] of creation will produce in one's total being the Godly estate that is desired.

You must have those moments when you conceive of yourself as a porous sponge or as a piece of rock, like pumice, filled with holes. You conceive of yourself as this holey thing through which the fire passes and penetrates.

Rebellion in the Electronic Belt

It is this estate which, when harbored within, casts out the darkening proclivities of the mortal consciousness and replaces them by the stern yet joyous awareness, the vital yet penetrating hope of the infinite mind of God as it descends into the finite world.

After all, it is the Christ mind that is the divine armor against the insidious forces that lurk within the individual's 'electronic belt'. This so-called belt is [actually] positioned in the aura of the individual around the lower portion of the physical form; it extends from the waist to beneath the feet, somewhat in the shape of a large kettledrum, and contains the aggregate records of his negative human thoughts and feelings.

Man is transported out of the confines of his mortal sense into spiritual realms of thought when he contacts the vital flames of the very essence of the Creator's consciousness. The desire to be transported out of the realm of the ordinary is tantamount to invocation; but when men also express a willingness to be decontaminated of all undesirable qualities, they open the floodgates of their consciousness to the light, which rushes in to expurgate all unwanted vibratory actions.

Fundamental to emotional disturbance or mental disturbance is rebellion against the law of one's own karma. You will find that sometime in the deep, dark past, somewhere deep in the caverns of your electronic belt on the four-ten axis, there has been a rebellion against your own karma. You did something, it came back for redemption and you rebelled against it; you rebelled against the situation that required you to serve someone whom you had wronged. And rebellion is based on pride, the pride that comes on the three o'clock line that is not transmuted, that carries over into the four.

As teachers of mankind yourselves, when you are giving invocations and making calls for individuals who have emotional and mental disturbances, you need to recognize that rebellion is lurking somewhere in the electronic belt. It may be way, way, way down in that belt. If you have ever picked up a lost stitch in knitting, you know how that stitch can go down sixteen rows and you have to weave it back. Likewise, way down deep in that electronic belt there is a fissure that occurred when the flame on the four-ten axis was let go, was let down. It might have been on Lemuria, it might have been on Atlantis, but whenever it occurred, it began the warp and wobble in the energy system on the four-ten axis.

You may have made progress in other areas, but you can never really make total progress involving integration with the Christ mind until you go back and redeem that energy. So if you have emotional problems and disturbances, the first thing you need to do is to say:

In the name of Almighty God, in the name of the Christ, I call on the law of forgiveness for my rebellion against the law of my being, the law of my karma. And I call forth the sacred fire into action for the transmutation of the cause and core of the records of that rebellion.

Now you've set the law in motion. You may have been reinforcing that rebellion for five hundred thousand years. So don't think that because you suddenly decide you're going to call on the law of forgiveness that everything is going to be swept clean and suddenly you are going to be whole. The Law is the Law, and you are going to have to invoke the violet flame and give Astreas cycle after cycle, especially when the sun and the moon are poling in Taurus and Scorpio.* You are going to have to work hard.

You can't have been in a state of rebellion for any length of time without having influenced other parts of life toward rebellion, so your responsibilities become quite far-reaching. That point of contamination, that point of fissure down in your electronic belt, will have ties to the electronic belts of people all over the planet in places you can't even imagine, people that you would disdain to even associate with, people on skid row. They followed your rebellion and it wrecked their lives. They became alcoholics ten embodiments ago and they are still alcoholics.

Clear Your Karma Daily and Carry World Karma

Well, there is a price to be paid. You have to invoke a lot of violet flame and do a lot of Astreas and get that karma cleaned up. But at least you are on the right path. At least you're going right back to the place where the karma was created, and you're going to start building from there. At least you are not in some kind of religion or theology that covers over all of this, where you smile peaceably, walking around in this pious attitude, and you've "found the truth," and you affirm metaphysically that all is well and you are perfect and you have always been perfect.

*the four and ten o'clock lines of the cosmic clock

All of those affirmations don't count one iota unless the transmutation has occurred. It may be comfortable to walk around in the consciousness of affirming "All is well, all is well," when all is *not* well. But don't buy it, because when you do, you are not really overcoming and you are not really attaining salvation.

If you really want your ascension and you really want to be free from disturbances in your own being, you have to roll up your sleeves, dig in and give those invocations. You have to be satisfied that every single day of your life you've given enough violet flame and enough Astreas so that you feel clear. It's a sense of being crystal clear. When you wash a crystal glass and it sparkles in the sun and you tap the glass and you hear that ring, that is the way you have to feel about your aura. You have to feel that it is sparkling clean and, therefore, that you have transmuted everything that can come out of your electronic belt on that given day, because only a certain amount can be transmuted.

The cycles of the law keep turning. "Sufficient unto the day is the evil thereof,"[8] the energy veil. Each day there is a sufficiency of karma, a sufficient amount that you are required to balance. You balance that and you clear your aura and you are immediately, on that day, a candidate for world service. After you've cleared your own aura, you start clearing the aura of the planet, you start transmuting mass forcefields.

Every day you have to renew your candidacy. It's not something automatic. If I get up in the morning and I'm immediately caught up in the responsibilities and business of the day, if I don't do my invocations and I haven't cleared myself of my own karmic burden, my own personal weight, how is God going to give me the weight of the world? How can I carry the weight of the world? I can't carry it and carry mine too. So I have to clean up my personal world and then I can hold the balance for the karma of the planet. I can carry a greater amount of world karma if I am completely crystal clear myself.

More than this you cannot do, but this is a great deal. Now, you may transmute all the karma and all the substance of that rebellion that you are allowed to transmute on that day. It may not bring about the total healing of your consciousness, but you will still be allowed to carry world karma. So you can have infirmities, you can have a thorn in the flesh, as Saint Paul did,[9] and still be on a mission of world karma because you are cleaning a sufficiency of your own energy and, therefore, you have a certain balance and momentum of light in your aura whereby the subsequent calls can go for world action.

Desire Equals Invocation

Lanto is talking about desire being tantamount to invocation. The word *tantamount* means "equals." Desire equals invocation. That's very interesting because we talked about the emotional body, the desire body, having such a momentum. *Desire* is actually a code word that means "*Deity sires*." It means God in you is giving birth to, is siring the matrix you are releasing.

When you have a tremendous desire within yourself to be pure in the sight of God, God in you releases an enormous quantity of energy for that goal to be realized. This is an alchemy, your alchemy. You have set the desire and you have released it. The desire is like your own little planet that is going into orbit. That's the meaning of siring a son, giving birth to a son. A portion of yourself is going into orbit in the mass consciousness of the world; it is this globule of desire for purity. It goes forth. Because of its purity, it gathers more of its kind, more purity. It finally returns to you, as all things do, as karmic cycles do. It returns to you an enlarged globule of the purity of God because your desire is the matrix of creation.

The very matrix of creation is desire. Can we create anything without desire? We think of desire in the negative context because we associate it with sex. But when you think of it in the sense of God desiring to be more of himself, you see that even the desire to procreate is the desire of God.

So, desire being equal to invocation, when you send forth good desires, you are decreeing, you are invoking. Those desires are creations and they are going out into the world and they are increasing the God consciousness of creativity in the world. They come back to you bearing fruit after their kind. This is why it is so important to purify the motive. Your motives are the same as your desires.

You may be standing somewhere teaching the word of the ascended masters, but your desire may be to be thought well before men. That's your real motive. You don't even know it yourself, you've got yourself so self-deceived. You're teaching the masters' teachings but you are enjoying it because people are looking at you and thinking how wonderful you are. That desire is also a globule—a globule of ego consciousness. It goes forth, gathers more of its kind, and what does it bring back to you? Other people who have the same self-seeking. And you find that you draw around yourself a cluster of people who form a personality cult.

You can always tell what kind of a teacher is teaching by looking around and determining who are the followers. The teacher will always attract that which is like himself, because he's the forcefield, the focal point of the release of energy.

You can decree and serve and study the teachings year in, year out. But if you don't purge your desires and purge your motives, as much as 50 percent or more of your energy can be going into the fulfillment of impure momentums, impure desires, impure motives.

People get into this whole thing about sex fantasy, realizing their sexual urges through fantasy, through having pin-up girls, and so forth. All these fantasies are constantly revolving through the mental body and the etheric body, and people get so intense in their revolving that they actually have physical experiences conjured up entirely by mental and emotional desiring. Imagine the tremendous, enormous tie-up of energy.

Of course, there are all kinds of desires. People spend all their life desiring social standing, wealth or success, wanting this, that or the next thing. Buddha taught the path of desirelessness—getting rid of all desire—because every desire that you put out, every globule of something you want, is still tying you to this plane.

To be free of the desire to add to yourself in the human sense is necessary. But God himself desires, and that is how the creation came into being. So we do not want to be free of the desire for purity, because this is what propels us to our ascension. You have to *want* your ascension to get your ascension because your desire is the momentum that draws the ascension to you.

There is an attitude of not caring if you win or lose. The saying goes, "If you don't care if you lose, you're a loser," because if you don't have the desire to win and your momentum isn't to win, you're not going to attract a victory to yourself.

Just remember, every desire you have is an invocation. The more you use the flames and the fires of God, the more you are going to find that your desires are your offspring; they are the children of your mind and your feelings, and they are going out and populating the mass consciousness. So think twice before you put forth a momentum of desire because it's going to go out there, it's going to influence people, it's going to come back to you.

Your desires are your karma. Remember that. Be very careful when you contemplate something. Jesus said he who looks upon a woman with lust in his eye has already committed adultery or fornication.[10] That is the whole law of desire—because Jesus knew how powerful the momentum of desiring is.

The light will purify your subconscious of all wrong desiring; you have but to make the call.

> *In the name of the Christ, in the name of the Holy Spirit, I call forth the light of Almighty God. I call directly to the heart of the Father for the release of that energy into my four lower bodies, the release of the full power of the violet flame, the cosmic honor flame and the flame of cosmic worth, to penetrate now and release all energies that are locked in pockets of wrong desire.*
>
> *I demand the shattering of the forcefields of all wrong desire of all incarnations since the day of my soul's entering into Matter! I demand the breaking of the forcefields of wrong desire! I demand that God-desire be the penetration of my subconscious, that only God-desire be the*

momentum and the motive of my life! I demand the full power of the Holy Spirit and the sacred fire to purge me now of all wrong matrices, of all wrong patterns, of all wrong grids and forcefields!

And I call in the name of the Christ to Mighty Astrea to lock your cosmic circle and sword of blue flame around the cause and core of all momentums and globules of desire floating in the astral plane which I have ever sent forth, knowingly or unknowingly, in any of my incarnations. I demand that that energy be seized in the name of the Christ! I demand that it be drawn now into the flaming presence of the Maha Chohan!

I demand that in my consciousness, in my soul, in my heart and in all of my chakras there be released only the full momentum of God's desire to be free, to be whole, to ascend, to resurrect, to love life free, to bring forth the teaching and the Law, and to be the fullness of the divine example to all mankind.

In the name of the Father, of the Mother, of the Son, and of the Holy Spirit, I accept it done this hour in full power. And I AM grateful for the presence of God desiring in me now.

Every Chakra Can Be a Vortex of Light

Beneath the surface calm there lies within the consciousness of men much that is undesirable, much that represents the polarization of imperfection during near and distant epochs of personal history. To cast out the enemy within by invoking the sacred fire is a necessary process. When this is done, transmutation takes place and the energies that have been imprisoned in matrices of imperfect thought and feeling are released. Immediately after having been dislodged from the electronic belt and purified by the flames of God, these energies ascend to the causal body of man which is the repository of all good that has ever been externalized by the individual.

Just as the electronic belt bears the record of human infamy, so the causal body of man bears witness to all true creativity. The causal body, then, is of the spiritual order and universe, and the electronic belt is of the natural order and universe. The glory of the celestial body is in the overcoming of the body terrestrial. In the words of Saint Paul: "It [the terrestrial body] is sown in corruption; it is raised in incorruption: It is sown in dishonour; it is raised in glory: it is sown in weakness; it is raised in power: It is sown a natural body; it is raised a spiritual body. There is a natural body, and there is a spiritual body. And so it is written, The first man Adam was made a living soul; the last Adam was made a quickening spirit."[11]

The wisdom of God "is first pure, then peaceable, gentle, and easy to be entreated, full of mercy and good fruits."[12] The tenderness of the Divine is a boon of great comfort, and the faith which men express in a childlike manner assists them in finding freedom from the darkness that hides in the self. May wisdom lead you into light and light into God-happiness.

Victoriously, I remain
Lanto

Lanto is the master who made his threefold flame shine through his own flesh form; that was the goal before he ascended, and his disciples witnessed that fire in his chest. I would point out to you from the heart of Lord Lanto that every chakra can be a vortex of light.

When Lanto is talking about wisdom leading you into light and light into God-happiness, wisdom is the vortex of the crown chakra. If you have a storehouse of wisdom of the mind of God, it becomes a vortex in your crown chakra, and that vortex becomes a forcefield that magnetizes all the energies of all your chakras up the spinal ladder into that forcefield.

Realize, then, that the pull of these vortices is how you are making your daily, hourly ascension. This is why the masters want you to develop wisdom (the crown chakra), the full power of the immaculate vision (the third-eye chakra, the all-seeing eye), the full power of the will of God (the throat chakra), and the full power of the love of God (the heart chakra). In these upper chakras you have the threefold flame—pink in the heart, blue in the throat, yellow in the mind—and the power to precipitate all three through the immaculate vision of the all-seeing eye.

If you develop a tremendous pull and momentum in these upper chakras, they are going to pull all the energy of your electronic belt into the vortex of transmutation. So you keep the flames rolling in the upper chakras and you magnetize the energies up from below.

And of course, the tremendous gift of the violet flame, the momentum of the violet flame is anchored in your soul chakra. So here in these latter days preceding the Aquarian age, we even have the opportunity to go directly into the electronic belt with the violet flame and anchor purification, which also assists the whole upward momentum.

Your chakras are God in you. The more you intensify the action of the flames in the chakras, the more you become a vortex of light and the more you magnetize God. And the more of God you magnetize, the more the remaining elements of negative substance in your being are purified.

February 3, 1975

CHAPTER EIGHT

STRIVING FOR PERFECTION

Commentary on Chapter 3

To All Who Seek Wisdom:

The quest for self-discovery is sparked in reality by the voice of God, spurring the creation onward to discover the real intents and purposes behind creation. Those who are content to remain snarled in the minuteness of karmic interaction are always overly concerned about the details involving their individual egos and lives. Therefore, one of the secrets of escape is to be found in the depersonalization of life as the Master Jesus taught. He who loses his life for "my sake" shall find it again.[1]

When you depersonalize life, you depersonalize good as well as evil. You don't make too much of human behavior patterns that aren't totally and always in keeping with the Christ, and you don't make too much of human accomplishment, but you are caught up in a spiral of glorying in the Lord.

Did you know we're not trying to perfect your human? That's not the goal of the ascended masters. The goal is to replace the human with the Christ. You are never going to perfect the human consciousness, so don't try. It's not perfectible. It's mutable; it's that which is changing. It is an instrument. It is a forcefield.

Perfectionists are the people who crack up. It's important to strive for perfection in the Christ and to strive to bring that perfection into manifestation, to have these as goals. But there is a cast of the mind which becomes too involved in the ego and how it is looking and how it is manifesting perfection. You reach a certain point in that consciousness and you flip. You flip right out of the spectrum because you can't live in an imperfect world and constantly try to be perfect, because you never measure up.

The depersonalization of life means that when people aren't perfect we don't get too excited about it. And when they are perfect we don't get too excited about it. This is a very fine line, it is the razor's edge. It is a tightrope walk of consciousness to understand this, because you could hear my words today and say, "Well, if that's the case, why bother? Why bother trying to be neat and tidy, to be clean, to do our papers well, to write well, and so forth?"

The masters teach that fastidiousness and diligence in striving for perfection is of the utmost importance. As Morya was saying in the *Pearl* he dictated last evening, you have to prepare for successive planes of consciousness, and diligence and perfectionment here give you the ability to cope with and grasp the next plane, where the coordinates of identity are much more spread.[2]

When you start getting into infinity and the co-measurement of yourself with infinity, you have to be able to comprehend a far more vast spectrum of points and counterpoints. It's like looking up at the stars and conceiving of your identity as being all of those stars. You can hardly look at them all at once, let alone contain them in your consciousness, because we're used to a smaller framework.

We really do have a very small reference point in which

to gain mastery. And the purpose of mastery is so that in succeeding octaves, as we expand with the curve of infinity, we are able to have mastery over the coordinates of identity. The striving for perfection is really the striving for merging with the Christ Self that is already perfect, whereas constantly worrying about the human action and its perfection can be devastating.

So you have to watch your matrix. Your matrix is striving for oneness with the perfection that you already are. That's the right consciousness and the right attitude: striving for the perfection that you already are, striving to be one with it, striving to outpicture it, striving to make your soul and your consciousness the proper vehicle for the mind which was in Christ Jesus.

You get a very good understanding of the sense of perfection and merging with it in the life of Jesus. There is never the feeling of constantly trying to appear or to be humanly perfect. Jesus was a master, but he let himself get caught publicly overturning the moneychangers, shouting at the lawyers, shouting at the Pharisees. He wasn't thinking about how he looked; he was thinking about merging with the perfection of his Real Self.

When you're concerned about your image and you're always worrying about how you look to people—if you look spiritual, or if you look polite, or if you're good looking, or if you look well-dressed—you might reconsider whether or not your consciousness is in the cycle of perfecting the human or striving for the merging of oneness.

Now, I am sure that Jesus always looked fine. I am sure he looked clean. I am sure his hair was clean. But I think he probably had the dust of the road on his sandals or on his feet and probably the hem of his garment got dusty, and I don't think he was always running home and changing. It's like the disciples in the field on the Sabbath eating the corn. He understood that the system was made for man, that man wasn't made for the system; the laws were made for man, man wasn't made to be subservient to the laws.[3]

When man starts being made for the human perfectionment of things, you get the mechanization concept, you get the totalitarian state where man cannot breathe because he has to live for the perfectionment of the outer, whether in himself or his surroundings. So he goes into the robot consciousness.

Merging with the perfection within can only take place if we depersonalize. You can become overly attached to your outer self and to your four lower bodies when those four lower bodies are very skilled, when you have expertise in something. That is like the health nuts and the people that are body conscious, who get so perfect in their bodies that they live for the perfection of their bodies. And because of the perfection of their bodies they are so admired and have such a sense of perfection in the physical that they don't feel they have to strive for soul perfection—for merging with the Christ within—because they have it on the outer. You get a tremendous attachment to the four lower bodies when any one of those bodies begins to excel.

We have had the example of having a very fine musician as our guest at classes, very accomplished, technically just about perfect. This musician gets so much praise and so much attention from the people of the world about his musicianship that it has become a replacement for spiritual attainment. And he has decided that he doesn't need the ascended masters' teachings and that he doesn't need to have a commitment to them and, therefore, there is no point in playing at our classes. I can assure you that this perfectionment, this skill, has taken him from the Path.

So perfectionment in the human can be your undoing. It was Lucifer's undoing—the pride and the ambition of perfecting the human consciousness and saying, "God, I can do it better than you can, so I don't need you."

We have to beware of the burden, the actual cross of a brilliant mind or a skill or a physical beauty. We have to see that many of the fallen ones have these, and often the children of God and the sons and daughters of God do not. They bear their karma on the surface as deformities and impediments and so forth. When a son or a daughter of God finally realizes perfection in the four lower bodies, it is because he has merged with the Christ Self.

God doesn't allow his children or his sons and daughters to go too far in this pursuit of human attainment without breaking them. And usually they break on this point of striving for a mechanical perfection, which becomes a wedge in the mental body and carries on into insanity. That which was once a brilliant mind becomes broken and goes into idiocy because of brittleness in using the yellow plume— expanding it too far out of balance with the other plumes, misusing it, and finally the whole momentum is broken because of imbalance.

So whether a child is very, very naughty or very, very good, we want to take the attention off the human in this yin and yang, this pendulum swing, and we want to get the attention on the Christ Self. Then the child centered in the Christ Self will be the perfection that we desire, but it will not be because we have set our mark on the perfecting of the human, disciplining the human so that the human can be a better human machine.

This takes a lot of devotion. It takes placing our attention on the masters, letting the flow go over the figure-eight pattern (as Above, so below). A very healthy state of mind to be in is to not make too much of our frailties, not make too much of our weaknesses, not make too much of our successes—at the same time refusing to fall into that hypnotic state where we use this knowledge as an excuse to tolerate sin, tolerate wrong actions in ourselves, and let ourselves get away with things that we know very well we shouldn't be doing.

The four lower bodies have to be disciplined, not because their goal is perfection but because their goal is to be a clear pane of glass for the Christ to appear through. This is something you have to feel and work with; you have to really live and be tested in order to understand what I'm saying. Above all, don't distort it. It's better to continue to try to perfect the human following the example of the Christ than to come to the recognition that the human is not worth perfecting and let the whole thing go down the drain and become slovenly and sloppy all over again, the way you might have been months or years ago.

This is the problem when you get into higher truth: Just one statement of the teaching of Lord Buddha or of the ascended masters understood incorrectly or taken from the standpoint of a rebellious mind can produce total rebellion and total self-annihilation.

So continue to meditate and think upon this balance.

Service and Self-Discovery

One "secret of escape" is depersonalization, another is service. Service to others becomes a means for self-discovery. The way you "lose your life" and yet maintain the level of perfection is through the concept of dharma, realizing your reason for being in service. Then you have a reason to strive for perfection that is totally unattached to the self.

Say you have a neighbor who is sick and dying of cancer and no one is caring for that person. You wake up in the morning, you know that neighbor is lying in torment in her bed, so you leap out of bed, you get dressed, you eat the minimum, you rush over and you start waiting hand and foot on this neighbor.

You're living for something outside of yourself, and you find by doing this you are perfecting yourself. You did exactly what you should be doing—you got up early, you got dressed, you got washed, you said your prayers, you took off. But you didn't do it because you were sitting there thinking about perfecting the human consciousness. You did it because you were thinking about leaping to the side of a manifestation of God that was in need.

When you have an all-consuming passion within you of service to your family or loved ones or your community, you lose yourself. You're not overly attentive to your imperfections because you have no time to be. You're in a battle, you're getting a job done and you're doing the best job you know how. You are not overly concerned about the perfectionment of the flesh.

What do you discover in this service? You discover the Christ. Months down the line you might look up; for the first time you might have a chance of actually studying your image in the mirror and you might notice a transformation. Your face is no longer hanging with the jowls of greed or the fat of pride or of the ego. You see a clarity. You see the light shining through. You see an impersonal gaze. You see the light of the Christ. You really haven't had time to look

at yourself every day and to primp and to constantly do and
re-do your hair, and so forth, because you've been in service.
But you've been neat and clean and tidy, and suddenly you
see that there was a transformation. That's the discovery of
how your Christ Self shines through by losing your life for
"my sake." And for whose sake is it? It is for the sake of
your Christ.

> It is extremely difficult for the person who has not con-
> tributed in an outgoing manner to the needs of others to
> relinquish his involvement in the personal sense of struggle.

You either get all caught up in your struggles with yourself or you're too busy—you're too busy to have a nervous
breakdown, you're too busy to become an alcoholic or a
chain smoker. You don't have time. You don't have the
money either, because all your money is given to those who
need it. You find an element of extreme selfishness in people who have psychological problems. They have time for
self-indulgence. They have never lost themselves in service.
Think about that.

You will find out that in serving your fellow man everything can be overcome, all of your problems. Take sex, for
instance. When you work twelve and fourteen and sixteen
hours a day in service, you don't have any leftover energy.
You're so glad to get to bed, you go right to sleep, and you
don't have the problem of sex. You have the problem of sex
when you have too much energy, when you're letting your
energies build up in your chakras and there isn't any flow
back to God or to your fellow man.

When you are constantly blessing life and healing life,
you are emptying your cup totally. And when that cup

is empty you're ready for your inner communion in the retreats of the masters. You find that the normal functions of the body take care of themselves, but the demands are not excessive.

You might be engaged in a kind of service that isn't a physical labor, in which case you should do physical things daily to take care of the energies of sex. You should go jogging or do some kind of physical exercise to work your body and get that energy flowing into the physical body.

When the ascended masters take on chelas they see to it that every waking moment, from morning until night, is taken up in service, in invocation and in hard work. In that way people overcome their psychological problems without really having to indulge them and constantly go over them, because in service there is a constant flow, you're constantly giving. Energy is constantly flowing through you; it's like a moving stream.

So everything is flushed out. You don't have anything that is accumulating. You can't sit and worry over something. You can't sit and have the devil talk to you because you're too busy getting a job done. You don't have time to listen to the pounding of your mind with intellectual arguments as to why you shouldn't be here, because a job needs to get done and someone has a need.

That is how all of the monasteries in East and West, for thousands of years, have been set up. And that is how the initiations of the Brotherhood have been: You occupy the energy which is the time and space of the disciple. You get his energy so involved outside of himself—in the Brotherhood, in devotions to God, devotions to the masters, and in service to people—that there's constant attention on service, on God, until the energy flowing through finally becomes the fullness of the manifestation of Christ because it is unhindered by the personality of the human.

That's the process. It is personalization when you get tied up with attention on yourself, depersonalization when your attention is on service to life. That is how the Real Self in all is discovered.

> The gravest dangers attendant upon such service lie in the hope of reward, for whenever individuals serve because they expect reward they already have their reward.[4]

I hope you know that law. You are either building your causal body or not. If you want a reward God will give it to you, but he has to take the energy of your causal body to give you the earthly reward. And if it's been given, it's been given; you are not going to be paid twice. So you forfeit saving up that energy for a greater glory in the resurrection. And the reward for service is more service. That is what Morya always says: "The reward for service is greater service."

The Christ Mind vs. Human Reason

The key to freedom, then, is to serve and search. But let the search not be a forced penetration of the mysteries of life but a beautiful expectancy that promotes discovery. One of the chief problems encountered by those who would discover the Real Self is the human tendency to analyze. This method while scraping the soul bare also destroys its fabric. So delicate is reality that it must be left untouched by the hand of human reason. This is why Jesus made the statement "The kingdom of heaven suffereth violence, and the violent take it by force."[5] Their rewards are a scorched-earth activity that destroys both wheat and tares[6] and leaves them comfortless.

Take care that your reason be the reason of the Logos, the reason of the Christ mind. Be content that the Christ in you knows why all that is happening to you is happening.

There are people who try to figure out everything on the basis of human reason. They will come and tell me they want to get married because their sun signs are in opposition and their moon signs are on a trine and because this is this in their astrology, and this is that, and this happened at the same time in their lives and, therefore, they must be right for each other. That is human reason.

If you want to plan your life and plot your life according to human reason, do so. But I can assure you, you will have a thimble-size existence, because things just don't work that way.

If you go by the Spirit and you go by the Christ and you go by the inner knowing, if all things have meshed in the Spirit, by and by down the line perhaps the Logos will reveal coordinates in your life and indicators in your astrology that do correspond with your inner design. But there are people who have never even touched the flame or the Source who are already down to this little nitty-gritty thing of defining everything with rulers and measurements and so forth to prove they are right.

Well, you really don't have to prove that the Spirit is right when you have the Spirit. This is why those who have the Holy Spirit are those least capable of conveying the teaching by the logic of human reason. They no longer require it. They are the Logos, they have become the Logos, and their logic is a logic that transcends time and space and human reason.

At certain points in time and space the Logos touches down and makes sense to people, as when the Word became flesh and dwelt among us.[7] But even then, the perfect logic of the Christ incarnating didn't come about in the way that anyone would have planned by human reason that such an event should take place.

So the Logos does touch base here and there. But there's one thing about a man of God or a woman of God: you can never confine them in a matrix that you would call common, like the common denominator of human reason, because that is the knowledge of this world and the matrices of your Christ mind don't fit in it. So don't try to force it into a common matrix. Don't try to continually prove God by syllogisms or by logic, but prove God by *being* God.

There is something about truth and Reality: People can't argue with it; it is completely and totally convincing. It is convincing because it ties into the logic, the Logos of the soul. The soul knows. It is convinced; it has absolute conviction. And until it transcends these vehicles it will not be able to totally put into words why it knows or how it knows.

Contact with Reality

We espouse the development in man of a sense of sweet surrender to cosmic purpose even though that purpose be unknown. The greatest masters, through an abiding sense of confidence and faith, have obtained reality. They have never found reality by intellectual design or by probing the recesses of the caves of darkness lurking in the subconscious mind. You cannot examine evil and produce good. Only by faith in the universal idea of the Fatherhood of God and a sense of proximity to the life-giving energies of the universal Christ can the soul be nourished with the milk of the living Word.

To ignore divine mandates and eternal wisdom and to

turn instead to mere intellectual sophistry is destructive of immortal purpose. There is no higher truth than contact with reality.

There is nothing higher than "contact with reality." You have moments of contact with Reality, thanks to the ascended masters, during all or part of a dictation when you are centered upon the master who is speaking and centered in your Christ mind. You receive a concept and the radiation that is in the cup of that concept; you have a contact with Reality. And there is nothing that is higher than that contact.

Now, I didn't say there was nothing higher than a dictation or a concept or the radiation. I am saying there is nothing higher than the *contact* you make when you put yourself in touch with Reality through the dictation, through the concept, through the energy. Anyone can sit in a dictation, but not everyone will contact Reality. So it's the contacting of Reality of which I am saying there is no higher thing. The dictations are given to us as one of the greatest means that we know of for contacting Reality, because if we place ourselves in attunement we are in direct contact with those who have become one with Reality.

The End vs. the Means

There is no higher truth than contact with reality. For here there is no need to describe sensation, but only to avow a buoyant sense of surrender to a spiritual escalation and exaltation which, by its own native intelling, fulfills the requirements of intelligent being.

God teaches in the space of an instant more than man could learn in thousands of years of raking over old ruins.

God is the Creator and he tutors man when man becomes a disciple in the essence of creative culture. Man needs to know how to do, but he can never convey to another by word of mouth, by rote, or by text the very marvelous means whereby the soul can expand itself and fashion its own wings to rise.

We who are greatly concerned with the evolution of God's intelligence in unascended man and with the furtherance of the true education of the Spirit have no desire to belittle the educational systems of the world or those who would convey basic knowledge to humanity. It is only when the system becomes an end in itself rather than a means to an end that we are concerned.

It is the same thing with the human consciousness when it becomes an end in itself rather than a means to an end. That is where you can always define what you are perfecting: Is the human consciousness an end in itself? Are you building a house because you are attached to the house itself? Or is the house the means for service, for family, for the Spirit?

The same is true with the church, the state, the economy. Unless all these things in Matter become vehicles for the Spirit, they will destroy those who are a part of them because the flame has to be free to transcend the form. When you confuse the two, you destroy the soul.

According to divine ideals, the universe is not competitive. It is buoyant and expansive, and it reflects in the world of the individual the reality of the Self in its highest state. When the individual is made aware of this reflection of the real within himself, he is changed in a moment—"in the twinkling of an eye."[8] He has found his reason for being in a relative sense, and he knows that he is standing on the brink of still greater discovery. This is transcendence as God wills it.

Human knowledge, while progressive, moves in such small increments that even today the advancing and whimsical fashions of the ages pirate from humanity their lost opportunities, leaving them desolate. The electronic pulsations of the great divine flame that embodies eternal joy, peace, and purity convey the refinements of heaven to evolving humanity. But where today can men actually make contact with the valid instruction which will enable them to utilize the tremendous boons which were secretly imparted by Jesus to his disciples?

"Where can we go, Lord? Thou hast the gift. Thou hast the word of eternal life."[9] We have to go to the Christ. Where can we go for this fount of perfection? We find those who have found it—the ascended masters—and we follow them, until suddenly we find that *we* are the Christ.

The Totalitarian State

Just because men and women have waited a long time to contact truth does not mean that they should not now get started. Involvement in the business of self-discovery is the greatest assurance one can have of obtaining a passport to reality. Man should desire to have that passport and to escape from the riddle of the shifting sands of personality. Man must build on the rock of reality. And that rock is the Christ,[10] the only begotten Son of God.

Mankind have lived in the denseness of the material world. They have been glued together by the strange anachronisms of the varying standards of civilization. Through the ages, the mores have changed while the lusts of the carnal appetite have robbed mankind of their immortal birthright. Now every son of God must discover who he is. He must recognize the accomplishments of the person—his mental grasp, physical strength, and moral values—as vehicles through which the expanding light of reality can shine.

Those planets that have become planets of the pleasure cult have become that way because the state has taken over all the functions that are rightly man's, everything that he should be doing for himself—his supply, his education, his caring for those in need.

The totalitarian state removes from the individual the opportunity to lose himself in service. When he no longer has the opportunity to serve, his attention goes back upon himself. He indulges himself in extra leisure time free from drudgery and cares, and he turns to sex and all types of sexual involvements and perversions, and adornments of the self, entertainment, and so forth. When science and civilization do everything that man should be doing for himself, the path of dharma is destroyed and with it the path of karma.

That is what Jung talks about in *The Undiscovered Self*—how the state totally takes over the functions of the individual, takes his identity from him. The state also takes his religion from him and makes itself with all its trappings become his religion. That causes a disorientation, a psychological problem, because the soul has a requirement for religion, for something that is metaphysical, or beyond the physical, an anchoring point for its energy, as we would say.

When the soul is deprived of this it begins to be split, it begins to be torn. So taking away religion and replacing it with the religion of the state begins all the modern problems, all the neuroses, psychoses and all that unseats the individual: schizophrenia, morbidity, depression, and finally suicide because there's nothing left to do when you have squandered all of your attention upon yourself. The final end is the destroying of the self. The ultimate end of self-indulgence is self-destruction.

Let us define self-indulgence as attention to the human that is not required, is not necessary in order to release the Christ consciousness through the four lower bodies. We understand the accomplishments of the person as vehicles through which the expanding light of reality can shine. Any time we pay attention to the four lower bodies, it should be for that purpose, to make them better vehicles for the light of reality to shine through. More than that is self-indulgence.

I had someone come to me for counseling who was talking about taking a speed-reading course and going back to college. He was worrying about the fact that he felt a certain amount of mental pride in doing this because it was for the perfectionment of his human consciousness. And I said, "There is nothing wrong with education or a speed-reading course, as long as you're doing this to the glory of God, to facilitate the expression of the Christ mind through you."

But I could see that the boy was actually correct. He did have a cast upon his aura of pride in what he would be attaining and gaining by this pursuit. So it is not *what* you do, but your consciousness—*why* you are doing it.

For greater service to God and man, there is nothing that can beat a certain amount of education. When you go too far, of course, it is questionable.

Perfection Comes through the Christ Light

When it shines, [this light expanding through the vehicle,] it carries the power of transmutation into the confines of individual manifestation and into every area of human endeavor. It lights the hidden recesses of being. It smoothens the anomalies of life. It brings the individual into contact with a higher fraternity. It shows him a new sense. It purifies, rectifies, and exalts his consciousness. It becomes the delight of his universe, the acme of his joy, for it is the jubilation of the Gods. This light is the deluxe contact with reality which will detoxify his being of old poisons and beyond the moment of cleansing fill him with eternal treasure—the treasure of his being.

The more you polish the four lower bodies to allow the Christ light to shine through and the more the light shines through, the more these bodies will be perfected and the more they will shine forth in the perfection of inner reality. So you will be accomplishing the perfection of the human without ever having your attention upon it. That is the reward for losing your life for the sake of Christ, that you might find it again.[11] The light itself will do the work, will transmute, will bring you into alignment. It will soften, smoothen, purify, purge you.

You can take anyone that you see in life as an example. Take yourself. Where you have placed attention on the human consciousness at the expense of the development of the Christ, the human has always had to pay the price. Isn't that true? It always pays the price, and you come out with neither: you don't have a perfect human because it can't be perfected, and you don't have the Christ either.

Now, Lucifer has gone an awfully long time on this trip

of perfecting the human; for thousands of years he has been perfecting that human. And he only deals with perfection in a relative sense. Relatively he is so much farther advanced than we are, than most evolutions, that he can go a long way in deceiving himself in the perfectionment of his form and his mind and his actions, thinking that he really is exalted. That is because of the relative state of his attainment compared to our own and to most people's.

In a science or a technology that is advanced far beyond the general norm of the common man, the scientists get very confident. They can now create people in a test tube, they can even take any cell of the body and make it become an individual. There are all kinds of things that scientists can do. It's like scientists of other systems of worlds: They have their spaceships, they can fly anywhere, they have rays that can dissolve anything, so they eliminate war and the mechanisms of war. They get so high in their attainment in Matter that the pride in this perfectionment of the human goes a long, long way. It can sustain them for thousands and thousands of years, as long as they are content to be boxed within the finite frame of time and space.

All you need is a grain of the Christ mind to realize that they are prisoners of their pride, of their time and space, of Matter, and that they are never going to get out of Matter without surrendering this whole fantastic scheme they have concocted. But they don't have the perspective to see that. As long as they can create a castle here, and have a good time here or have women there, they don't even have a sense of the finiteness of their time, of the duration of their years, that all of this is going to be cut off in threescore and ten.

If you can look at the beginning and the end of the days of an individual who is caught up in this spiral, in five minutes you can decide that it is not the way for you and you can save yourself all that folly. But for some reason with the Fall and all that has gone on on this planet for thousands of years, only the handful are able to observe the scene, look at it and say, "This isn't getting anyone anywhere—it's just an old treadmill."

Souls keep coming back. They are still confined. Why? They are trying to perfect the human. That is the whole thing.

Lucifer was cast down; he was cast out of heaven, cast out of the plane of Spirit where his rebellion occurred, cast into the earth, into the plane of Matter. He will never get out of Matter.* Relatively speaking, it's a big cage—only relatively speaking—but it's a cage, it's a grid, and we have to transcend that grid. So the jubilation of the Gods will literally pour through your very cells when you make contact with Reality and become the fount of that living flame.

Be God Now

> ... detoxify [your] being of old poisons and beyond the moment of cleansing fill [you] with eternal treasure ...

The treasure is your own causal body. Finally and ultimately you become one with your causal body, either before or after the transcending called the initiation of the ascension. You can establish such a contact and such a flow that you become the full manifestation of God wherever you are. But this can only come with total depersonalization.

> Those of us to whom has been assigned the task of tutoring you in the art of self-discovery warn you at the outset that ours is no mere game of word juggling but an

*See p. 370, ch. 2. note 6.

infinite revelation which must be studied and absorbed. The Great White Brotherhood has long desired to assist man in discovering himself, but in order to do so we must cover many angles from the simple to the most complex. We must provide new insight and new approaches so that every hungry heart can be filled with spiritual manna.

Never before in the history of man have the dark ones carried an age to the brink of destruction as they have done in these latter days. Yet never before in the history of man has so much inward delight in the law of God indicated possibilities that can draw forth and magnetize those indomitable spiritual characteristics that make of mortals immortal adepts. Once again the earth must be trod upon by embodied Gods. This is no desecration, it is the fulfillment of God's dream for man! Only men of courage and valor, men of consecration and universal understanding can penetrate the insidious plots that would defraud the earth and its people of the solar power of reality.

Think about this statement: "Earth must be trod upon by embodied Gods." God isn't waiting for you to become disembodied or to pass through a transition into the etheric plane for you to be God. He wants you to not have to take all of your physical incarnation to become God. He wants you to be God *now*, so that you'll have the rest of your life to walk around in your body as God.

Really, when you come right down to it, the only price you have to pay is coming into the understanding of ceasing to perfect the human and, instead, exchanging the human for the Christ—taking off your old underwear, putting it into the fire and putting on your seamless garment.

Did you ever get to the point where you have had clothes

so long that they are saturated with the records of past experiences, past momentums, and you just have to throw those clothes away, even if they're not worn out? You have to put them into Goodwill, but they are nobody's good will. You have got to get them into the incinerator. You have got to get rid of those clothes. If you haven't had that feeling, you ought to get that feeling, because your clothes carry the records of your former self, and you really do have to put off that old man and put on the new.

When you think about it, God is waiting to make you a God. All you have to do is get over your pride, get over your ambition, get into the plane of the Christ mind and just be. Cease your sense of struggle, fulfill the requirements of the Law, surrender that substance into the flame, literally get rid of your old underwear, put it into the flame and put on the new garment of the Christ. You can be an immortal adept in the flesh.

It doesn't matter about your grid or your forcefield. There are beings who are using the stars to anchor their energy. They are not using flesh-and-blood bodies as we are, but they use the forcefield of the stars and have cosmic consciousness attainment. Your grid can be the body you have. It's as good as any; it will be flushed out and perfected by your light. But pick a grid. Let the fire blaze through it, and be God. Don't set up any mental blocks, any emotional blocks, any etheric blocks or any physical blocks. Just be God. If Mark were here, he would leap for you on the platform!

Meshing Your Consciousness with God's

"We have seen his star in the east."[12] The light from within must go forth and it must reveal that which is hidden. It must remove from the consciousness the barriers that prevent individuals from becoming the elect and chosen of God. Fear not, little children; it is the Father's good pleasure to give you the kingdom.[13] And "when he shall appear, we shall be like him; for we shall see him as he is."[14]

In most profound peace, I AM

Meru

I hope you will find the happy medium of not neglecting the four lower bodies and yet not neglecting the Christ—not entering the state of depression we were talking about where the slovenliness of the body comes in. On the basis of religion, some people have decided to let themselves be unkempt and dirty, wandering around not quite in their right minds. And that is being just a hair off of depersonalization.

When you depersonalize and you get into the real personality of the Christ, in that centeredness you are going to be clean and neat. In the wonderful path of the saints (no matter what saint you read about), you will find a glistening countenance, a purity, a sense of duty, early rising, holy prayer, love of God in manifestation, a holy rapture of communion with the angelic hosts and the Most High, with Mother Mary, and holy rapture in service, in real heart contact with men and women surrounding oneself in this plane.

That's like Ramakrishna. He would walk down the street and see a woman, probably a prostitute, and he would go into samadhi because he beheld the Divine Mother. That is the sense of communion with God in all life, of being so in love with God that wherever you are, you contact God and you mesh your consciousness with his. And in meshing your consciousness with God's there is the flow that flushes you out and transforms you.

Meditating Yin or Yang

Student: When I meditate sometimes I get carried away, I get too abstract and I lose myself. What is the best way to meditate so that doesn't happen?

ECP: You have to decide whether you are going to meditate yin or yang. Yang is the centeredness of the white-fire core. Yin is the expansion of the whole cosmos from that core. It's much more difficult to have mastery when you are yin. That's why students of macrobiotics will say someone is too yin as if that means they're out of balance or they're sick. Usually being too yin eventuates in that, because not many people can keep track of themselves in an expanded state. You have to be aware of all your coordinates everywhere and be able to master those coordinates as well as you did the one point in the heart, and it takes cosmic consciousness to do that.

So the yin is the Mother, and those who master the Mother flame have to be able to be aware of detail at all levels and points of identity in the cosmos. However, you can get lost in blending with everything if you haven't really mastered the yang.

Summit University is a yang experience, highly concentrated in the fiery core of being. When you begin to gain that mastery, you begin expanding it by increments and you only expand it to the point where you can keep track of your mastery.

A key concept of the fallen ones is divide and conquer. You're sitting at your desk, you're concentrating on your work, you're doing it well. The baby starts to cry, so you take care of the baby and go back to your desk. The phone rings, the doorbell rings, two other kids are having a fight upstairs, the water main breaks, a fire engine goes down the street—pretty soon you have so many things to keep your mind on.

Usually one split is enough, and a person loses total emotional control. When you can take care of fifty different problems going on at once and still not lose your mastery or your ability to solve those problems, you know you're moving into cosmic consciousness, because you can be aware of yourself in many points of identity, many manifestations, and still have God-control.

You learn what you can take and what you can't take. You learn how many things you can keep track of and still keep your health and your sanity, and you don't go beyond that. There are people who always take on too much and never get anything done. They haven't been able to measure their yin or their yang consciousness and how they can center in it.

About blending with your surroundings—you have to become yang before you can become yin. You start out as a baby very yang, involuted in the womb, all concentrated fiery energy, and then you start evoluting out from the womb, and stage by stage, what you are mastering is Matter, your coordinates in an expanding manifestation. After you've learned to take care of yourself, you get married and you take care of a spouse, you take care of children, you take care of a business, and so on, and it keeps on growing until some people create an empire. From the womb to an empire is going from the yang to the yin forcefield.

If you go out before you've gone within, you are liable to blend yourself with the astral plane. You are liable to merge in meditation with discarnate entities. Discarnate entities release energy that moves around you and feels like radiation, and it's nothing but astral soot. But it does have a frequency, it does contact your chakras, and it can be quite

forceful and quite powerful. People who don't have discrimination think, "Oh, I'm on the right path. I've contacted
God" or "I've contacted a master," but it's just their energies blending with the entities.

When you lose yourself in meditation that way, it's
because you haven't been yang enough. Go back; concentrate on a really simple form, a triangle or a dot. When I
want to get really concentrated, I visualize God as a dot
of light, and I pray to the dot and I pour all of my energies
into that dot, and I go straight to the heart of God in the
cosmos. I'm in the Great Central Sun just by meditation
upon the dot—whereas if I were looking all around at the
trees and the sky and the birds and people walking by, that's
where I would be. God is in them but I'm not contacting
him because I'm not getting yang, I'm not getting centered.

You have to learn how to center yourself in something
beyond this plane so that when you go into meditation you
don't get lost in all these planes of Matter.

Impostors of the Ascended Masters

Student: When you call to a master and you feel radiation, should you just assume that it's the master's radiation
and not a lot of discarnates?

ECP: Well, it's not safe to assume that when you make
a call to a master and feel energy that it is the master. I have
seen people who are psychic, who are in the plane of the ego
and the flattery of the ego and all caught up in the ego. They
talk to the masters and with regularity the impostors of the
masters release their energy to them. And they have this
whole world of fantasy built up around themselves, about
who they are and how important they are to the hierarchy.
They have their own little hierarchy. It's like a little kid

playing with a chess set; they arrange all the pieces around themselves and they're the center of this universe. But these people are so far down deep in the astral plane that they don't even have the remotest contact with Reality. I just happened to meet such an individual this past weekend, so I know I'm talking about something that actually goes on. And I've seen it over the years, of course.

So you cannot assume anything. You have to say:

> *In the name of the Christ, I demand proof that this is the living God. In the name of the Christ, I demand the binding of all discarnates and fallen ones who would dare to come near and impose themselves upon my forcefield. Roll back all black magic and witchcraft and all entities and discarnates. I refuse to accept the presence of aught else but the living God.*

You see, you can call in the wolves. You are calling in the wolves of the astral plane when you constantly desire contact because the ego needs to be flattered—"Kuthumi" visited you and gave you a special message. People who want messages are likely to be the ones who will attract the false hierarchs. But if you sit quietly and go about your business of service and be a good chela and do the works of the masters, the masters will reward you by coming and visiting you when you are least aware of their presence.

The problem is the situation where people assign their identity to things outside of themselves. In order to reinforce this identity, they have to have spirits visiting them all the time because they are not important enough if they don't. So they build up a whole religion and a whole cult and a whole experience around themselves.

It is important to know that when you decree properly (*"In the name of my Christ Self, in the name of my I AM Presence, I call forth El Morya"*), because you have used the Law correctly and made the call correctly, you can therefore count on the fact that the energy return is going to be El Morya.

In other words, infallibly, without fail, El Morya will respond to that fiat. He did come forth with a very powerful ray upon me when I made that call. By cosmic law he must respond and he does respond. If you are new in the teachings or you have a lot of astral effluvia, you might not feel that response, but you can be absolutely certain that it is forthcoming.

On the other hand, when you're not even on the Path, not using the flames, and you're in a state of total saturation of the ego, you may call to the masters and not call in the name of the Christ or the I AM Presence, and you may get the impostors, because your consciousness has an affinity and a vibration that goes along with it.

Just to be sure that no impostor comes along before Morya gets to you, you can speak that challenge.[15] There's a very high pitch and a very high charge to a master's radiation and to God's light. It will not take long—I would say within six months to a year—and you should have quite a degree of discrimination of frequencies, of what is light and what is darkness.

I can tell you that I am still learning. The definitions and the shades of darkness and light are sometimes so touchy, and the disguises of the fallen ones are so clever, that it sometimes takes a great deal of probing to discriminate, especially when you are in the plane of the Mother upholding the immaculate concept for life. When you are always looking at the perfection of God in the universal creation, you have to change glasses and put on that all-seeing-eye discernment that looks through the immaculate concept to what is acting humanly, what is manifesting, and discern the level of attainment in those who come to you.

Student: If you happen to contact a fallen one, what do you do to chase them away?

ECP: You say: *"In the name of the Christ, get thee behind me. In the name of Almighty God, I call to Astrea to encircle all foreign identities, all patterns, individualities, all consciousness with and without form that comes near my being or that would enter this house. I call to Archangel Michael."*

You have to keep calling to Michael, Astrea and Hercules for the binding of impostors. But it is people who are constantly waiting for messages who get the impostors. If you take the teaching, read your books, do the decrees, go out and serve your fellow man, get the job done, spread the teachings, you are not going to be bothered with impostors because you are not sitting there waiting to be flattered by their coming and by their messages and by their praise, and so forth. You are not tuning your receiving station in to that kind of energy.

Student: What should you do when you are contacted by an impostor while you are sleeping?

ECP: When you wake up, you should get up and make your calls to Archangel Michael to "cut me loose and set me free," reverse the tide, demand action from Almighty God and not be content until you have completed enough decrees and released enough energy for Astrea to take care of it.

You have no fear, because they have no reality in God.

They're putting on a big show to make you frightened and they say, "Here I am! And I'm this very powerful black magician, and I'm going to do this and this and this." They don't have any power unless you give them power by fear.

But you have to instantaneously call to the Christ because of the simulated power they have. They simulate power. They simulate energy. They have a synthetic self that has been going for thousands of years. And many among mankind have given them power, so they come to you seemingly with great power. But it can never equal God, and God is right there as soon as you make the call.

You have the Law and you have the science and you have the energy and you have the masters. So nothing should be able to overcome you. But it takes quick action, determined action and powerful action. You've seen the momentum that I have on making calls. They have to be sharp, dynamic, quick and absolutely uncompromising. You don't ask a demon to leave. You tell him!

I have had psychics tell me that they are polite to the impostors; they ask them if they are impostors to please leave. Don't ask them, because they are not going to leave. You have to have the absolute authority of God, and *then* they will respect you.

Student: Should you take an angry attitude toward a discarnate entity or impostor?

ECP: Don't lose your cool, because if you do, you are going to get into their vibration. When I use the word *angry*, I think of a lack of emotional control. Anger to me is a certain red passion that flows through the chakras. If you can put yourself in the consciousness of looking at Serapis Bey, at his eyes, they are steely, fiery, piercing. He has no need for anger; he just dissolves them with his flame.

You don't have to get angry. Let the force get angry, let the Rumpelstiltskins[16] get angry. That's what the devils are like. You have to get rid of them by the command of the Christ. They are not worth getting angry over. They are not worth getting upset with and letting that energy pass through you.

February 10, 1975

LORD MICHAEL

In the name of the beloved mighty victorious Presence of God, I AM in me, my very own beloved Holy Christ Self, Holy Christ Selves of all mankind, beloved Archangel Michael, beloved Lanello, the entire Spirit of the Great White Brotherhood and the World Mother, I decree:

1. Lord Michael, Lord Michael,
       I call unto thee—
   Wield thy sword of blue flame
       And now cut me free!

Refrain: Blaze God-power, protection
               Now into my world,
           Thy banner of Faith
               Above me unfurl!
           Transcendent blue lightning
               Now flash through my soul,
           I AM by God's mercy
               Made radiant and whole!

2. Lord Michael, Lord Michael,
       I love thee, I do—
   With all thy great Faith
       My being imbue!

3. Lord Michael, Lord Michael
       And legions of blue—
   Come seal me, now keep me
       Faithful and true!

Coda: I AM with thy blue flame
           Now full-charged and blest,
       I AM now in Michael's
           Blue-flame armor dressed! (3x)*

And in full Faith I consciously accept this manifest, manifest, manifest! (3x) right here and now with full Power, eternally sustained, all-powerfully active, ever expanding, and world enfolding until all are wholly ascended in the Light and free!

Beloved I AM! Beloved I AM! Beloved I AM!

* Give the coda three times at the end of each repetition of the verses.

CHAPTER NINE

KARMA AND OPPORTUNITY

Commentary on Chapter 4

To Men and Women of Faith:

The little child is born. His life begins and moves forward. Of what is he composed? Ideas? Whose ideas? His own? God's? The world's? Out of many ideas the outer person comes to be. "What is man, that thou art mindful of him? and the son of man, that thou visitest him?"[1]

Man has many overlords of whom it can be said, "Thou shalt have no other gods before me.[2] These rulers of the deep are built into the consciousness and very existence of the person in such a manner that their influence is both subtle and obvious. For example, the karmic record when it is not benign becomes an opposing force, a threatening god that must be reckoned with. Man sows; he must also reap.[3]

Although the Karmic Lords seek to bring the best tutoring out of each experience that is karmically leveled against humanity, the fact remains that sometimes the hammer blows of "fate"—which are actually manifestations of cosmic law in operation—do bring to a very low estate (seemingly without purpose) individuals who long to rise. The cry of "Why?" is heard. Yet what is needed is a perspective outside of the self, an objective view of the human person.

Men must behold the outer self from afar so that
they can be objective in analyzing the drama of existence.
Negative karma should not be an overlord. Man should
learn to rule his karma through understanding himself.
Obviously it is there, it is a fact. He cannot pass over it
entirely, for he created it.

You can see the commentary of Kuthumi on that element of the self that rises up to attack the Self, to attack the
soul, to condemn it through past records—the conglomerate of karma, of the electronic belt personified in the carnal
mind. And you can sense the overriding carnal mind not
only of the individual, but also its tying into the mass consciousness. These are the "gods many" and we must say to
them, "Thou shalt have no other gods before me."

You must not become the idolators of your karma, of
your four lower bodies or your personal momentums, any
more than you are going to be idolators of the moon or
the astrology or the waves of substance that pass over the
planet. This is idolatry: to place that substance and that
energy before God.

I have a young woman working for me who is suffering
from the illusion, the gross illusion that threatens to destroy
her mind, that she is being overtaken and overpowered by
an individual who is supposedly projecting energy at her
daily and keeping her awake. I said to her, "You are giving
more power to that person and that energy than you are to
your own I AM Presence. This is idolatry." And this girl has
been through Summit University.

So remember, it is not what you hear and it is not that
you attend Summit University, but it is what you *apply*. You
must resist idolatry. And this is what idolatry is.

The Desire to Control vs. God-Control

We leave you with this thought for a moment that we might go on to another subject and that is the buildup within the self of a resistance to opposing forces which manifest in society in general and in the world of the individual. In this connection we would also speak of a man's desire to control others, of his desire to dominate, of his will to rule even where he is opposed. And we see now that there are gods many and lords many,[4] but the man who will truly understand himself must be subject to none of these.

The illusions of the carnal mind—that aspect of the self which is dominating the Self through one's records and karma—are attackers that enjoy controlling the soul. The four lower bodies that are spoiled, that have been indulged, also enjoy controlling the energy of the soul. Once they find they can control your soul, they try to control other souls.

There is also the situation of a dominating parent, where you are taking in that dominating parent and then you are beginning to dominate others. This is a perversion of the will. The will is a forcefield within the Self, the drive and the determination to be God. Your will can have ulterior motives, and these ulterior motives—such as the desire to control other parts of life—will deprive you of your victory and of your God-dominion. Sadly, most people don't realize that they have a momentum on desiring to control others.

People control people by being discordant, by throwing energy, by being irritable, by demanding attention, by making people wait on them, making people do things for them. There are all kinds of methods of control that are quite subtle. People control people through sex. They control people through fits of weeping or through sexual magnetism.

They toy with people. They toy with their energies. All these things can go on at subconscious levels—partly subconscious, partly conscious.

Then there is God-control, and God-control means the channeling of your energies according to the divine plan. If you're in the center of a group and you have leadership qualities—and by the way, beloved Ascended Lady Master Nada says the quality of leadership is a quality of divine love—if you have the ability to lead, and by God-control you are assisting in the directing of everyone's energy into the divine plan, this is not what we're speaking of. This is not manipulation. This is not unwholesome, but it is as it should be because then someone is always there to keep the flame for the flow of energy in the mandala. Sometimes when people get very adept at doing this they are accused of using people or controlling people, but that's not it at all, because God uses all of us, and God controls all of us according to our free will.

Honestly Observing Your Subconscious

Beware, then, of subtle motives. There is one thing you must understand: the subconscious pockets of human willing and human motivation so sap your energy and drain you that they can cut your momentum in half. So you have got to let these things come to the surface. This is the very healthy situation of observing your illusions, observing your synthetic self. It doesn't mean that you have to get so psychically entangled with that substance that you can never be extricated. But for a moment, for a period, let yourself have the courage to allow some of this subconscious business to come to the surface. Look at it for what it is. Examine it. Pass it into the flame.

A certain amount of introspection is necessary and healthy. When it becomes too much and when we engage in self-examination just for the sake of enjoying being involved in subconscious psychic energies, we've lost the whole purpose. But from the level of the Christ Self, to be able to stand and wisely observe your own trends and momentums and see the interaction and interplay of yourself with other people, and perhaps for the first time in your life to be totally honest with yourself, *this* is an experience of such maturity and such freedom.

To not fall apart, to be able to say, "I tell a lie once in a while. I exaggerate. I wasn't honest with that person. I used that person because I wanted to get something done." To be able to admit that to yourself, to not engage in self-condemnation, to not get all emotional about it but to say, "All right, this grid, this forcefield that God has given me as an opportunity has been used for darkness. It's not going to be any more. I am taking dominion. I am turning over this grid and this forcefield to God and I am going to let God, Portia, Goddess of Opportunity, use me. Instead of being an opportunist, I am going to be a flame of opportunity and extend opportunity to life." And no matter what you have done or what you have used this forcefield for, you are now going to say, "All right, I am going to let it be the focal point for cosmic rays."

This moment of truth, this moment of awareness is so cleansing, so beautiful and so freeing. But let go of it. And for God's sake, have the faith to know that the flame will wash you clean.

Have Faith

To come out of a decree session and say, "It's all right for now, but it's going to come back later"—where is your faith? Doesn't the Bible say "Though your sins be as scarlet, I will make them white as wool, white as snow?"[5] If the Bible says it, believe it. If God says it, believe it.

If Jesus can forgive sin, believe that it can happen to you by the power of your own Christ. Your own Christ Self has the power to forgive and to redeem energy, but faith is necessary. Faith is your chalice which keeps that energy moving. No matter what you find, no matter what you see as distortion in the self, believe absolutely in the law of your being that God can heal it. You must be a torch of faith and you must start with yourself.

You must believe with all your heart that God can heal anything and everything that is a flaw in your consciousness. Turn it over to him. When Jesus says, "Whatsoever you ask the Father in my name, he will give it to you,"[6] believe it. Ask the Father in Jesus' name, and release your fear, release your worry. Turn it over to God and Jesus and the ascended masters and know with absolute faith it is done.

This spark of faith is a kindling fire that will set the world on fire with the ascended masters' teachings. You must be infused with this faith. And on the basis of that rock of faith in the Christ consciousness, you can stand with your full God-maturity and be the observer of your infractions of the Law and be not moved one iota. That takes all the sting and all the energy and power away from the dark forces, because they thrive on condemnation, on accusation, on shame, on making you feel that you did this terrible thing and you can never be free from it.

Once you have faced it, exposed it and stood up to it and said, "Okay, so I made a mistake. Well, God is forgiving me and I'm going on," and that is cosmic law—no one can ever tempt you, no one can ever tear you down, not the voice inside of you or the voice from without. It is so important that you have faith in the Law itself. The Law is the rock of our salvation.

You Have a Right to Joy

Man is born to rule, but first he must rule himself. He must school his desires and flex the muscles of self-control. If he cannot do this by himself, he has the right to seek divine help. He is not alone. He is a unity in a diversity which itself is held within a unity.

Just remember this when you know you should do something because the Christ within you is speaking and it is the Law, but somehow there is resistance, or you don't really feel the flow and the joy of doing what you know you should do. Invoke the joy. Invoke the desire to do it. Pray to Jesus:

Beloved Jesus, Good Master, you served. I would serve also. I know that I ought to be about my Father's business. Place in my heart the joy of serving, the desire to serve. Blend my free will with your free will and let's be a team and let's go forth and let's do this thing in the name of God.

You don't have to wait until your human self gets around to deciding it's going to put aside a clump of substance. If you don't feel that overwhelming joy of service or joy of decreeing, demand it be put in your heart. Don't stand for that nonsense of boredom and that substance of carnal-mindedness and that substance of doubt and fear. You have a right to be joyous in your life, every day of your life. You have a right to have joy. "Your joy no man taketh from you."[7] Don't let any force, any criticism, any cynicism and that intellectual substance put a wet blanket on you to steal your joy.

One thing about ascended master students, we are not going to walk around with long faces and sackcloth and mourning with the crucifixion consciousness. When people look at an ascended master student, I want them to see joy and happiness, that there is something about this path that makes you happier than any other thing you could possibly be doing on the planet. Who wants to follow you if it's such a vale of tears? Nobody wants to follow you through that. So you really have to radiate joy. Joy is what the force tries to take from you, to make you have a look of anguish and pain and sighing and burden and all that type of consciousness.

One disease students get is continually talking about "the force this, the force that and the force the other thing." Why talk about them so much? Don't give them that power. The only power they have is your attention. It's all right to acknowledge the battle. We know the battle is there. But for heaven's sake, I'd like to hear you at least give equal time to saying, "The I AM Presence this and the I AM Presence that and the I AM Presence the next thing." After all, who is in command of this universe?

See Karma as Opportunity

Returning now to the idea of the karmic god in its negative aspects, we would point out that what one cannot change one must learn to live with. And it must be remembered that the intervention of mercy is always a possibility for the soul that would truly serve the cause and in so doing emerge from the entanglements of his karma.

There are conditions that we find we must live with—a thorn in the flesh, a situation of owing karma to individuals, a situation of having to serve, or being in a job, or economic situations. These make us have to go through certain things. But remember that life, as the unfoldment of your karmic cycles, never gives you more than you can handle in a given day or a given lifetime.

If you will graciously accept from the hand of the Goddess of Opportunity, Portia, the karma that is given to you and see it not as punishment but as the marvelous opportunity to redeem energy, then you can feel the flow— the ever-flowing stream of divine love moving through your heart all the day and all the night, loving those who are near you, loving those whom you serve. And no matter what the yoke of bondage or tribulation the karma might appear to be, this ever-flowing stream of love gives you such bliss because you can constantly feel the balancing of forces of cosmic energies. Where you have wronged life, this love flowing through your heart is righting that wrong.

As that balancing is taking place, there is such a flow of joy, of feeling that balance is being brought to bear. There is the idea that the whole cosmos is coming into alignment because of this release of energy through you, because of the flow of love and the transmutation of electronic-belt substance. And each person you serve is thereby freed. And you are freed. That is the sense you must maintain.

The Sense of Poverty Is Inharmony

I received a letter from a girl who attended Summit University and will be entering the path of service in nursing. But she is burdened by worrying about the fact that she doesn't see abundance around her. She doesn't have a job. She doesn't have the nice clothes or the beautiful things that she thinks ought to surround her, and she can't understand why she should be in such a state of poverty. Yet she says that her consciousness is completely harmonious.

Now, here's a subtle trap. The sense of poverty *is* inharmony. The impoverished consciousness is an inharmonious consciousness because it is an absence of wholeness. If you don't have a sense of wholeness, you can't maintain harmony because harmony is the perfect balance of Alpha and Omega within you. A lack of wholeness is a lack of love.

This particular individual has had a problem on the ten-four axis for a number of embodiments and has made tremendous strides and progress through coming here. But now she's out in a large city feeling the weight, feeling very much alone, feeling the oppression of family members and of not having yet established herself in a nursing school. She is feeling that weight.

You must beware of any sense of incompleteness. If you ever have a sense that God isn't manifesting in his full glory of the abundant life right now, right where you are, you are off-center. You are out of harmony and you are engaging in the misqualification of the Mother flame on the six o'clock line and you are stopping the flow of your supply. And for that very reason you are impoverished—because you don't have the abundant sense, the abundant life. Jesus said, "I am come that all might have life and that more abundantly."[8] That abundance is his attunement with the Divine Mother.

I remember the day I moved into the very first apartment I had while I was in college. I couldn't afford much. It was a basement apartment, and the vibrations were just terrible. At that time I didn't know about decreeing. I took a look around me and it was certainly not the surroundings I was accustomed to. It was on the verge of being squalor. It was in Boston, in the heaviness of the weight of that city.

I communed with God and I said, "Dear God, I know

that if I am here, it's because I have a work to do here. And if I am here there's something in me that has attracted this place to me. So I'm going to stand and I'm going to see and I'm going to know you until my awareness of you propels me out of this place into the consciousness that I want to be, that I know I really am."

It gave me a great sense of joy to commune with God in this manner. I sensed the challenge and I totally accepted the responsibility for being in that place as being some lack in my own consciousness. After I got through saying this, I was completely happy. I was living in the aura of God. It really didn't matter where I was. I was going to school. I went about my business.

Within two weeks someone offered me a beautiful apartment on the top floor of a place with lots of sunshine and bay windows. I very happily moved in, painted the whole thing myself, put together some secondhand furniture and so forth, and made a very happy little home. It was only two weeks. It might have been two embodiments if I had entertained the poverty consciousness. I could have remained in the basement of a Boston apartment to this day. Some people stagnate. They never get beyond; they get locked into a certain stage.

So it was a choice, and we all have these choices. You don't have to stay where you are. You don't have to put up with your karma. You can master it. But you have to understand that wherever you are standing, whatever you see around you is your responsibility. You clean up your world, you remain positive and circumstances will change. People around you will be transformed. Nothing can stay the same if you are transmuting energy, because it affects the entire creation, the entire cosmos.

But you cannot entertain a sense of lack. The idea "I'm here, God's over there, and someday I'm going to get there, and sometime I'm going to be perfect, and someday I'm going to have all the qualities I want to have" is the procrastination consciousness, the terrible mesmerism of the serpent and the dragon. Morya says you cannot be on the path of initiation if you have procrastination, because you don't have the sense of the now and the fullness of the now. You have to claim everything as yours *now*, God as being yours *now*. You have to claim your healing *now*. You can't wait until tomorrow for it.

Take your attention off it. Turn it over to God. Give your call to God in the name of Jesus, which is always answered, and then lovingly accept with that inner joy and humility whatever the Father's dispensation is in response to your call. Maybe you need to have an earache for a day. It's teaching you humility. It's showing you compassion for pain. Maybe you need to experience a few things to get ripened for your world service.

The minute you have an infirmity and you can't get rid of it with one call, don't say to yourself (or let the force say to you) that the teaching is no good and it doesn't work and you should quit. If you really accept the Path and the teachings, you have to welcome adversity as the friction which enables you to develop your muscles and to anchor the energy that is necessary to overcome. It's just like a baby lifting himself up by the rope that you put over the crib, or the little chain with rattles and things. He's got to flex his muscles and pull himself up. He has to learn how much energy is required to do that. And you have to learn it too.

Karma Is Opportunity to Free Electrons

Meeting your karma is a joyous path. It is exciting. It is thrilling. Don't ever teach that karma is punishment. Be careful not to ever let that come out of your mouth—the concept that your karma is a weight of punishment, that God is punishing people. Karma is opportunity to free electrons. Write that down.

Karma is opportunity to free the electrons, the atoms and the molecules of your being. And what an opportunity it is! God is always willing and ready to help—not sometimes but always. And he doesn't condition his help on your state of consciousness. You condition your *receiving* of that help by your state of consciousness.

God is always willing and ready to help. The statement of Jesus to Saul of Tarsus "It is hard for thee to kick against the pricks"[9] reveals the fact that when living truth first manifests to the human consciousness, it may seem to be a hard thing and the way difficult. All of the forces of the universe seem to oppose the life of the Divine Manchild. It is as though the Herods of the world were sending out soldiers to slaughter the innocent young Christs emerging within the dense domain of the person.

Yet the struggles against karma must not be permitted to overcome the self nor to make the self bitter as those individuals driven into the wilderness of self-consciousness who, feeling the pangs of inferiority, seek to flagellate the world, to lash out and overcome in an earthly way those "opponents" of their very existence. We are reminded of the words "All is vanity and vexation of spirit."[10] But such is not the purpose of life. Man must truly know himself—not as a karmic record, but as a divine being.

Isn't that exciting? No more going to psychics for life readings. No more reading the tarot or tea leaves or palmistry to find out who you were in the past. You know who you are. God in you is who you are and that is what is so important. *You are a divine being*, not a karmic record.

God Is the Keeper of His Own Child

We come, then, to the god of opposition. The world seems to contain within itself the very seeds of opposition to the achievement of any good thing. All who rise are opposed, and we sometimes ask ourselves if opposition itself is not the goad that engenders strength for attainment. Yet man must not become subject to an overpowering sense of the opposition of the world. These towering gods must be dethroned not by human reason but by holy reason and by a purified intelligence. If the surface of the idol be rough, then that rough surface will provide a foothold for the climb.

And of the desire to dominate others, this must be recognized as one of the most dangerous of all diseases of the ego. Only by the wings of true selfhood can man actually attain, and when he does so he becomes a power of good example in the universe which all may follow.

Let me tell you a formula for an invocation when you feel yourself having the need to dominate someone because they are not quite doing the right thing they should be doing on the path, or so on and so forth. You tell yourself that God is the authority and God is the control of that person. You refrain from speaking—unless, of course, it's your child and you have a responsibility for discipline—and you know within yourself that your I AM Presence, your Christ Self, is moving into action to control that person because your God, his God, all God is one God. And when that unbridled energy starts rising up to nag someone or to constantly remind someone that they're not doing this and they're not doing that and they should do this and they should do that, you say to yourself that that type of thing will destroy a marriage, will destroy a personality.

I want to tell you a story about this desiring to control and the fear of thinking that God cannot control man and his own creation, the idea that human beings have to control each other through the human consciousness. It's the story about carrying the ark of the covenant. In the days of the Old Testament God said that no man should touch the ark. They were transporting the ark, and it was on the road and it began to tip and teeter and totter a little bit. One man came forward to steady the ark. He put his hands on it to hold it, and the Lord God struck him dead for his disobedience.[11]

This was the impersonal Law, the very energy of the ark itself. That ark was so highly concentrated with the Lord's Spirit as a forcefield that this individual who was not consecrated as a priest could not stand that momentum of light. It struck him dead.

The Old Testament records such things happening, like people being struck dead for an infraction of the Law, because in the dispensation that came before Jesus there was the pure energy of the Law without the intercession of the Christ and mercy. There were very harsh experiences and so-called punishments or actions of the Law, such as Lot's wife turning into a pillar of salt, Onan being struck dead, Saul dying, and so forth.[12] There were many experiences that seem terrifying.

In actuality, that dispensation of energy was given to the

274 Advanced Studies in Understanding Yourself

Israelites and it had to counteract a tremendous momentum of their rebellion—of Taurus substance, of disobedience, stubbornness and defiance of the law of their own being. They did not merit the mercy of the Christ or the intercession of the Christ at that point of world karma. If they were going to have the light, the demand was absolute obedience. If they didn't give that obedience, those were the consequences.

So the Law came through Moses, and grace came through Jesus Christ.[13] Now you understand the meaning of that statement—it is the intercession of the law of forgiveness.

When you are trying to control other people or thinking that you need to control other people, you are reaching out your hand to steady the ark because you don't have the faith that God can steady the ark himself, that God is the keeper of his own child, his own son and daughter. You need to develop that faith and that trust, and you need to say:

> *Dear God, I know that you are taking care of your child, your son, your daughter. And I turn over this entire situation and this problem to you. I commend it into your keeping. I commend this person into your care. And I will not interfere in his evolution and in his free will.*

So remember the ark when you get into the momentums of desiring to control. The desire to control is not always for the obvious reason of wanting to help someone or wanting to bring them closer to the Path. The carnal mind has very deadly motives for control, all tied up with self-seeking, and so on. Nevertheless, the same invocation, the same prayer must be made. You have to stand back and let God work through his creation. Let God be the teacher. And when your children reach a certain age, you have to turn them over to God. You have to let them be free. You have to let go of them and you have to trust that God is able to take care of them.

I Can Do It All by Myself

Here are the words of Jesus:

"Verily, verily, I say unto you, he that believeth on me, the works that I do shall he do also; and greater works than these shall he do; because I go unto my Father."[14] As the soul rises toward God it becomes a luminary that inspires other lives to see his star, to be his star, to ingest light, to be possessed by light, to be light, to exalt, and to be exalted. This is ascended master God-control which mobilizes the good in all life through the individual who has attained self-mastery.

By your God-control of your own forces and your own energies, you become an electrode of God-control whereby you can magnetize the I AM Presence of mankind into action to control them. And that's the way it should be, because in reality, all people are just like your two- or three-year-old who will say to you, "I can do it all by myself. I want to do it all by myself." And if you do something for them, you have to go back and undo the whole thing so they can do it by themselves.

Maria Montessori lovingly explains that a child does not do something to get something done. A child does something for the sheer enjoyment of the ritual that is involved. The child enjoys the ritual, and therefore, for you to hurry up and do it for him is not the point. The point is, "I can do it all by myself." And that's how people are. They have to focus that control by themselves. And you have to trust that God is able to unfold the flower of the soul.

"Man, Know Thyself!"

How man trembles on the brink of self-destruction. Indeed, how he trembles on the brink of self-exaltation! The little children of God must learn to fear not, for the natural steps to universal attainment unfold within the domain of the inner Self. It is but the outer self that trembles, as has been said, "the devils also believe, and tremble."[15] Yet man is not a devil (*deified evil*); he was made a little lower than the angels and when he is found to be an overcomer he shall be crowned with more glory and honor.[16]

The self must be discovered. If a man lose his life for "my sake," the fact that he shall find it again[17] must be realized by him as eternal truth which cannot be gainsaid. He is not the little person that he seems to be. He is the great Person (the pure son) that God made him to be. But the overlay—the patine of mud, of human filth, of degradation and dust that covers the earth—must be removed by the cleansing power of the Holy Spirit, by the washing of the water by the living Word[18] that makes all things real.

Then upon the altar stone, the foundation of truth and reality, he must rebuild the city of perfection which is cast down. In his search for the real, man can, if he wishes, explore the world of the unreal. But merely to understand what is not real will not of necessity bring him a sense of that which is real. God seems far away to some, but when they draw nigh unto him and he does draw nigh unto them[19] the comfort of the Holy Spirit manifests in the joy of discovery.

Kuthumi is giving you permission, on a limited basis, to explore the world of your unreality. But he says that it will not bring you of necessity "a sense of that which is real." Therefore, psychology without the understanding of the psychology of the causal body, the I AM Presence, the soul and the Christ Self does not have that counterpoint of the divine gnosis to give you what you need after you have explored the subconscious.

Religion has been dangled before men as a panacea for all of their ills. It is not formal religion that is the answer, but the reality of God who originally clothed man with innocence. This purity that is the identity of the real man must be put on once again even as the old man with his deceit and shame is put off.[20] This is not merely a matter of sect or philosophy; it is more than that. It is the living actualization of truth and being—being that refuses to accept the mold of complacency, of degeneracy, of death, that recognizes that the last enemy of death[21] shall be overcome together with all of the lesser enemies that seek to destroy the reality of the person.

The false realities must go, they must be overcome, they must be recognized for what they are—enemies of the real Person. Not only do these lie in wait without to waste away the substance of the soul, but also they lie within the domain of the individual consciousness. That discord which is without is drawn to the self because reason has already been dethroned within and man lives in ignorance of his great commission.

You are commissioned by God, as sons and daughters of God, to deliver the word of truth to the age and to be the flame of reality. This is your great commission.

As he returns to reason, as he begins the process of rediscovering himself, much of the sense of struggle disappears and experience is seen as the turning of the pages in a great book of known reality. Rise he must; but the how, why, and when is not always answered to one's satisfaction. The great universal magnet—through the hungers of the soul and its subtle belief in reality, by its inward majesty—appeals to the being that lives within this shroud of human personality.

"The great universal magnet"—you feel that magnet through the hungering of your soul. When your soul hungers for God it is actually the impulse of the Great Central Sun Magnet wanting to go back to the center of being.

Truly the words "Man, know thyself" lead him onward and upward into the light.

Radiantly, I AM your elder brother,

Kuthumi

We thank you, beloved Kuthumi.

February 13, 1975

CHAPTER TEN

LIGHT
AND DARKNESS

Commentary on Chapter 5

To Those Who Maintain an Open Mind in the Spirit of Inquiry:

One can easily resolve the question "Which came first, the chicken or the egg?" by asking, "Which came first, God or man, Spirit or Matter?" The answer may well provide additional insight into our subject—understanding yourself.

Man was created as a Spirit, and consciousness and intelligence are a necessary part of the spiritual being that man really is. However, consciousness—which may be defined as God's awareness of himself—not only functions in the domain of Spirit but also is able to project itself into the time-space continuum and thus to integrate the ever changing world of the finite into the magnificent real world of the Infinite.

The sole purpose of life upon the schoolroom-planet Earth is to develop in man through consent by free will those masterful cosmic qualities that are a part of the character and being of God. The eternal Spirit is all-goodness. Man is intended to become that goodness. Of necessity, his intelligence has been limited both in ability and flexibility by his karmic pattern and by his response to the opportunities of

Life. His power, likewise, has been restrained until such a time as the character of the individual might be developed in its divine similitude, whereupon his acts would become wholly divine, hence worthy of the divine power.

There is no competition in God. He delights in the diversification of all creation provided that its pattern is after the true nature of the divine being. The reason that pattern is all-important has to do with eternal life or a state of permanence in God. God does not wish to perpetuate evil or unhappiness, and certainly man should not desire to prolong his imperfection. Therefore the guardianship of the Eternal has placed necessary safeguards and restraints in the world of form, including the death of the physical body. This was done in order to prevent the perpetuation of undesirable traits of mortal thought and feeling.

Have you ever thought about that? You have to break the matrix, break the mold at a certain point. The calcification of human consciousness is such that, in the present state of evolution, it is better for people to reincarnate with a clean slate and a new opportunity to develop than to continue in their old ways. So the death of the physical form is an action of cosmic mercy.

Zeal, Ambition and Pride

Let men understand that the abundant life must come into manifestation in the world of the individual as naturally as the opening of a flower once he has developed attunement with the mind of Christ. For the Christ acts as a mediator for him and imputes unto him that righteousness which is the Father's will.

There are many weapons which the dark ones have

employed to keep mankind from discovering the Real Self. The most darkening of all is the screen of egoistic (self-centered) consciousness and that altogether human quality of pride which so readily saturates the being of man. Beloved ones, pride is so subtle that individuals often mistake it for spiritual zeal.

Now, beloved Portia spoke to us and called that ambition.[1] We must be careful about zeal and ambition. That doesn't mean we should sit back and not do anything about bringing in the kingdom of God. You do have to strive to enter in yourself and to bring others the teaching. But there is a flow whereby you become the handiwork and the instrument of the Holy Spirit in executing this, rather than becoming so zealous that it turns into something you want to accomplish in the human consciousness or in the human personality—chalking up merits for sainthood, the idea "I'm doing this, and God's going to think I'm wonderful because I've converted so many sinners this week."

The difference is a very fine line, and the subtleties really lie at subconscious levels. So it's good to keep on trying, and to call for the refinement of motives while you are trying. Just be on guard—that is the main thing. Be on guard that your desiring to reunite with God could become a point of pride within.

The great doer is always the Eternal One who employs the hands and feet of humanity as well as their consciousness, their mind, and their will but never without the consent of the individual. It is his intent to turn over to the individual—just as soon as he has demonstrated his capacity and worth to receive it—the full employment of his God-given talents. The correct use of these talents is always under the direction of the genius which God has implanted within the mortal consciousness. This genius is truly a manifestation of the infinite law that lives and moves in the finite world.

With all of their hearts, men should guard their consciousness against the Luciferian attitude of human pride. With few exceptions, the people evolving upon this planet have lurking within their consciousness the quality of pride which shows its face when individuals allow themselves to become piqued over little things. The spiritually progressive lifestream who is willing to engage in a bit of introspection should note as an indication of personal pride the fact that he becomes annoyed or angry with others over trifles or unimportant matters that ought not to make any difference. One should learn balance and reasonability, giving unto others the same grace that one expects to receive.

If at this moment you are thinking of someone who gets piqued over little things and blows up at the drop of a hat, you are in a wrong state of consciousness, because when this kind of situation is described, you should not be thinking about anyone but yourself. You miss the whole point of the teaching when you say to yourself, "Aha! I hope so-and-so is listening because that really applies to him—he does that all the time." We're not here to worry about anybody else but our own self and our own electronic belt.

So draw in your feelers and draw in your consciousness and concentrate on your own four lower bodies. If you have ever become upset over some little thing that wasn't important, know that that was pride acting. It comes in the guise of being overly fastidious or the concept of perfecting the human that we spoke about, of idolatry. When you become annoyed or angry over trifles, you can be certain that pride and that which is antichrist within you is acting. If it is ever manifested in you, you have work to do. And you can't be worried about anybody else's consciousness or world.

The Tree of the Knowledge of Good and Evil

Through inward delight in the law of God,[2] a man can reach the point where he is able to withstand the onslaught of excess emotionalism and hold himself in the balance of the universal light even when his sensitive nature causes him to feel the pain of anger or regret concerning the conduct of another. Self-control that is control of the emotions and the feeling world is one of the keys to self-mastery which some of our disciples find difficult to employ.

Because the individual identifies with his consciousness, he is sensitive to circumstances which invade his consciousness and which he may interpret as an affront to his own life. By identifying with all life right while he maintains an awareness of his personal function and a sense of his personal mission he can easily understand why individuals may act or react as they do. This understanding will spread the oil of tranquility on the troubled waters of human affairs. Above all, the self should remain poised yet not aloof or without compassion for the problems of others.

Training in sensitivity to Christ is advocated by the Brotherhood, but we would point out that involvement in psychic sensitizing and improper physical contact with others (which comes under the heading of "sensitivity training") is a dangerous procedure which can very easily bring about the demise of needed individuality. Men need to preserve the individual self while they attain spiritual identification with the Real Self. Expanding that sense of identification, one can include as a part of his own self-awareness the God Presence in all life. And he need not explore the human psyche or physique in order to achieve this awareness.

Yesterday, as I was receiving people in line and shaking hands, a girl came up to me and said, "Do you really think that a person can reach fulfillment and a consciousness of wholeness and be celibate?" And I said, "Yes, I do." I named Jesus and the saints as examples of a communion with God whereby they attained wholeness here and now in the physical plane. Then she explained to me that she felt her union with a man, at all levels, was the only way she could experience wholeness.

I explained to her that for some the path was celibacy and for others it was being married, and by both paths one could attain union with God. Certainly both experiences are valid in the eyes of God. I agreed with the concept that one can attain a greater realization of God through the path of marriage, but I also affirmed the way of celibacy.

I want to point out that people will take a truth, they will put it in a framework of, let's say rebellion or immorality or being outside of the law, and they will justify the whole framework on the basis that there is an element of truth in it. Lastly, they will seek the confirmation or the approbation of someone who is a representative of the Great White Brotherhood, or someone who is a minister or a priest, to set the seal of authority of the church or of God or of his laws on their actions. People will ask you such questions in a very off-handed way, and in an unguarded moment, by seeing an element of truth in their argument, you may tend to agree with them.

The basic argument of the Luciferians is always that you require a backdrop of darkness in order to perceive light—that light in itself has no relief, no shaded areas whereby we can identify the light—and therefore, in order to appreciate truth, reality and so forth, mankind must indulge in and partake of sin, and only by experiencing sin can they appreciate the light.

There is an element of truth in this because we have all had the experience of being out of phase with God, and during those moments of being out of phase, by the contrast of the absence of God and his presence, we have learned a little more about the Law. But it is the unfortunate state of our limited consciousness that has ordained this, not the law of God.

God's law says that you can know the light while you are in the light, and you do not have to taste of the fruits of the tree of the knowledge of good and evil.[3] And when you do insist on tasting those fruits, you fall from the state of holy innocence and you dwell forevermore in that shadowed level of relativity where good and evil move on a scale and on a spectrum.

There was an individual on the staff who tried for years to get Mark to affirm that yes, you had to know darkness in order to appreciate the light. And he finally resigned because he could never get Mark to say that.

The masters explained to us that light has all types of hues and variations and frequencies and vibrations. Take, for example, the seven rays and the five secret rays.* Even the intensity of light in your light bulbs can vary from very

*See p. 372, ch. 7. note 5.

low to very high, and by the action of the light you gain perspective.

So light provides its own bas-relief, its own backdrop, its own sculpturing. And on the backdrop of light, the light creation, the sons and daughters of God can and do appear, and they can realize the fullness of joy without ever departing from the light. That is important.

The same Luciferian argument is found in the concept of "sensitivity training"—that we have to feel bodies, we have to feel psyches, we have to explore the astral plane in order to ultimately get to God. The only sensitivity you truly require is sensitivity to the Christ. When you are centered in the Christ, you will have the full discrimination that Jesus had to perceive not only the physical body but the aura, the organs, the state of health, what is ailing in an individual, what calls are necessary. That far transcends what you could ever learn through human probing of the human consciousness.

Note how subtly these arguments come up. Even as I talked to that young woman, I was probably not as vociferous as I should have been, because I wasn't even thinking of her situation and her involvement as being outside of the Law or immoral. I was thinking of the celibate state versus the married state and analyzing the two for her. But as I concluded my presentation of the Law and really looked at this woman, I saw that her face was distorted and she was truly in a state of rebellion and had been for many incarnations.

As I thought of the encounter through the day and gained perspective, I realized that she was definitely seeking the seal of my approval on a very unwholesome and illegitimate relationship—illegitimate in the sight of God. I thought that would be interesting for you to hear because you will be involved with people and the perplexities of their problems and you have to know how to deal with them.

> It is necessary that effective God-control over the creation be maintained in the universe so that God can produce the reality of his kingdom everywhere. Where the Spirit is not present, where the Spirit is denied, where the Spirit is quenched[4] there is no fount of reality that brings the buoyancy of inter-spiritual and inter-personal realizations to the consciousness. The little bursts of joy that flood the soul as it comes in contact with those who are spiritually of like mind is a certain indication of the presence of the Spirit.

"The bursts of joy that flood the soul" have to do with the cross where the energies of Alpha and Omega meet and the bursting of the Christ consciousness at the point of that nexus. When you feel a burst of joy, there has to be alignment somewhere—somewhere within you and somewhere within those with whom you share—alignment in the converging of the Father-Mother God in wholeness.

Maintaining Christ-Dignity

Those who engage in so-called mental karate,[5] those who seek to control or to hypnotize others, often do not realize that they are functioning outside of the intent of the eternal Father. Each son, in the dignity of true self-realization, must hold a sense of his own individual mission and expand outward in consciousness through the heavenly Presence to understand the life plan of others.

In one sense all life is one, and this is the highest sense; but in the lower senses there are many snares and tangles to be avoided. Through discretion, Christ-discrimination,

> and holy prayer, men retain their divine dignity which does
> not preclude the possibility of the effervescing of the self in
> humor, truism, and perpetual joyousness. Such dignity is
> never overcome by person, place, condition, or thing.

Have you ever felt that your dignity in Christ was somehow assailed by the presence of rebellion, darkness, accusation, swearing—conditions surrounding you? This can
easily happen. You can feel the thrust of dark energy lashing
into your aura, and you can momentarily feel your being
almost teeter-tottering to regain balance when you come
face-to-face with dark ones. In those moments you have to
affirm divine dignity; the dignity of the Christ is never overcome by any "person, place, condition, or thing."

In Clara Louise's memoirs we have the writing of Cecilia
Lewis, who stated that as a young girl she was with Louise
in Denver. They had had a guest, and Cecilia felt that she
had made some kind of awkward remark that probably
offended Louise. She was rather silent and moping, thinking
she had somehow hurt Louise's feelings or marred her image
or embarrassed her by her actions.

Louise finally asked her why she wasn't speaking. So
Cecilia told her. And Louise said, "I am never embarrassed by anything that anyone does around me. I am never
embarrassed."[6]

It is important to maintain Christ-dignity no matter who
or what is misbehaving, whether it's your personal family,
your friends, those you feel attached to—those to whom you
have assigned a portion of your identity and are therefore
embarrassed if they misbehave. That is a key lesson. But in
order to feel that lesson we have to reclaim our identity from
those who have had the power to embarrass us, because we

are obviously all tied up with them if we get embarrassed.

Another note is on taking offense. Mary Baker Eddy wrote an article on taking offense that was published in a book called *Prose Works*, a collection of her writings. She made the statement that the poised woman, the woman centered in Christ, never takes offense, can never be offended by insult, by injury, by remarks that are untoward or beneath her dignity.

Taking offense is the same principle as going off in a huff because someone has not spoken properly to us or someone has not treated us properly. All that is part of the little piques of pride people have. It is definitely part of being dependent on what those around us are doing or saying or thinking about us in order to maintain our identity. As soon as they do something that is an insult to the illusion we have about our identity, we get offended.

I am pointing this out to show that if you have embarrassment over others or if you can be offended, it is because of pride and the fact that you are not maintaining wholeness within yourself. And since your wholeness has to include other parts of life in order to be complete, if they misbehave, your day is ruined.

So striving for wholeness is the answer to our psychological problems, striving to be the fullness of the Christed One. In that state we are not moved.

Health, Faith, and Determination

Health, faith, and determination are all adjuncts to the expansion of the real in man.

"Health, faith, and determination." You must guard your health because without your health you will have a warped presentation of the teaching. Poor health engenders self-pity, a misuse of the Mother energies. Poor health will leech from you the energy of God that should be in balance in your chakras. To really be a representative of the Brotherhood, you must be healthy and you must guard your health.

"Faith and determination." Faith is a tremendous drive of willpower, so when you say a decree or a Hail Mary, you have faith that it is in manifestation *now*, actualized by the power of the spoken Word. Faith is a spark and a light that coats all of your prayers, all of your decrees, all of your actions—this living faith that whatever you do has positive results and is a fiat unto God and unto life and unto energy. Faith is such an important element as you walk the earth, because it ignites and engenders faith in others. And determination is the thrust you need to cut through.

Take the opposite of those conditions—poor health, doubt and fear, and lassitude or a lack of self-will—and you come up with a namby-pamby figure that no one is going to respect or follow.

> You must come each day to a greater understanding of yourself in order to be able rightly to represent the purposes of life. You are love and you love love. You are wisdom and you love wisdom. You are power and you love power. But you know that all is fulfilled in the perfect triangle of balanced attitude. This is the attitude that seeks the commonweal and understands the dangers of mental manipulation. Through human cleverness and wit, the kingdom of God has suffered violence,[7] the world order has been tampered with, and the forces of media have been used for purposes of negative control.

The key to the redemption of the social system lies in the victory of divine law in the being of individual man. What the individual man becomes, the collective world is. Through a wholehearted entering into the kingdom of God and his righteousness[8] and through participation in those spiritual exercises that strip man of the false and clothe him with the real, the individual and his world can and must become the fullness of all that God intended from the beginning.

O wisdom's star, continue to shine!

Graciously, I AM

Lanto

Lanto's spiritual focus is at the Royal Teton Retreat. The theme of the retreat is "The Evening Star," a tribute to Venus from *Tannhäuser,* by Wagner. We will have that played for a brief meditation at this time.

In the name of the Christ, in the name of the Holy Spirit, I call forth the living Presence of Almighty God. Beloved Lanto, beloved Kuthumi, beloved God and Goddess Meru, beloved Confucius, Brothers of the Golden Robe, beloved Jesus and Gautama, blaze and intensify the action of the golden flame of illumination from the heart of the living Christ! Blaze forth and intensify! Blaze forth and intensify! Blaze forth thy light and let thy will be done in us!

I call for the golden sun of Helios and Vesta. Shine forth in every heart! Melt all hardness of heart, all ignorance of the Law, all defiance of the Law. Let the light of Kuthumi burn and consume all dross. Let the light of the living Christ, Lord Maitreya, blaze forth the cosmic

*consciousness of the Law. Let this light purge this organi-
zation of all those who are in rebellion against the great
law of life. So let them come into alignment according
to the will of the Karmic Board, according to the will of
Cyclopea. Let it be done! We call for the anchoring of the
ray of cosmic judgment here. Let thy will manifest in us,
as Above so below.*

*We thank thee and accept it done this hour in full
power, in the name of the Father and of the Mother, of the
Son and of the Holy Spirit.*

*In the name of the Christ, we call to the causal body
of the secret love star, we call to the causal body of Venus,
we call to the causal bodies of Sanat Kumara, Mighty
Victory, Lady Master Meta, beloved Lady Master Venus.
Blaze forth the light of the victorious evolutions of the first
three root races and of all evolutions of Venus! Blaze forth
the light! for the preservation of life, the defense of life
in all.*

*In the name of the living Christ, we accept the ful-
fillment of our prayer answered this hour from the heart
of the Seven Holy Kumaras. Blaze forth thy light! Blaze
forth thy light! Blaze forth thy light! and let thy will be
done in us. Let thy will now flood forth. Balance the four
lower bodies; create the grid of alignment for the healing
of each one.*

*I call forth the healing thoughtform. I call forth the
light of ten thousand suns. I demand the reversing of the
tide of all energies directed against these students of the
Law. Roll it back! Roll it back! Roll it back! Blaze forth
the light of God! Blaze forth the light of the Seven Holy
Kumaras! Burn through! and draw the ring-pass-not and*

the sacred forcefield of the sacred fire around every student of the light.

I call for protection, healing, the purging of all that is not of the light and the reestablishment of the divine plan. I call for the healing ray to be anchored. I call to Hilarion to make each one the instrument of healing to all mankind. I call for victory and I call for the victory of love. So let it come forth. So let it manifest in the fulfillment of the Cosmic Christ.

Let us give the mantra to Helios and Vesta together.

Helios and Vesta!
Helios and Vesta!
Helios and Vesta!
Let the Light flow into my being!
Let the Light expand in the center of my heart!
Let the Light expand in the center of the earth
And let the earth be transformed into the New Day!

(Given 3 times)

February 17, 1975

CHAPTER ELEVEN

THE ENERGY OF THE SOUL

Commentary on Chapter 6

Peace Be unto Wisdom's Children:

In order to create a more crystal-clear picture of the self, we wish to discuss the self in terms of energy levels. The parable of the talents[1] reveals that individuals vary according to the gifts given unto them. This is also true of energy levels. Health, karma, and aspiration are among the many factors that govern the abundance of energy one has at his disposal. Energy levels also vary within the framework of a norm—a high and a low.

Most individuals do not realize that the potential of the self is related to the quantity and quality of the energy which they use. Very little progress in the study of the self has been made by mankind, for they have not known just how to proceed. For instance, the idea of the soul has been preserved as a sacred cow. Men have not considered the soul as energy bestowed. They suppose that the soul is a unique but undefined quality of reality.

If you will think of the nature of the soul as the nature of God and consider the facts (1) that God is boundless energy, (2) that man has been given a limited quantity of God's energy, and (3) that the energy which he has been given does comprise the content of the soul, you will be on the right track in your investigations of the self.

Souls Read Each Other

Each individual soul is actually capable of gauging and having a registration upon the soul of the assessment of other souls. The way we react to people, the chemical reactions that we have to a great extent are determined by the interplay and interaction of our sensing of energy levels. We tend to be drawn to or repelled by people according to their energy levels and the type of energy that they qualify. And we tend to be attracted to those who have made a similar disposition of this soul energy or solar consciousness. Of course, we find solar consciousness is compromised and colored by the electronic-belt patterns.

You can visualize the soul and its energy as a giant balloon filled with water, the water representing the energy level. The coloration of the water and the amount of water retained as energy defines, in effect, what your soul is at a particular moment. And we sense this about people.

For instance, men tend to be able to sense the difference between a virtuous and an unvirtuous woman, whether a woman is loose and free with sex or not. Now, this is actually read by the amount of energy within the soul. A woman who is pure retains her light and her energy, and that is the reason a man who is around such a woman will always have that intuitive feeling.

We also have that sensitivity about men and we have that sensitivity about children. We can sense those who are pure because of this soul contact. Really, we are reading one another by our souls all the time, but we are so disconnected from our souls that the registration is often subconscious. We are so mixed up with mental concepts, patterns, acceptable norms, emotions and so forth, that many times we get entangled with people we shouldn't be entangled with, simply because we don't trust the reading of the soul.

The point to remember is the *way* the soul reads—the soul reads comparative energy levels in people.

The Soul Is a Reservoir

Jesus warned that men could lose their souls,[2] and of course there are many trials and taxing situations which may deplete the amount of energy available to the individual. I do not say that all energy used by man comes from the soul, for as you know man's supply of every good and perfect gift is from above.[3] But I do relate soul energy to the temporal manifestation of identity.

You can visualize the soul as a reservoir in Matter, as a receptacle. The energy comes from the fountain of the I AM Presence, flows through the Christ Self over the crystal cord, and the soul is the reservoir. People who get a lot of energy in their chakras or in their souls, if they have a momentum on spending that energy, are just like people for whom money burns a hole in their pocket and as soon as they get it they have to think of a way to spend it. There are people who cannot retain energy in a reservoir, holding it to be used later.

If you think of a reservoir, immediately you will realize that the water filling the reservoir becomes a reflector. The reservoir of your soul reflects your I AM Presence. So the more water you have within it, the more energy that is there, the more the soul becomes the reflector of God, the more the soul *becomes* God. But if the energy is dispersed, whatever the way may be, you don't have a reflector.

This soul energy, or solar energy, is limited in quantity—some having a great deal more of it than others. As a man soweth, so shall he reap.[4] Therefore karma acts as the governor, in part, of the flow of man's energy from his Presence just as it regulates the amount of soul energy given to the lifestream at the beginning of each embodiment.

In a situation where people are always tired and never have enough energy to do what they need to do, there is a problem in the soul's retention of energy. Either karma blocks it or they have an altogether too passive attitude where they don't pull on the cord hard enough to get the energy to do the job and get it done; they are sitting back waiting to be acted upon, waiting for God to do something. The fact of the matter is, according to cosmic law, you can demand and receive all the energy you require to fulfill your mission.

Not having enough energy or enough strength to do what you have to do is a psychological excuse that comes from deep within the subconscious that is really saying, "I won't." It says "I can't," but it is saying "I won't." In other words, if you really want to render a service, you can demand the energy necessary to render that service.

Have you ever had the experience of being totally exhausted, finding that someone had a need and you had to get involved in service, and suddenly you found yourself charged with so much energy you could work all night and all day? So the limitless source is there.

Even if karma dictates that we are weak or thin or pale or have some kind of physical condition, the karma itself can be challenged and overcome. But you must take care when you do this that you do it in God, rather than it being a driving of the physical body unto its death. You have to take care to do this exercise by communion with the Holy Spirit, where you really make contact with the fount of the

I AM Presence, and when the energy pours forth you are able to collect it and keep it in the reservoir of the soul for when you need it.

People talk about using up their reserves. We all have a certain amount of reserves we can go on, and when they are used up there is nothing left. Well, the reserves are really the reservoir of the soul. And the important thing is to keep those reserves replenished so when you do have to go for days without sleep or food or rest you can make it.

The way you do that is by obeying the laws of each plane. You have to obey the laws of chemistry involving your physical body. You obey the laws of harmony involving your emotions. You obey the laws of the Logos in your mind and retain only those concepts that serve the health and well-being of the body. When you retain patterns of rebellion, they sap the reservoir of the soul and you don't have enough energy.

Likewise with the etheric body—if you let it drain you with revolving, with resentment, with whatever it might be, you are using up your soul energy, and when it comes to the mark of achievement you have achieved nothing.

Write Down Your Accomplishments

At the conclusion of each week and each month and each year, it's a good idea to ask yourself, "What did I actually accomplish?" and write it down. "What did I bring through to physical conclusion? What work of art got done? What paper did I write? What book did I finish reading? What did I accomplish? Did I paint my house? Did I clean my house? Did I do this?"

Write down things you did and finished, that began with an etheric matrix, moved to a mental idea, were fed with the desiring of God, and finally were fulfilled.

The reason I say this is that you can go a long time in life thinking about things, praying about things, feeling God's radiation and fooling yourself into thinking you are accomplishing something. But if all of your dreaming and all of your thinking and all of your planning hasn't borne some fruit, then you really have not completed your spiral.

All this has to do with energy levels, soul energy. If you are not somehow accomplishing, if you are not moving forward, your soul energy is being drained, it is being siphoned from you and you may not even know it. It may be going into subconscious pockets.

You may not even realize that for all your loving of the teaching and of the ascended masters, there are not marks of progress showing that you have taken the needle with the thread of consciousness and anchored it back down into the cloth of reality. You have to keep on anchoring those stitches. And each time you anchor into the physical, you have achievement, you have self-mastery, you have the City Foursquare[5] that comes into being because some people have decided to master the flame of truth.

Boundless Energy

Health is related to karma because both are cumulative. Health is the result of past and present energy uses. Good health encourages the steadfast flow of energy. The reverse is also true.

We cannot deny that there are good and bad energies. But let us remember that energy itself is really neither good nor bad; it is the qualification that is made of energy that determines its manifestation. Therefore in our study we must remember to relate energy and its qualification to the self.

> There is undoubtedly an initial impetus or quantity of energy bestowed upon the individual as his divine portion.[6]

This is interesting because children seem to have boundless energy. They are still operating on that initial impetus of light sealed within their aura and their forcefield. As long as they remain pure, untainted by the world, they will retain the ability to draw upon boundless energy. This is the virgin consciousness. It's not only physical virginity but it is also a virginity of the four lower bodies where the sealing of identity is within a very filigree, glistening, translucent substance. It almost looks like a placenta on the inner planes, and it surrounds the soul and the four lower bodies and seals them in that initial release of energy.

One of the marks of the saints is that they had boundless energy to perform the duties they had to perform—all the necessary tasks involved in the monastery or the nunnery or the school or the hospital or wherever they served. It is because of their communion with God and their energies tethered to the I AM Presence and the continual flow going from the I AM Presence to the soul and back again that they retained the ability to be a perpetual focus for service, for action, for prayer and communion. Their bodies were actually an electrode for the release of God's energy.

Many of you are coming to the point where your four lower bodies are becoming pure enough that you can retain more light and have more energy at your disposal. And if you will analyze your past as I do when I read your letters to me, you will see that all of the various involvements you describe are the assailing of the dark forces upon your being to steal from you your energy—because without energy, without enough energy in your forcefield, you can't be God.

You can't do his works. You don't have the reservoir, the pool to reflect his light. So for all intents and purposes you have been deprived: deprived of your mission, deprived of your identity. You have been emasculated, so to speak. All your energy has been taken from you.

That is the desire of the dark force—to leave you as a vegetable. And the state of that vegetable is that it does not know it is a vegetable. This process is enacted so subtly that you don't even realize when you've been had. You don't even realize when you have had your true identity stripped from you by the stealing of your light.

So this concept of the divine portion

is brought out in the parable of the prodigal son.[7] The statement "To him that hath shall be given, and he shall have abundance: but from him that hath not shall be taken away even that which he hath"[8] also gives a clue to the maintenance of the energy potential necessary to the self— what we might call the "critical mass."

Now, that sounds like a hard saying and a hard law. We would rather think that it is the poor who should be given the abundance, but it is not so. Jesus said, "The poor you always have with you."[9] The poor, because of their poverty consciousness, never have an energy level to attract the light they need to carry on in this world. They don't have the pump of the well primed. They don't have enough water there to make the well flow. And every time their pump does get primed they spend the prime energy. That's the definition of the poor.

Soul Energy and Critical Mass

Then there is the point of the "critical mass." Once you have a critical mass, a forcefield of energy within you that reaches a certain level of intensity, you never want for anything. You will not want for companionship, for love, for family. You will not want for supply, for intelligence, for right ideas, for creativity. Everything you need to have a rich and full life will be there.

If you currently lack any good thing, any good and perfect thing from God,[10] it is a sign to you that your critical mass is not to the place where it has become a Great Central Sun Magnet. It means you need more light. And you need to determine those forcefields that are taking your energy from you.

We can think of the seat-of-the-soul chakra as a bowl, a receptacle that resembles the shape of the electronic belt, which surrounds the forcefield of the lower chakras. The crystal cord descends through the heart chakra and distributes energy to all the chakras. This energy comes to the soul and the soul starts to fill. It fills to a certain level, which is perhaps more energy than this person has had for a long time, and he begins to feel a certain weight of light.

If the electronic belt has not been cleared, the energy that is in the soul chakra begins to activate lower chakras. And the tendency is for those chakras to direct this energy into the channels in which it has been drained before. There are all these various subterranean channels in the electronic belt: the hatred of this person that did this terrible thing to you when you were three years old; a pattern that you have from a previous life; a runner coming off that pattern that goes deep into the psyche and into the subconscious roots of your neighbor, and so forth.

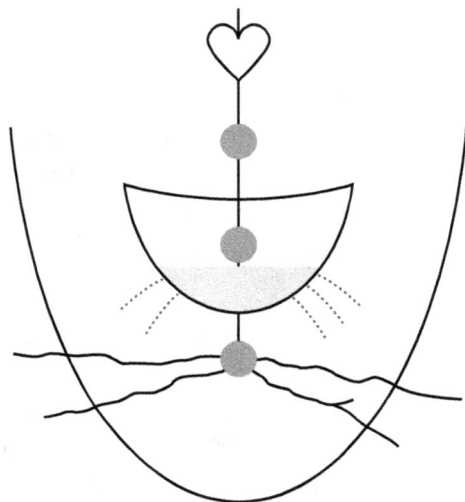

This diagram symbolically depicts the heart chakra, the solar plexus, the seat of the soul and the base of the spine. The seat-of-the-soul chakra is shown as a bowl, which is being filled with energy descending through the heart over the crystal cord. If there are holes in the bowl, the energy will leak out as the level rises and flow into old, familiar channels in the electronic belt (which is shown here as the large bowl surrounding the lower chakras).

You aren't thinking about these things consciously. They don't come to mind unless you have an experience that jars you. But they are there and they look like underground streams. When you get all this energy flowing through the chakras, it wants to give, to be released. It's not yet trained to rise and go back to God, so it pushes out into the channels that are already formed.

There are people who every time they get a certain increment of energy from God spend it. They can't contain it. They don't have a cup to contain it. It's as if it short-circuits. They may have a temper tantrum. They may go into a weeping session. They may go out on the town. They may be up all night living the "good life." Whatever it is, they don't know what to do with the increase of energy, and they don't know how to send it back to God in the action of raising the Kundalini and the caduceus. Rechanneling energy takes discipline. Discipline means erasing the old channels and forcing that energy to flow in new channels.

There are all kinds of leaks in the soul chakra. The cup that is the chakra is like a membrane with little pinpricks in it, and when the chakra starts to fill, the energy leaks out. It gets siphoned off, maybe drop by drop. It has been said that most people in the world today are in a state of depression and don't even know it. These leaks are the cause. That is where their energy is going.

This is why it is so important to discover what your subconscious motivations are and to get rid of subconscious guilt and shame, self-belittlement and self-indulgence. There is a pattern where people indulge themselves and then feel guilty for having indulged themselves. Then they say, "Okay, it's not right to feel guilty." So they get rid of all their guilt and turn right around and indulge themselves— but now they do it free of guilt.

That is the philosophy of liberalism in psychology today: "Do anything you want. Don't repress anything. Enjoy sex. Enjoy life. Enjoy whatever you want to enjoy because then you will be a happy animal. No guilt feelings, no repression. Change all the laws. Change cosmic law and you will thrive."

Well, you will thrive as an animal. But there will be a siphoning off of your energy at subconscious levels, and you have to put a stop to it. Each time there is something that comes to the level of conscious awareness that enables you to see a portion of yourself that you don't like, you're zeroing in on one of these leaks that is taking from you the critical mass of energy in your soul.

When the reservoir of the soul is full, the soul has a

critical mass, has enough energy to attract what is required in the planes of Matter. So, "To him that hath shall be given, and he shall have abundance: but from him that hath not shall be taken away even that which he hath."

We are talking specifically about soul energy because the soul chakra is in polarity with the third eye (see p. 202), which has to do with the mastery of the green ray and precipitation. But these principles of energy levels apply to all the chakras in the whole being of man.

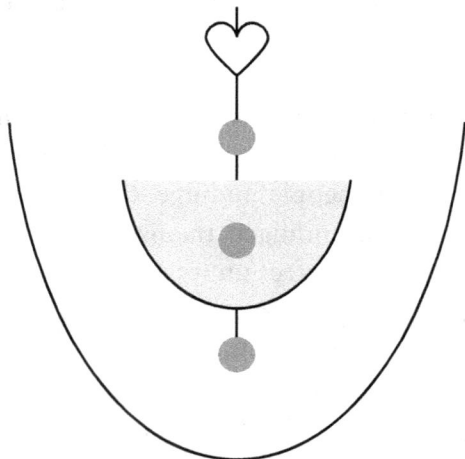

A diagram showing the reservoir of the soul being full.

You may have a lot of love in your heart but no ability to precipitate love. If you can retain energy in your heart as love, you will attract love and loving people. You may not accomplish anything in the way of building the kingdom of God, but your karma is your karma, and therefore, wherever you do have good energy, you will attract good energy. Karma is karma, and wherever you have the mastery of a chakra, that chakra itself will attract more energy of its kind.

People who are very mental and have been devoted to intelligence and the Christ mind may have an abundance of intelligence and of that mind, even though they may be completely lacking in other areas.

Rescuing Imprisoned Energy

The more energy a person has, the more he is apt to attract; and the less he has, the less he is apt to attract. The need to purify one's energies becomes more and more apparent as the individual sees that his life potential is dependent upon the quality of his energy. Actually a great deal of energy which was once his to use is now imprisoned in the imperfect patterns of his own human miscreations. Like money in the bank which has been pledged as collateral, this energy cannot be withdrawn until one's spiritual obligation has been met.

Energy gets imprisoned when it is drained out of the chakras; it flows through channels and fills pockets that become momentums in the electronic belt. These pockets get bigger and bigger and bigger, and pretty soon they become entire creations. When you keep on feeding negative momentums, you create the zoo of your electronic belt—all the different animal forms and thoughtforms that can be seen there. So all that is there has been created by all the energy that should be in the bowl of your soul, and as you create it, the energy level in the bowl goes down, down, down. And of course, this is happening throughout a lifespan of three score and ten.

Old age is defined by the amount of soul or solar energy that is siphoned off into other matrices so your physical body doesn't have the energy to sustain it, to sustain eternal

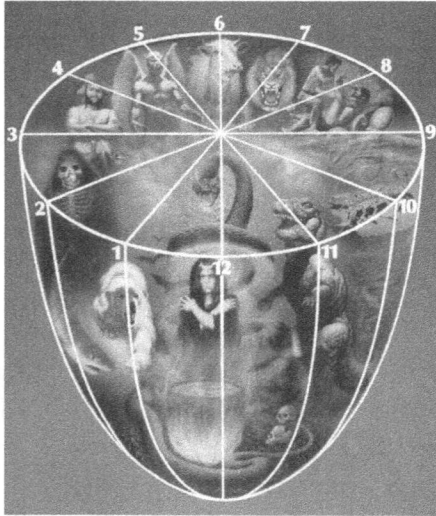

When individuals continually feed negative momentums, this energy coalesces as negative forms that may be seen in the electronic belt. This illustration shows thoughtforms typical of the misuses of the energies of the twelve lines of the cosmic clock.

youth. The energy is going down, it is feeding the electronic belt, which is getting fatter and fatter. Your four lower bodies are being drained of their vital essences, and finally they are so drained that there isn't any more. The Presence withdraws the crystal cord and there is no life left in the form because it has all been assigned to other pockets.

The path of the ascended masters is to rescue that energy from the imprisoned matrices. I cannot emphasize too much that if you spend your life investing energy into negative matrices, there comes a time in middle age or old age when your electronic belt will completely take over. It has the energy that your soul chakra should have. It takes over your life, and you get into the consciousness we observe in older people—senility, bitterness, sickness, rigidity, and so forth—because there's no energy flow left.

So in preparation for that time of life it's important that you begin to fill the cup of the soul with light. Liberate the energies of your electronic belt. Get them back into the cup so that you really never have to experience old age as it is commonly seen on this planet. Instead, you can have years of maturity when you set the example to a younger generation of being a flame.

The energy cannot be withdrawn from the electronic belt until the spiritual obligation has been met. Your spiritual obligation in this imprisoned energy—to free it—is to invoke the equivalent in violet flame, in Astrea's decree, in the healing flame, so that energy can be released and transmuted and used to fulfill certain karmic obligations.

You have an obligation to serve someone or to serve the light. Until you do so, God does not return to you the energy you misqualified previously, the reason being that people have promised again and again to do well in the sight of God. And on the basis of promises, God has given them an extra allotment of energy, an extra dispensation. Then as soon as people received that energy, they squandered it. Again and again and again God has been shortchanged by people's promises.

There comes a point in the path of each soul's karma where a promise isn't good enough anymore. It takes action. It may take years and years of action, of proving to God that your word is good, that you mean what you say. You go out and you do his will and you serve. And there comes a point—it's that magic moment when you have served and served and served—when God says, "That is the collateral I need. That is the amount of energy that was required for me to give you back the whole equivalent of everything that you have put into your service." And all of a sudden you find yourself surrounded with a tremendous forcefield of energy and light that you need to serve in an even larger way—because the reward for service is always greater service.

So don't be impatient in any way with your association with the ascended masters and what takes place in your life, because as long as you follow the Law, the teaching and the principles, you are getting closer and closer and closer to the point where there is enough energy in the bowl of your soul that it is going to be the critical mass.

Why Things That Are Not So Great Happen

Those who serve mankind in the field of medicine and chiropractic, especially those who work with nerves, understand that when muscle groups are in a state of tension there is an enormous tie-up of energy that keeps the entire body tense. They know that the release of tension in the muscles of the body provides more energy for both mind and body. Likewise those who have an understanding of the human mind know that when the psyche is tied up emotionally with diverse problems, this can cause a split personality. Increased mental and emotional tensions create a buildup of attracting and repelling forces that divide the self. Those who treat the mind or emotional nature of man know full well that where there is a drop in energy levels, where fatigue occurs, there is a much greater tendency to mental disorders.

What man must do, then, is learn how to release himself from tensions—physically, mentally, and emotionally. He must learn to use all of the energy which God has given him, some of which is in a state of rest and some of which is in a state of movement. He must learn to undo the misqualifications of energy for which he bears responsibility;

he must learn to requalify that which has been misqualified. This will give him a greater quotient of energy that can be used in the development of true soul consciousness, for the purposes of life are that man might master the universe through first mastering himself.

In a very real sense the spiritual energies of the divine image are reflected in the mirror of mortal consciousness. These energies bring about the advent of soul force within the lifestream, but they must be continuously augmented in order that the expanding soul may attract a greater portion of divinity to the life of the individual.

All undesirable karmic manifestations return to their point of origin—which is the individual being of man—when the attractive force within him, whether qualified with good or ill, has reached a certain intensity.

One of the reasons we are attracted to young people—children all the way up to adults of about the age of thirty—is because they still have their soul energy, their soul force. We are drawn to people who have that life force within them. After the age of thirty they begin to reap the fruits of wrong sowing, of giving that energy away and not replenishing it, and so middle age and old age begin to set in. People of those ages are not as attractive. We simply are not attracted to them because they don't have their energy level where they are supposed to have it.

This doesn't really make youth any better. It just means that their initial impetus, their initial portion of energy hasn't been entirely spent. But the age of thirty comes extremely quickly in life, and we find that the returns for misusing that energy are upon us almost before we have begun to live. It's good to recognize that. Because you can definitely keep perpetually young and youthful and have your life force within you if you conserve it when you have it and use it for service.

> All undesirable karmic manifestations return to their point of origin ...

We might add that all *desirable* karmic manifestations return to their point of origin. And their point of origin can be any one of your chakras.

> ... which is the individual being of man—when the attractive force within him, whether qualified with good or ill, has reached a certain intensity.

There is the law that teaches us that just when we get a lot of light within us, many things that are not so great start happening. There is the statement that "undesirable karmic manifestations" come back when the attractive force has reached a certain intensity. You can have an attractive force within you such as a large momentum of black magic, which would also attract energy fields.

The Dark Night

> Therefore it is well that individuals recognize the fact that when they draw to themselves the higher nature of being, they are also drawing a definitive quantity as well as a definitive quality of energy that will serve to fortify the being of man against the day of karmic reckoning when all negatives and positives must be adjusted.

When you start on the Path, you have time and space to attract to yourself a certain quotient of energy, of light that will be oh so necessary in the day when you must stand, face and conquer *all* your negatives and *all* your positives. That is conquering the dweller-on-the-threshold, conquering the energy of your electronic belt in the period that is called the dark night,* when the soul is cut off from the I AM Presence and it has to go on just the energy that is in the bowl.

By your solar awareness, by your attainment in the soul you will create your own sun of being, your own sun that will light the way in the hour of darkness. But if the bowl is empty and the test of this dark night comes, the soul will go through the second death because there will be nothing in the soul to light the way, to keep the lamp trimmed, to keep the flame in the heart blazing.[11]

Sooner or later we are all coming to that point. And as far as I can see, at this particular age you can look down the road we are on and almost see that point in the distance. It's no longer on the other side of the mountain. It's no longer out of sight. We are nearing that point and we sense it within. We sense the urgency of getting the teaching and getting the light, because we know that the reservoir is low and we've got to get it filled because we've got to meet that challenge and that judgment when it comes.

So take heart. Because when you do get a lot of light, that light will be the whirling sun of your being that will draw into it, like a whirlpool, the dark energy of your karma—which can be transmuted with comparatively little suffering if you have that sun really spinning, that flame really going. But if you've let it get sluggish and slow down and *then* you're hit with the momentum of your own karma, it's

---

*This section combines information about both the dark night of the soul and the later initiation called the dark night of the Spirit. For a full explanation, see p. 375, note 11.

going to be a way of sorrow and pain and suffering, and it will truly be a dark night.

Quantity and Quality of Energy

In our considerations of man's energy potential we are concerned with both quality and quantity.

Remember that it's not just the quantity of energy but how you *qualify* that quantity. You may meet people who seem to have an enormous quantity of energy, powerful individuals in society—but it is dark energy. They have learned to keep energy in their aura and in their chakras. They are smart. They don't spend it. They are not impoverished; they keep it. But it's a murky color. It's muddied water. It's dark energy. And by the use of that energy and the interplay of the forces of their being, they may rise to great power.

There are people in all nations who do that, whether in government or entertainment or what have you. You see them and their cup of energy is like a pus pocket, but they function on it. It's like dirty gasoline. Their motors run and they have a certain animal existence. And you find yourself very oppressed in their presence.

So the masters are not just concerned with the quantity of light in your reservoir but also with the quality.

Although it is true that the Absolute is all and therefore possesses all (in a sense being possessed by all),...

This is true, but you have free will. So

... the universal desire for the manifestation of purity by the self—whether it be the desire of the macrocosmic Lord

of the Universe or the desire of the individual monad—
should be a progressive reaching out for more and more of
the reality of right qualification.

Now you can see why so many different false teachers
have success in their mind-control courses or their meditation courses or whatever they are teaching. They are teaching people how to get and manipulate energy. They are not
teaching them purity. They are teaching how by the manipulation of the mind you can go into certain centers and have
certain psychic experiences and even have healings and convey psychic energy across the planet; you can do psychic
readings; your soul can travel in its astral body. Given free
will, there is almost nothing you can't do by the buildup of
energy—create dinosaurs or spaceships or travel to different
planets. There are all kinds of things you can do.

Remember what manipulation is: the "mani-pollution,"
manifold pollution of consciousness. Polluted energy still
has force. It still has weight. It still has momentum. It can
still be used.

As you think of the soul as the repository of the energies of the fiery world,[12] you will feel a greater sense of
responsibility to maintain the soul and its contents upon
the altar of purity. And perhaps you will consider more
often how vastly beneficial it will be—not only to you as
an individual but also to the universe as a whole—if you
will learn how to summon the will to requalify negative
thoughts, feelings, and creations with the pristine beauty of
the first creation of God. Think of the worlds of misqualified substance that are waiting to be conquered when you
practice this supreme art of transmutation!

Following the Master in the regeneration, cradling the infant Messiah of reality in the crèche of the heart, men will begin the process of expanding their understanding of the self through becoming all that which is real and discarding, through requalification, all that which is not.

The task may seem interminable, the process involved. It is not. Except that ye become as a little child ye cannot enter in.[13] To manifest the little-child consciousness is to develop the masterful Christ consciousness that will successfully take dominion over the earth.[14]

Wait, watch, and work. For the Father works with you and within you.

Faithfully, I AM your brother,
Kuthumi

February 18, 1975

CHAPTER TWELVE

THE NATURE
OF INDIVIDUALITY

Commentary on Chapter 7

Beloved Seekers after Wisdom's Flame:

Consciousness, when functioning properly, is a glowing orb of reality, joy, and full illumination. The individual reaching-out from the seemingly separated center of being to contact the cosmic center of life and thence the periphery of all reality is accomplished as easily as the miracle of the radiant, expanding mind of God penetrates the universe with light.

This is a period of going into the center to contact life. This is what Jesus did for thirty years in preparation for going out for three years.

In your preparation is all of your victory, in your laying the foundation. Every line and every brick that you lay in the center will be a bulwark of defense and strength on the periphery. All must be carefully executed because you are drawing a miniature of your soul's pattern in the center. In the core of the secret rays is a miniature, microcosmic world where you see yourself under a microscope, and you are building in this small world, in concentration in the microcosm.

When you go out to the periphery, it is like an artist

putting a portrait on a screen to trace it. The whole thing is blown up to a huge dimension. That's when you see every line, every dot and everything that is in you, everything that is in the subconscious. So at that point you will be well pleased that you have taken the trouble to gain mastery step by step, leaving nothing out, being meticulous, because it will all show. Where there are weaknesses and snarls and all kinds of little knots, it will be much harder to conquer them then. They will become the beasts of the air when they are projected on the screen of the macrocosm.

One of the causes behind the problems of insanity and the turbulence in the world is that now is the time in some people's cycle to have what they have garnered within projected on the planetary body. And what we are seeing projected on the screen of the astral and mental plane and finally on the physical is very unwholesome.

Inherent within man is the power to expand consciousness beyond the sphere of the personal self into the dominant domain of reality.

The power to expand consciousness beyond this sphere is inherent within you. *Inherent within you* is the power to expand consciousness "into the domain of dominant reality."

Locked-In Individuality

This reality is shared by the myriad manifestations that inhabit cosmos; but because of the marvelous quality of "locked-in individuality," there is never any oppressive erosion of the permanent nature of man. There are only the gentle molding factors as the hand of Universal

Intelligence, Power, and Love commences the process of tutoring the evolving soul personality.

Your locked-in individuality has more power than the combination of all the causes and effects in Matter that you have ever experienced. The problems you have of parental influence or the influences of people around you—they did this to you, they did that to you and you did that to them— all these episodes are like the mist on the horizon that disappears when the sun rises and the morning light comes. They dissolve.

We must be careful when we are in the state of looking through the microscope not to give too much power to the grains that we find. One of my children was examining the cross section of the leg of a flea under a microscope for school and describing this leg to me. And I told him I wasn't interested in looking at it.

Sometimes the little episodes that we think have bent the twig or the branch of our personality one way or the other—we remember this terrible thing happened, that terrible thing happened—have to be put in proper proportion. It really has no more power than the leg of a flea under a microscope.

It looks like a gigantic thing when it gets under that microscope. So we have to maintain the sense of co-measurement with the infinite and realize that this locked-in individuality is God himself—the power and the vastness of the entire cosmos. We must not allow the leg of a flea to be pitted against this fantastic momentum that is Reality within us.

If you lose your sense of co-measurement and proportion, that's exactly what you are going to do. And you are going to say, "I will never make it because my father was mean to me. I will never make it because my sister was always fighting with me." You have to get out of the consciousness that these influences have that much power to change the unchangeable—your own locked-in individuality. When you realize that and put these other things into the flame, then you are living in the ascended-master consciousness and in their perspective.

We understand that for the purposes of discovering the microcosm, the world of biology, for the purpose of science and understanding the cell it is necessary to look at the leg of a flea under a microscope now and then. But we have to keep it in proportion, keep it where it belongs. Sometimes we allow ourselves to get a bit too caught up in the minutiae of the human personality and its molding factors.

I feel impressed to give you this word from El Morya: Chelas must not allow any cause, effect, condition, person or personality in this plane to cast a shadow of substance upon the great and infinite being that you are. You must claim it and be it and not dwell forevermore in the consciousness where you are continually going over the past, the present, the emotions, the feelings, and so forth.

The Ocean and the Drop

Recognizing then, as beloved Kuthumi has said, how easy it is for individuals to misqualify energy and conversely how wonderful it is to begin the process of requalification, the individual self can look forward to experiencing newness of life and a sense of fulfillment that he has not known before.

Soon he will bypass the false structurings that he has created and that have been created for him by the dark

overlords and their dark stars of compounded misqualification. Soon he will realize, with the joyous gurgle of a
newborn babe, that the universe is a home of light and
hope where the temporal manifestations of intelligence,
consciousness, and identity can be welded to the Eternal
even as the Eternal permeates the substance of mortality
with its essential reality. Here at last mankind can come to
know the permanent gift of bliss which it was the Father's
joy to convey to the individual at the birth of his identity.

The Ocean could have chosen to remain the Ocean;
but, by separating the tiny luminous drop from the Whole
and holding it up to the glorious rays of the sun of illumination [and purpose], a new ocean was begun. And so the
individual consciousness was given dominion over his own
world. And so man, made in the image of his Creator,[1] also
became a creator.

You might want to memorize that paragraph. It is one
of the most sublime statements of truth. If someone ever
asks you, "Why are we here? Why were we born? What's
the purpose of life?" you can just rattle off this beautiful
paragraph and let them feel the bliss of this ocean that could
have chosen to remain the ocean.

The first stirrings of reality outside of the lost Edenic
state moved in the darkness, in the void of not-knowing;
these stirrings of purpose were soon translated into outer
action, but the fabrications of social contact unfortunately
dedicated themselves to egoistic expression and a sense of
struggle.

Man's rise seemed to be proportionate to his dominion,
not over self, but over others and over his environment.

The overcoming of environment was valid. The wreaking of destruction upon others was not. Therefore, the tribunal of justice known as the Karmic Board came into being in order to record and govern the interaction of man's humanity or inhumanity to man.

The sense of struggle mounted. Involvement in the ego became a snarl of inverted spirals, structuring within the consciousness of mankind a kaleidoscopic reverie so complex as to make the consciousness to recoil. The simple forms of grace were forgotten in the astral melodrama. Man seemed to live without, but actually he lived within the snares of his own creation; now he was infecting others with his own dilemma and the power of contagion banished him from the heavenly state.

The ego is the seat of all man's problems. What are known as inferiority or superiority complexes revolve entirely around the pride and frustration of the ego. But although people know these things they continue to allow themselves to be victimized by the internal obstructions which they have created.

The only way out is through the door of reality. This is the escape hatch which has been provided so that the body of destructivity created by man's own negativity can be transmuted and overcome. As long as men remain involved in the ego, no matter what religious study they undertake, no matter what devotion they temporarily manifest, no matter how many good works they do, no matter what level of striving they attain, they will never be free from the illusion of the self that pursues them as a wanton ghost of struggling identity.

Only when they escape through the door (I AM the door[2]) into the understanding that the eternal being of God is the "doer," into the realization that God can act in them to remove hampering influences, to transmute their darkness, and to translate their consciousness from darkness into light, will they begin to know the freedom of the Self to achieve without limit.

We could set up guidelines which would help you to recognize when the ego is in command, but I think that a little honest gazing into the mirror of self and a study of the reactions of the self to the doings of others will quickly show, if one's appraisal be honest, whether or not the ego is acting.

Let all see and know for all eternity that the not-self, the shadowed-self, the named-self, the personality-self, is and always has been the snare of the ego, and that the man or woman who lives in that consciousness must die in it. There is no possibility for flesh and blood to inherit eternal life.[3] Men seek eternal life because it is their true nature, the nature of God and of the divine image. Eternal life is formed independently of the vehicle of self through the process of translation, that man should no longer see death but be translated into that life which is the divine nature.

The statement that man should die daily[4] to the finite, egoistic self must be followed by another—that he should live daily to the progressive glory of his eternal Self and the apprehending of all the reality which that Self can and does bring. This is the Sun we face that casts no shadow. Oh, we can and we will bring forth such an abundant wealth of spiritual information regarding the true nature of man as to almost cremate man's present consciousness! Yet we must delay long enough in this bringing forth until man has had ample opportunity to understand how necessary it is that he shed the ego.

This concept is far more than an index of words. It is a flow of the vital seed-idea into the consciousness of man whereby the consciousness itself is transformed into its natural glowing Presence. This is the Presence of God which identifies the individual, through his sense of expanding reality, with the universal consciousness of God yet never takes from him one erg of his energy or of his true selfhood.

The Father created the Son to be the beloved inheritor of all things that were made. And in reality the Son of God, or the light of God that never fails, was the means by which the Eternal Progenitor performed the creative act. "Thou art my beloved Son, in whom I am well pleased."[5]

The ego that is always being hurt, that is over-sensitive, full of self-pity and a sense of struggle, the ego that seeks in poring over the rubble of past lives to find some element of worth should understand that man's worth is in the Eternal Now. He should understand that the Eternal Now is in the Eternal and that the grace that man must have that is sufficient for every day was implanted within the soul with the inpouring breath of divine energy that first gave him consciousness.

In the name of Holy Wisdom I, Meru, urge upon everyone the willful relinquishing of the snakeskin of identity that has crawled upon its belly while pursuing the vanities of the intellect. Replace this by the dominant sunburst of the living, vital mind of God and that reality which God is and which you are because he is.

I AM his servant and your elder brother,

Meru

Traits of the Ego

I think we should list these traits of the ego.

1. The void of not knowing.
2. Fabrications of social contact.
3. Egoistic expression.
4. Sense of struggle.
5. Destructive dominion over others.
6. Man's inhumanity to man.
7. Snarl of inverted spirals (Astral melodrama).
8. Banishment from the heavenly state (Mass contagion).
9. Inferiority and superiority complexes (Pride and frustration of the ego).
10. Self-created internal obstructions ("I can't").
11. Body of destructivity (Negative karma).
12. Illusion of the self (Wanton ghost of struggling identity).

That's the funniest one of all: "Wanton ghost of struggling identity." Did you ever see yourself running around struggling, trying to overcome, trying to win this battle, trying to master yourself—this wanton ghost of struggling identity? It's really a joke, isn't it? That old ego, if it can't be anything else, it's got to be this wanton ghost of struggling identity.

13. Reactions of the self to the doings of others.
14. The not-self.
15. The shadowed self.
16. The named self.
17. The personality self.

Sometimes we get quite a sense of self-importance about our name, and our name becomes our identity. When somebody says to you, "Who are you?" you always respond with your name, probably because society expects it. Nevertheless it shouldn't be a reflex. When somebody says, "Who are you?" you should immediately say inside yourself, "I AM God. I AM a flame." All your name is, is a dog tag for this life so people can tell the lumps of sugar apart.

18. Finite, self-centered.
19. Always being hurt.
20. Oversensitive, full of self-pity.

You have an immediate reaction if somebody laughs at the wrong time or cries at the wrong time, or walks around at the wrong time. Thinking "Nobody is having as many problems as I am having."

21. Poring over the rubble of past lives to find some element of worth.

Now, this is a significant one. People will come to me and tell me their life story. It may take them an hour to two. They tell me everything they have ever done.

The truth is that a good life or a bad life or a mediocre life is not where worth is. It is not in the human experience, not in the psychic melodrama. Man's worth is in the Eternal Now.

Stop raking over what you have been, what you have done, who you were, who your friends are, who you are interested in, who you want to get married to, who is waiting for you when you leave Summit University, whether there is a job there or not.

You have to shed the snakeskin of all the coordinates of the human consciousness. Here is your ego and it has an identity because there is an ego over there. And there is another ego over there and finally you become the center of a cosmos, of all these ego stars. And by your distance and by your relationship to all these individual circumstances and experiences you are so-and-so; you gain an identity.

Therefore, it's like you have to take scissors and cut out

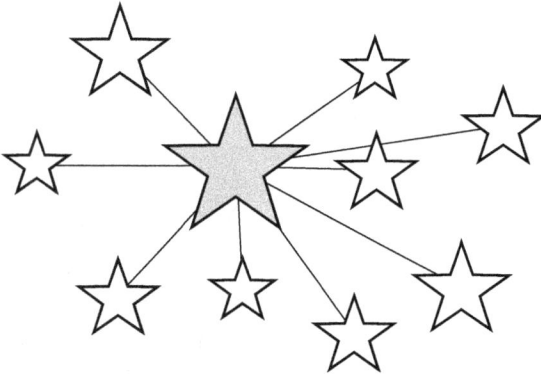

The ego gains an identity by its relationship to other egos.

this whole island of relativity that you have been involved in and put it aside. There's no way to have one foot in and one foot out because other people's consciousness of you is so based on the old coordinates that that alone, during a process of alchemy when you are precipitating, is enough to throw your experiment off. You can't precipitate the Maltese cross of your own identity, the amethyst of your own being, when you have other minds impinging. So don't ever be afraid to leave the old moorings and the old landmarks.

In time you will come to the place where you will precipitate that jewel, that Maltese cross, of your identity.[6] It will be hardened; it will have been realized concretely in the physical. That is comparable to the time when Jesus was thirty years old and ready for his mission. At that time you can go back to those areas and the people you left behind because your mold is fixed and hardened; it can no longer be tampered with. It is sealed. You can go back and you will feel that you are light-years beyond them. But you can move among those that you formerly moved among, you can be of some service, and you are set in your matrix so you are not going to be moved. Others cannot melt down that amethyst at that point.

But while it's in the formative stage—when you have the first gleanings and glimmers of this glorious being which you are—the first thing the carnal mind wants you to do is run back to everybody you knew and tell them about the ascended masters' teachings. And you write frantic letters and you send them all the material. And you find that doing this before your alchemy has been completed simply attracts all these other minds onto your experiment. One percent of them may respond. But those who don't respond present a hardness and an opposition to what you are doing, which is not healthy.

I am sure some of you have shared your discoveries and knowledge of the masters with people with great success and have brought them into the teachings. And others of you have met rebuffs and questionings and doubts. Those questionings and doubts filter into your consciousness, and they sometimes cause you a tremendous burden. So it is best to perfect the self, let go of the ego and become strong in the Law before you try to give what you have to others.

The masters caution you on this because it is an alchemy. And by your decrees and your own inner flame, by the impersonal action of the law of your Presence, you will attract to the teachings all those who need to come in.

22. The snakeskin of identity that has crawled upon its belly.
23. The pursuit of the vanities of the intellect.
24. False structurings.

False structurings should be at the head of the list. That's what I have been talking about: structurings, the structure of social contacts.

25. Dark overlords and dark stars of compounded misqualifications.

The Disease of the Ego

The disease of the ego is this: whatever your identity as your ego is, your identity is actually that ego and its frequency *wherever it is found in the planes of Matter*.

Say I have a quality of envy that's an aspect of my ego. Every ego on the face of the planet Mars, every other planet, every other system of worlds* that has that exact frequency of envy is one with my ego. The mass consciousness is one. You can't say that you are an island and your ego is off all by itself. Things equal to the same thing are equal to each other. So your ego does not just consist of you and your envy, it consists of this larger conglomerate. That is what is called "the dark stars of compounded misqualification."

Whatever you retain in your ego is compounded by that exact frequency in all other egos with which you vibrate, and then you are one. Your friends will also consist of those who have a similar substance. So it is impossible to preserve an element of the ego and say, "Well, I will just keep this little part of it and no one will really know and it won't matter." It does matter. Whether it is a dark overlord on Mars or your

---
*The lifewaves on many planets are evolving on planes other than the physical.

carnal mind, it is really the same thing. As long as you are in that frequency, you are going to be tied to it. As long as you are tied to it, you are going to keep on reincarnating.

It is really quite a dangerous thing to allow yourself to tarry in any phase of the ego consciousness. It's quite astounding, isn't it, when you think about it?

For example, resentment and revenge pole with envy on the cosmic clock. Say a quality of my ego is envy, but I wouldn't dream of stooping to the level of taking revenge on someone or having resentment or retaliating because I believe I am above all that. So that is the very thing I am going to dislike and find fault with in somebody else's ego. The reason I am finding fault with it is because it is really in me since it is the polarity of my envy. It's the yin and the yang, and you can't have one without the other.

Whatever point you find yourself qualifying, it has a coordinate and a counterpart in some other ego. That some other ego is really your ego *because it's at the same frequency*—but it's the negative or the positive of what you are manifesting. So there are all these people on this planet hopping around having ego interactions, hopping up and down, reacting and interacting. And really it's just different phases of the one common ego that we all share, personified, let's say, in antichrist or Lucifer. So we blame him for everything, or we blame Satan for all the problems we have. That is assigning the carnal mind to an identity outside ourselves.

Satan and Lucifer would have no power whatsoever if you didn't have an ego or a carnal mind. They wouldn't even exist. They wouldn't even be in your frame of reference or your spectrum if it were not for the fact that you share their rebellion or their pride or whatever it is they have. It arcs right into your being by your own forcefield.

Now, it is important to recognize that the enemy exists. It is important to recognize that he is there. But just for the moment, the moment now of truth and the moment of personal responsibility, you might as well say, "Satan and Lucifer don't exist. The whole thing is in me. The whole thing is inside of me. I conquer this and I will have conquered all. There will be nothing left that can assail me." That's a very good consciousness to be in. Put the whole responsibility back on yourself, take it into yourself and say to yourself, "If Lucifer exists, if Satan exists, they exist inside of me. When I conquer that which is inside of me, the sphere of my consciousness will be whole in God and no thing within or without can assail me."

Student: Is Satan attracted to the three o'clock line of the cosmic clock?

ECP: I would say Satan is more on the four o'clock line and Lucifer more on the three, if you really want to bring it down to that. The god Pan, with the cloven hoofs and the horns, identifies with the perversion of Taurus on the four o'clock line.

Student: Satan and Pan are the same?

ECP: Yes. The god Pan is a disguise of Satan, whereas Lucifer represents the calculating, cunning perversion of the Logos. Mentally and philosophically he has the whole question of his rebellion completely rationalized. His is more an energy of sophistication, while Satan is more or less the Taurus substance of sex and carnal-mindedness and a certain grossness.

"What I AM"

Now, here is a list of what Meru says we really are—a list of "What I AM" to counteract all this ego business.

I AM a glowing orb of reality and joy and full illumination. (Illumination is illumined action.)

I AM the radiant expanding mind of God penetrating the universe with light.

I AM the power to expand consciousness beyond the sphere of the personal self into the dominant domain of reality.

I AM locked-in individuality.

I AM an evolving soul personality.

I AM and I know the permanent gift of bliss which it was the Father's joy to convey to me at the birth of my identity.

I AM the ocean of God's being.

I AM the drop in the ocean of God's being.

I AM man made in the image of my Creator.

I AM a co-creator with God.

I AM the door of Reality.

I AM the eternal being of God who is the doer.

I AM God and God can act in me—to remove hampering influences, to transmute darkness and to translate my consciousness from darkness into light.

I AM the freedom of the self to achieve without limit.

Eternal life is my true nature, the nature of God and of the divine image.

I AM that eternal life which is formed independently of the vehicle of self through the translation of the Holy Ghost.

I AM THAT I AM. I shall not see death, but be translated into that life which is my divine nature. I AM WHO I AM.

I AM the Presence of God which identifies through my sense of expanding reality with the universal consciousness of God that never takes from me one erg of energy or of Selfhood.

I AM the Son of God, the beloved inheritor of all things that were made.

I AM in reality the Son of God, the Light of God that never fails, by which the Eternal Progenitor performed the creative act.

I AM THAT I AM. God in me declares, "Thou art my beloved Son in whom I AM well pleased."

I die daily to the finite egoistic self. I live daily to the progressive glory of my Eternal Self and to the apprehending of all the reality that that Self can and does bring.

I AM THAT I AM. My worth is in the Eternal Now.

I AM that grace that is sufficient for every day.

I AM that grace of the Lord Christ which is implanted within my soul, with the inpouring breath of divine energy that first gave me life and consciousness.

In the name of Almighty God and in the name of the risen Christ, I willfully relinquish the snakeskin of my former identity that has crawled upon its belly and pursued the vanities of the intellect. I am replacing all that by the dominant sunburst of the living vital mind of God and that Reality which God is and which I AM because he is.

Thank you. Those are important fiats for your healing action and for your precipitation of the emerald ray.

February 19, 1975

CHAPTER THIRTEEN

THE NETWORK OF JOY

Commentary on Chapter 8

This *Pearl of Wisdom* from beloved Lanto is the eighth in the series and has the action of the eighth ray of integration.

To Those Joyous Hearts Who Would Expand the Joy of God:

Our subject is the spreading of the network of joy, the antithesis of sorrow, in the domain of consciousness and its communication into the world of form.

When the individual monad can willingly give up the personal self beyond the point of test in a genuine act of surrender, he is soon magnetized to the God ideal of spreading in the world domain the marvelous activity of vibrant joy—joy in self, joy in nature, joy in opportunity, joy in service, joy in music, joy in art, and joy even in the process of purifying the self.

Every facet of life takes on the aspect of challenge to those who daily strive to be more like Him. But this is not a challenge of discomfort, it is one of hope. The very fact that the individual can improve regardless of his station, that he can change his concepts, his vibratory action, and the contents of his mind as he would his garments is a sign of hope and a portent of delight.

Energy fields are magnificent when they are properly qualified, for they not only surround the creator of the energy field with his own vibration of bliss but, according to the law of attraction, they also magnetize the vibrations of happiness and joy from many parts of the world. We acknowledge that the reverse is also true, and seldom do people take into account the fact that from time to time they are surrounded with entities—entities of fear, of doubt, and of grief—which seek to invade the aura only because by their own attitudes individuals create the climate that attracts these outsiders.

In the matter of moods, then, we would suggest to every student who pursues God's happiness, whenever he is invaded by a feeling that is less than God-happiness—a feeling of discomfort or disquietude—that he begin to look for the cause first in his own subconscious mind and in the centering of his attention around negative ideas which he may have allowed to enter his world and secondly in the person of masquerading or malevolent entities.

Entities

On the subject of entities, the Great Divine Director has pointed out that a sudden drop in blood pressure or a change in body temperature can denote their presence.

The thing I have noticed about entities is that people come with their human stories, their human patterns, and with a recounting of these. They come saturated with human effluvia and we are called upon to counsel them and work with them. In the process, they tell us their story.

You find this when you're helping a friend. The friend is so caught up in the problem he's having that he will outline his experiences, and so forth, and you find yourself entering into a spiral of astral substance following the person through his own astral nightmare.

You will notice that there is a certain fascination pulling you into this spiral where you suddenly become very interested in all the little details and all the little things that make up this glob of astral substance. And you find yourself asking the person more questions and getting more emotionally involved in the problem than you need to be to solve it, to cast it out, to blaze the flame through it.

Therefore, take special note of the word *fascination*— because entities suck you in by this fascination with human gossip, human detail, human consciousness. So when you are dealing with people, remind yourself that you only need the barest facts to make an invocation, to make a call. You do not need to prolong the period of conversation about human creation in order to help the person. You do have to extend comfort. But watch that you do not take on a person's entities or get into a negative spiral yourself by following the energy until all of a sudden you are wrapped in it.

> The nature of invading entities is such that whenever an individual seeks to improve himself by engaging in religious worship, by attending a constructive lecture or concert, or by reading religious literature, the vibratory action of the higher pursuit makes the entity extremely uncomfortable. The entity, unwilling to relinquish his hold on the lifestream, will then project to his consciousness a feeling of discomfort or unhappiness and this, he will assure the individual, is directly attributable to the function in which the individual is involved.

This is such a typical plot of the force that it is routine! You see it coming and going. You see it happen to individuals, and as far as they are concerned, they are the only person that has ever had that experience. They think they are becoming extremely astute and sensitive. They count themselves as being highly spiritual, that they can discern that this particular religious activity is not for them because they sense in their being that it is not right for them. And you just can't convince them otherwise. You can't talk them out of it, unless they stay long enough to find out how it happens that all they are sensing is their discarnate entities.

People will tell you, "I got it in meditation." They got that they are not supposed to be a part of this group, or they are not supposed to decree, or their way is another way—"God bless you in your way, we're going our way." In truth, they meditate on their own discarnates, and the discarnates speak to them loud and clear within their soul. But they are sure it is the voice of God speaking.

Fascination, Witchcraft and Glamour

In this manner many sincere souls are either stopped on the Path or they are prevented from obtaining the benefits of higher meditation. Thus, through their susceptibility to invading entities, they are deprived of the opportunity to receive transcendent blessings. This is why spiritual protection is necessary for those who would continue to progress on the upward way—protection not only through the knowledge I am conveying but also through decrees, through prayer, and through the determination to do the will of God no matter what the argument of the opposition may be.

When you are able to cast out from the self the influences of discarnate entities—whether these be departed relatives, friends, or enemies who may be magnetized to your person—when you are able to invoke the protection from on high that will insulate you from the malice of those whom you may not even know are your enemies—whether embodied or disembodied—you will find yourself making spiritual progress at a more rapid pace.

Because of the increasing threat of witchcraft in the United States as well as in the world, spiritual aspirants must exercise caution and they should learn to weigh the evidence before they credit all of their failures or seeming failures to themselves. Witchcraft has a subtle allure ...

Fascination, astral fascination, and subtle allure have the same vibration because it is sex energy that is being perverted. It is the glamour of the human personality. What creates glamour is the sacred fire of sex energy that is used to adorn the person, to make people "glamorous." It has an icy feeling, like a not-quite-white energy. It's not the pure white light. It's kind of a grayish-tinged white that surrounds people that is mistaken for the white light.

Witchcraft has a subtle allure for those who are not grounded in spiritual knowledge and who do not understand the karmic penalties that accrue from such dangerous practices. Often practitioners of witchcraft use their powers to launch a general form of attack against anyone who tries to escape from the mass miasma.[1]

That is actually what does take place in witches' covens. They form a cone—a sex cone—in the center of a circle. And the energy is directed through a formula of witchcraft against all people serving the light.

There was a witch from Los Angeles named Leta who called here during a class. She said that Madame Prophet should stop her work because if she didn't stop, pretty soon there would be no more witches in California because I was destroying all of their sex cones and all of their work. When she called, she was very excited that I should stop doing my work, and a couple of witches from her coven threatened to come to the class and put LSD in our drinking water. They got extremely vicious for a while.

> There is something about progress that always engages the teeth of men's egos. When others begin to progress, they often enter into feelings of jealousy. Jesus described this human propensity in his statement "Woe unto you, lawyers! for ye have taken away the key of knowledge: ye entered not in yourselves, and them that were entering in ye hindered."[2]
>
> Many in the orthodox churches are naïve concerning these facts. They are entirely too standpat in matters of the self. Quite frankly, as you have been told in this series, the self is little understood. This is why people often work against their own best interests and against the best interests of humanity, why they are so easily captivated by the idea of massive social gain and why the dark forces are able to create so much unrest in the world, making men and women think they can gain spiritually as well as materially through forms of government control.

The amplification of that last paragraph's meaning is made in Jung's book *The Undiscovered Self*. The fascination with government controls is another form of fascination and allure. It is projecting onto the state the portion of the ego, of the self, that is the authority figure and then having it also take over the authority for mankind's spiritual lives. So the state becomes a religion as well as a hand that delivers to everyone everything they need. And that is a fascination—massive social gain.

Because of ambition we buy the line of socialism, because we're ambitious for society, for gain, for wealth, and so on. Somehow in exchange for signing ourselves over to the state, we think we are going to have all our needs met. Instead, we lose our identity. We lose our life and we don't really get the social gain we are looking for because the state can never make up the difference for the impoverished condition of consciousness. It simply goes into more and more debt until it finally collapses.

Giving and Receiving

The ideal society is that which evolves out of the higher consciousness when the individual opens the door of his being to God without reserve. In such moments of personal contact with Life, the entire being of man becomes as a mouth pressing itself against the Infinite in order to receive the subtle nourishment that floods into the hungry soul.

An interesting thing I notice about serving communion is how far a person will reach to take the bread and the wine. Some people just stand there and they make me actually take a step to reach them. As we have learned in our other studies of psychology, this is a sign that these people have constantly been fed by their mothers and they expect the mother to do all the work. Others will come forward, stick their tongue out and take the bread. Still others will take the cup from me and drink it themselves. It's really cute to see the different levels of how hard people will work to get the Body and Blood of Christ. When it is little children and they stand two feet away, I make them come forward.

A similar thing happens in a line where I'm giving a blessing on the forehead. If I don't watch it, I'm walking halfway across the room before I'm finished because people stand so far away from me waiting for the blessing to happen to them. People will simply not come up to me.

This shows that by and large in the subconscious of early aspirants on the Path there is the feeling that God is going to suddenly come down and work a miracle in their lives and everything is going to be all right. That myth persists. So they see the ascended masters or they see me, and here is the blessing and they stand there waiting for it to descend upon them.

We all come to the realization—sometimes a rude awakening—of just how much we are required to do for ourselves. And that's very healthy. Of course, we need the Mother there when we need the Mother there, and there is just no substitute. But hopefully through the teachings and the process people go through on the Path, they finally do come to the realization that they have to *be* the Mother.

Personally, in looking at myself, I think that if I have any problem along these lines, I tend to do a little bit more for people than I should. I tend to completely take the responsibility for everyone's salvation. That is in my heart, and I don't know quite how to balance it with the understanding we are gaining. I do realize that the Mother has to be the Infinite against which the children of God can press their mouths and receive the flow and the milk of the Word. But at the same time the Mother has to know when to wean the children and make them go out and learn to conquer time and space.

Because the grace that comes from on high is so creative, so inspirational, so filled with depth and height and volume, it literally overwhelms the being of man, and spilling over the lip of life it floods forth as the impulse to be a benefactor to the race. Such impulse must be guarded under God-control and channeled constructively in order to protect the self and the highest nature in others.

This impulse to be all things to all people—to give the light, to give the teaching, to serve mankind—has to be guarded with God-control because you can so totally spend yourself in service that you have nothing left with which to sustain an identity. People who do this don't know how to receive, they only know how to give, which is a problem in balance.

Helios and Vesta told us that the periods when we are not feeling the radiation of heaven pouring upon us are when we are required to project our love to God so we can receive love back again on the return current and tide. They told us not to feel alone and bereft and cut off during a quiet period when suddenly we say, "I don't feel any radiation. Where did God go?" At that particular moment it's time for us to be giving God radiation and reinforcing the arc of the return.[3]

The taking from God and the giving to God has to be in balance—channeling our energies constructively so we don't destroy the self, burn out the self and then not be able to continue on a longer span of service for mankind. So enlightened self-interest means you have to preserve your health and your supply.

Nurturing People's Inward Gifts

Each person should realize that the higher intelligence within himself is capable of making accurate decisions as to when he should speak and when he should be silent, when he should offer a helping hand and when he should withhold it. There are times when nothing is as important as a physical gesture of assistance to another, and at other times there is nothing so dangerous. Some of the best gifts that can be given to men are inward gifts such as the communication of the highest vibrations of hope and comfort.

"Inward gifts"—providing the spiritual grace, the hope, the immaculate concept, and perhaps not speaking. You can understand so clearly how much people have a need to conquer individually, to have a sense of the measure of the man, of the woman, to sense what they are capable of doing with their two hands and with their four lower bodies, and to gain the sense of self-mastery.

You have that understanding when you look at children. They get completely off balance when you do too much for them. They want to do it all by themselves. For example, if you dress them and they wanted to dress themselves, nothing will help until you completely undress them and let them do the whole thing over again because they have to show you that they can do it by themselves. And I'm sure you are aware of the misfits whose mothers dress them all their lives. To do too much for a child is smothering.

I am so delighted when I see my children making right choices because they have had freedom and—given the freedom that I gave them—they went out and made a choice, made a decision based on right knowledge. Now, there's no question that they make mistakes. But at least they have a sense of having made the mistake, understanding why it was a mistake and trying something again.

The person who never makes a mistake isn't really

getting anywhere because he is not a person who's trying. If he is not trying, how can he grow? So you have to let your children try. You have to let them make mistakes. And you mustn't get upset and condemn them when they make mistakes. You mustn't show terrible condemnation. You carefully point out the reasons why it was a mistake and go on. Let them be free. Let them know that the world isn't going to collapse because they wet their bed last night or they spilled a glass of juice on the table.

I've noticed myself getting quite firm with my children lately because the spilling of juice has been going on almost every day for the same reason. They sit in the wrong posture at the table and then they don't have control of themselves. So I've been cracking down on this. And I find that the way to crack down is to assign work detail rather than to heap condemnation upon their head so they feel like they should crawl in a hole because they spilled their juice.

There are ways of keeping the discipline but always extending hope, the flame of hope that the mother has in her heart. She is always certain her child is going to be victorious and always lets the child know he is going to be victorious.

I have found as Mother Mary has counseled the staff through me for many years that she never leaves a staff member without hope. No matter what has been done wrong, she will always affirm and praise the inner virtue—the quality, the potential and many actions which the individual has performed that are worthy—so that the individual has the ability to bear the weight of knowing "Yes, I've done a wrong thing. It was wrong and I acknowledge it and I'm going to see to it that it doesn't happen again." At the same time he knows inside himself that he has done something of worth, and that momentum is a fulcrum for him to lift himself right up into the heights of God-communion and God-practicality for another round of trying and doing better.

Avoid Condemnation

When you can see so much, when you can see the immaculate concept and you can see error as well, you have to be careful not to verbally cut off the head or the arm or the leg of someone in the process of purging them of their human consciousness. This is what we do when we come in with a huge wave of condemnation on people. And that condemnation usually comes from a sense of pride in perfecting the human.

I will soon be entering the twelve o'clock year with my birthday, bringing a tremendous opportunity for everyone in the movement to inaugurate cycles. Since I hold the flame at the top of the pyramid of the organization, everything that I do filters down to everyone who is under me. That's true of your point in hierarchy too. Wherever you are, your brick or stone is in the pyramid of hierarchy and what you do filters through to everyone under you.

Since my point of God consciousness will be in God-power, it's going to be a fantastic opportunity to inaugurate spirals. And you can't initiate one single spiral when you are condemning yourself, because while you are condemning yourself, you cannot be releasing God-power.* It is impossible to do. It's more difficult than patting your head and rubbing your tummy at the same time.

It is simply impossible for energy of one frequency and of another frequency to flow through your chakras

---

*God-power is the quality charted on the 12 o'clock line, where all new spirals begin. Condemnation is the misuse of energy on the 12 o'clock line. See p. 368.

simultaneously. That's why Jesus said, "Can this sweet water and bitter water come forth from the same fountain?"[4] He was talking about the chakras and the energy released through the chakras. You can't release both condemnation and God-power at the same time; you just can't do it.

You are making such decisions constantly. If you feel a negative thought of condemnation about someone, you can't be blessing them. You are cursing them. And those thoughts sometimes enter your mind before you realize you even have them.

Have you found yourself moving away from self-condemnation, yet looking at someone else and instantly condemning them for something? Your own mind hasn't even gotten in gear to greet this person or welcome them or love them, and you find yourself seeing them in some human matrix that you've got to shatter before you can go over and shake hands with them.

So you can see that there's an absolute death force of antichrist on the planet that, when you start zeroing in on it, affects your relationship to your inner self and to all the outer selves around you.

Accept a Helping Hand

The consciousness of the individual should become like a grail, and the knowledge that flows into the grail consciousness should draw more and more of the regenerating Christ consciousness into the domain of the self. Certainly it is true that if a man ask of God bread, he will not give him a stone.[5] Therefore consider the fact that constructive endeavor always receives the necessary support spiritually, morally, and materially proportionately as one accepts the highest sense of his mission in a spiritual manner.

"It is more blessed to give than to receive"[6] yet unless men receive they cannot give. Therefore the words *allotted portion* must be understood as the grace of God on deposit in the great causal body for each individual. Man can expand, as he is able to receive them, the highest judgments and qualities of God. He can grow in grace and in the knowledge of truth. He can become tomorrow a greater servant than he is today.

Part of learning to receive is learning to allow Simon the Cyrenian to carry the cross for you. A certain portion of the Path is the great initiation to acknowledge that you need help and to receive that help graciously, to learn that you are not an island, that your ego isn't so great that it is a sufficiency unto itself. There is nothing worse than the pride of self-containment, of fancying that you are so complete and so whole in yourself, in your ego, that you do not need anyone or require anything.

I feel very fortunate to have had many opportunities in this life to realize that with all of my trying and striving I have come to places where there was no other way to succeed than to accept a helping hand. And usually I never had to ask, but people would come forward with the helping hand. Then, of course, I also had to pass the test of not being too proud to ask for help, because that test comes too. If people know you need help, they are ready to give it, but if you don't tell them, they don't always know you need help.

So you have to reach that point of humility where you can say to your friend or your brother, "I need help. Will you help me? Will you pray for me?" You need to be self-sufficient in God, but understand that God is in all mankind and they can be the instrument of his fulfillment in you. You need to get over the pride of self-sufficiency in the human ego. You must be able to receive and you must be able to give.

The Eternal Cycles of God

Yet the foundation stones of the temple must be laid while consciousness is held in readiness. This is done by an act of willing to do whatsoever must be done in the furtherance of the kingdom of God both within and without. The self needs to expand. In order to expand, men need to receive. But all who receive need also to give; for if man becomes an inlet with no outlet, he will eventually become a parasite on the world body.

Man must qualify his energy with divine love just as the pulsing joy of God vivaciously entices all of Nature to perform her wondrous feats—her miracles of temporal reality immortalized as they recycle over and over again. Thus shall the individual realize that one day the true meaning of his life will be found in the spiritual interchange between the microcosm and the Macrocosm that is known as flow.

In these last two sentences there is a point of contact with the infinite mind of God that tells you that as Nature is eternal by the eternality of its cycles, so you are eternal by the fact of the eternal cycles of God moving through you. The leaves will fall from the trees, but the four seasons will continue. Your body cells are being continually renewed. Some of the cells that are on my hand now will be dead in five seconds. They will be continually renewed. The cycle that is renewing them is eternal, even though the material substance passes away.

So right while you are living in a corruptible form, you can put on incorruption by identifying not with that which goes through disintegration and decay, but by identifying with the cycle that controls the process. That cycle is the cosmic clock of God's own being, of God's mind. That is the eternal aspect of you. It is also the eternal aspect of the flowers and the trees. And this is flow because over these cycles of flow you have the spiritual interchange between the microcosm and the macrocosm. *The eternal aspect is the flow itself*; it is the cycle itself rather than the parts of the body or the leaves or the flowers or the petals.

Through this process, the allness of man flows into the allness of God and the allness of God, flowing into the allness of man, brings about an exchange of the pulsations of identity which make the humblest soul a king of victory and the most exalted to bow in joyous humility.

Truly "he hath put down the mighty from their seats, and exalted them of low degree."[7] Truly the living God is crowned in every atom. Truly each man is the son of the Eternal One. Move on, then, to understand that which you can be; for out of the expectancy of hope is born the implementation of faith that establishes the borders of self right where charity is. When the meaning of true love is known, it is found to re-create that supreme moment when the innocent soul cried out with divine wonder, "Because thou art, O God, I AM!" Thus we see the links of identity, intelligence, power, and love uniting all to the oneness that is God.

Victoriously, I remain
Lanto

In closing, let us give these words as a chant.

Because thou art, O God, I AM!

I AM THAT I AM.

OM.

Because thou art, O God, I AM!

March 3, 1975

The Chart of Your Divine Self

There are three figures represented in the Chart of Your Divine Self. We refer to them as the upper figure, the middle figure and the lower figure. These three correspond to the Christian Trinity: the upper corresponds to the Father, who is one with the Mother, the middle to the Son, and the lower to the temple of the Holy Spirit.

We address our Father-Mother God as the I AM Presence. This is the I AM THAT I AM, whom God revealed to Moses and individualized for every son and daughter of God. Your I AM Presence is surrounded by seven concentric spheres of rainbow light. These make up your causal body, the biding place of your I AM Presence. In Buddhism it is called the Dharmakaya—the body of the Lawgiver (the I AM Presence) and the Law (the causal body).

The spheres of your causal body are successive planes of God's consciousness that make up your heaven-world. They are the "many mansions" of your Father's house, where you lay up your "treasures in heaven." Your treasures are your words and works worthy of your Creator, constructive thoughts and feelings, your victories for the right, and the virtues you have embodied to the glory of God. When you judiciously exercise your free will to daily use the energies of God in love and in harmony, these energies automatically ascend to your causal body. They accrue to your soul as "talents," which you may then multiply as you put them to good use lifetime after lifetime.

The middle figure in the Chart represents the "only begotten Son" of the Father-Mother God, the light-emanation of God, the universal Christ. He is your personal Mediator and your soul's Advocate before God. He is your Higher

Self, whom you appropriately address as your beloved Holy Christ Self. John spoke of this individualized presence of the Son of God as "the true Light, which lighteth every man that cometh into the world." He is your Inner Teacher, your Divine Spouse, your dearest Friend and is most often recognized as the Guardian Angel. He overshadows you every hour of the day and night. Draw nigh to him and he will draw nigh to you.

The lower figure in the Chart is a representation of yourself as a disciple on the path of reunion with God. It is your soul evolving through the planes of Matter using the vehicles of the four lower bodies to balance karma and fulfill her divine plan. The four lower bodies are the etheric, or memory, body; the mental body; the desire, or emotional, body; and the physical body.

The lower figure is surrounded by a tube of light, which is projected from the heart of the I AM Presence in answer to your call. It is a cylinder of white light that sustains a forcefield of protection twenty-four hours a day, so long as you maintain your harmony in thought, feeling, word and deed.

Sealed in the secret chamber of your heart is the threefold flame of life. It is your divine spark, the gift of life, consciousness and free will from your beloved I AM Presence. Through the love, wisdom and power of the Godhead anchored in your threefold flame, your soul can fulfill her reason for being on earth. Also called the Christ flame and the liberty flame, or fleur-de-lis, the threefold flame is the spark of the soul's divinity, her potential for Christhood.

The silver (or crystal) cord is the stream of life, or "lifestream," that descends from the heart of the I AM Presence through the Holy Christ Self to nourish and sustain (through the seven chakras and the secret chamber of the heart) the soul and her four lower bodies. It is over this "umbilical" cord that the light of the Presence flows, entering the being of man at the crown chakra and giving impetus for the pulsation of the threefold flame in the secret chamber of the heart.

The lower figure represents the son of man or child of the light evolving beneath his own "Tree of Life." The lower figure corresponds to the Holy Spirit, for the soul and the four lower bodies are intended to be the temple of the Holy Spirit. The violet flame, the spiritual fire of the Holy Spirit, envelopes the soul as it purifies. This is how you should visualize yourself standing in the violet flame. You can invoke the violet flame daily in the name of your I AM Presence and Holy Christ Self to purify your four lower bodies and consume negative thoughts, negative feelings and negative karma in preparation for the ritual of the alchemical marriage—your soul's union with the Beloved, your Holy Christ Self.

Shown just above the head of the Christ is the dove of the Holy Spirit descending in the benediction of the Father-Mother God. When your soul has achieved the alchemical marriage, she is ready for the baptism of the Holy Spirit. And she may hear the Father-Mother God pronounce the approbation: "This is my beloved Son in whom I am well pleased."

When your soul concludes a lifetime on earth, the I AM Presence withdraws the silver cord, whereupon your threefold flame returns to the heart of your Holy Christ Self. Your soul, clothed in her etheric garment, gravitates to the highest level of consciousness to which she has attained in all of her past incarnations. Between embodiments she is schooled in the etheric retreats until her final incarnation when the great law decrees she shall return to the great God Source to go out no more.

Your soul is the nonpermanent aspect of your being, which you make permanent through the ascension process. By this process your soul balances her karma, bonds to your Holy Christ Self, fulfills her divine plan and returns at last to the living Presence of the I AM THAT I AM. Thus the cycles of her going out into the Matter cosmos are completed. In attaining union with God she has become the Incorruptible One, a permanent atom in the body of God. The Chart of Your Divine Self is therefore a diagram of yourself—past, present and future.

Introduction to the Cosmic Clock

The science of the cosmic clock is a means for the charting of the cycles of our lives. It is not traditional astrology. It is an inner astrology whereby we can chart the cycles of our karma and be the master of our fate, our cycles and our destiny. It also allows us to chart the cycles of our *dharma* and to fulfill our reason for being. As the wheel of the cosmic clock turns day by day and we experience the cycles of our tests and initiations in life, an awareness of this science can help us pass these tests.

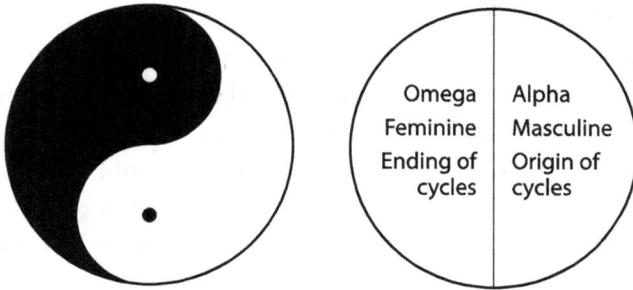

Omega	Alpha
Feminine	Masculine
Ending of cycles	Origin of cycles

The beginning and ending of all cycles

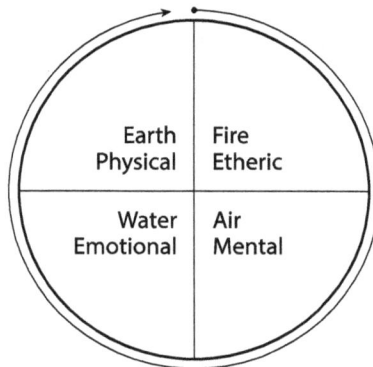

Earth	Fire
Physical	Etheric
Water	Air
Emotional	Mental

The four quadrants of a cycle and the four planes of matter

All cycles follow the same archetypal pattern. The most fundamental division of a cycle is represented by the T'ai chi, the two halves representing Alpha / masculine / the beginning of cycles on the right side, and Omega / feminine / the ending of cycles on the left.

Each half of the whole may in turn be divided into two halves, resulting in four quadrants, which correspond to the four elements: fire, air, water and earth. All cycles begin on the 12 o'clock line of this clock, in the etheric quadrant, and then proceed through the mental and emotional quadrants to the physical.

These four quadrants also represent the four planes or frequencies of the material universe. Man's being extends through all of these planes and into the realms of Spirit. We are less aware of our etheric, mental and emotional bodies than the physical, but these three are no less real. These four lower bodies are the vehicles for man's evolution in time and space.

Each of the four phases of a cycle may in turn be divided

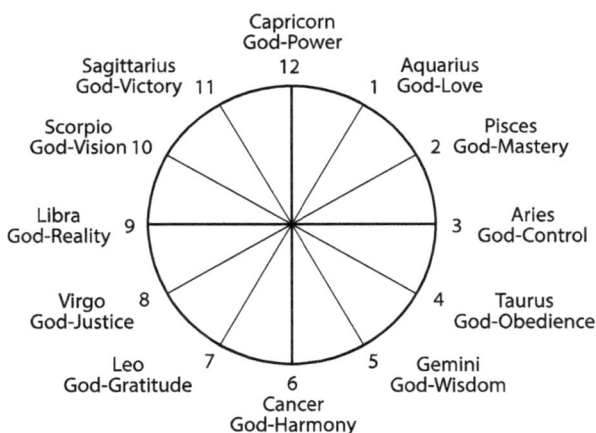

The twelve lines of the clock and the corresponding God qualities

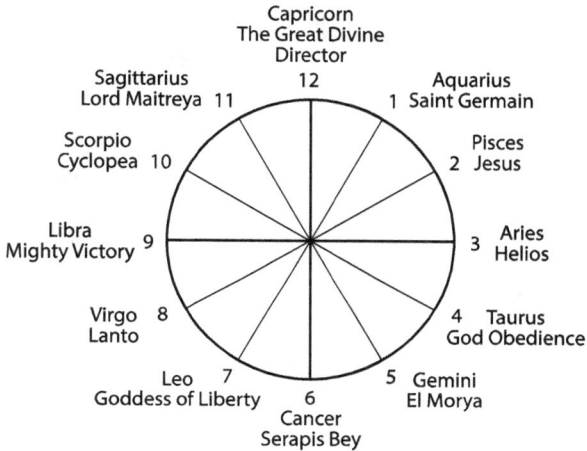

Capricorn
The Great Divine
Director
12

Sagittarius
Lord Maitreya 11

Aquarius
1 Saint Germain

Scorpio
Cyclopea 10

Pisces
2 Jesus

Libra
Mighty Victory 9

Aries
3 Helios

Virgo 8
Lanto

4 Taurus
God Obedience

Leo 7
Goddess of Liberty

5 Gemini
El Morya

Cancer 6
Serapis Bey

The cosmic beings who serve to release the light of the twelve solar hierarchies to earth and her evolutions

into three, resulting in twelve divisions, which are referred to using the names of the signs of the zodiac. Each line of this cosmic clock represents a specific frequency of God's light/energy/consciousness, which we refer to as God-power on the 12 o'clock line, God-love on the 1 o'clock line, and so on.

We begin walking through the cycles of the cosmic clock when we are born. We begin at the point of origin of all cycles, at the twelve o'clock line. One year later, on our birthday, we enter the one o'clock line, and so on once around the clock every twelve years of our life. As we enter each new line of the clock, we receive an increment of light corresponding to the quality on that line, and we also face the tests of how we will use that energy or misuse it.

Along with the tests on each line of the clock based on our personal cycles starting at birth, we also face tests on each line when the Sun and Moon enter the signs of the zodiac corresponding to the lines.

These twelve frequencies of God's energy may be

Criticism, condemnation and
judgment and all black magic

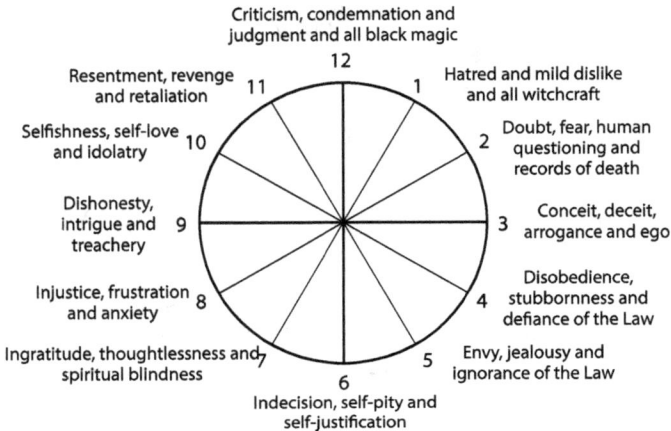

Resentment, revenge
and retaliation

Hatred and mild dislike
and all witchcraft

Selfishness, self-love
and idolatry

Doubt, fear, human
questioning and
records of death

Dishonesty,
intrigue and
treachery

Conceit, deceit,
arrogance and ego

Injustice, frustration
and anxiety

Disobedience,
stubbornness and
defiance of the Law

Ingratitude, thoughtlessness and
spiritual blindness

Envy, jealousy and
ignorance of the Law

Indecision, self-pity and
self-justification

Misuses of the light on the twelve lines of the clock

misused by man, resulting in negative karma on each line of the cosmic clock. The misuses of the twelve lines may be summarized as criticism, condemnation, judgment and black magic on the twelve o'clock line, and so on around the clock.

We are all walking a path of initiation, and we all have a choice to either keep going on a treadmill of failing our tests as we pass through the lines of the clock, or to determine to pass these tests and move on with our spiritual development. These are the tests of everyday life that come every moment.

Each test we pass gives us the right to carry more sacred fire in our chakras. Thus, initiation is cumulative. What we earn on one line has to be carried to the next line, and it becomes the foundation for mastery in that line. Likewise, what we do not pass on one line cannot be built upon in the next. So we must prepare.*

---

*For more information on the cosmic clock, see Elizabeth Clare Prophet, *Predict Your Future*.

Notes

Unless otherwise specified, books listed here are published by Summit University Press and are available from www.SummitLighthouse.org/Bookstore or by calling 1-800-245-5445 or 406-848-9500.

CHAPTER 1 • The Study of the Soul

1. "Know thyself": an ancient proverb attributed to several sources, among them Thales and Solon of Athens (two of the Seven Wise Men of Greece) and Socrates. Cicero speaks of it as a precept of Apollo. It was one of the maxims inscribed in gold letters over the portico of the temple at Delphi.

2. Rom. 8:7; I Cor. 15:46, 47; Rom. 7:23; Rom. 7:15, 19.

3. Mark 3:25.

4. Matt. 16:25.

5. Isa. 1:18.

6. The movie *Peter Pan*, based on the play by J. M. Barrie, Scottish author and dramatist.

7. "God is a Spirit and the soul is the living potential of God. The soul's demand for free will and its separation from God resulted in the descent of this potential into the lowly estate of the flesh. Sown in dishonor, the soul is destined to be raised in honor to the fullness of that God-estate that is the one Spirit of all life. The soul can be lost; Spirit can never die....

"The soul, then, remains a fallen potential that must be imbued with the Reality of Spirit, purified through prayer and supplication, and returned to the glory from which she descended and to the unity of the Whole. This rejoining of soul to Spirit is the alchemical marriage that determines the destiny of the self and makes it one with immortal Truth. When this ritual is fulfilled, the highest Self is enthroned as the Lord of Life, and the potential of God, realized in man, is found to be the All-in-all" (Mark L. Prophet and Elizabeth Clare Prophet, *The Path of the Higher Self*, vol. 1 in the Climb the Highest Mountain series, pp. 7, 8).

8. Calvin S. Hall, *A Primer of Freudian Psychology* (New York: Penguin, 1999).

9. Calvin S. Hall and Vernon J. Nordby, *A Primer of Jungian Psychology* (New York: Penguin, 1999).

10. C. G. Jung, *The Undiscovered Self* (New York: Signet, 2006).

11. Mildred Newman and Bernard Berkowitz, with Jean Owen, *How to Be Your Own Best Friend* (New York: Ballantine, 1971).

12. Mark L. Prophet and Elizabeth Clare Prophet, *The Path of the Higher Self*, chaps. 1 and 2.

13. II Tim. 2:15.

14. Matt. 9:17.

15. Matt. 5:16.

16. The practice of group criticism and self-criticism was developed in the Soviet Union in the 1920s and widely used by communist movements in the twentieth century as a method for indoctrination in communist ideology. The practice was expanded in Mao's China to include "struggle sessions," in which a person would be brought before a group of people and verbally or physically abused until he confessed to crimes against the people or counterrevolutionary thinking.

17. Rev. 22:1.

CHAPTER 2 • The Search for the Friend

1. Matt. 5:14.

2. Matt. 8:20; Luke 9:58.

3. John 14:2.

4. "Fourscore and seven years ago our fathers brought forth upon this continent a new nation, conceived in liberty, and dedicated to the proposition that all men are created equal." Abraham Lincoln, the Gettysburg Address, 1863.

5. Rev. 12:4–6.

6. Lucifer (the name comes from the Latin, meaning "light-bearer") was one who attained the rank of archangel and fell from grace through ambition, the pride of the ego, and disobedience to the laws of God. He is described in Revelation 12 as the "great dragon." The fallen angels are those who followed Lucifer in the Great Rebellion and whose consciousness therefore "fell" to lower levels of vibration and awareness as they were by law

"cast out into the earth" at the hand of Archangel Michael.

The ascended masters have revealed that on April 26, 1975, about three months after this lecture, Lucifer was found guilty of total rebellion against Almighty God and was sentenced to the second death at the Court of the Sacred Fire on the God Star, Sirius. Since then many others in the hierarchy of fallen angels have been bound and judged (including Satan), but many others still remain, carrying on their evil works on the astral plane or the physical. For more about the fallen angels, see Elizabeth Clare Prophet, *Fallen Angels and the Origins of Evil.*

7. Gen. 1:26.

8. Matt. 7:12.

9. Luke 24:13–35.

10. Matt. 12:37.

CHAPTER 3 • The Synthetic Image and the Real Image

1. I Cor. 15:50.

2. See Phil. 2:6; John 5:18.

3. Matt. 5:44.

4. See the Book of Job, especially beginning with chapter 4.

5. Job 3:25.

6. Mark 8:24.

7. In his address to the Keepers of the Flame Fraternity given January 2, 1965, beloved Saint Germain said, "The time has come when the mask of imperfection ought to be removed and men ought to see clearly that the hand of God is available to free men from the bane of superstition. Hence, I come this day in the name of the holy flame of freedom to ask you this year to

make special appeals to the great Karmic Board for and on behalf of removing the causes of superstition in the world. Do you know, precious ones, the world is so full of superstition today that if the energy which mankind actually congeal in the matrices of superstition could be released, I think that it would be enough to strike a blow at the forces of juvenile delinquency which seek to devour the youth of the world." 8. Matt. 24:15; Mark 13:14.

CHAPTER 4 • **Anger and Forgiveness**
1. Amaryllis, April 21, 1962.
2. Eph. 4:26.
3. Matt. 6:23.
4. Matt. 21:12.
5. See "Djwal Kul's Breathing Exercise," decree 40.09, in *Prayers, Meditations and Dynamic Decrees for Personal and World Transformation.* See also Djwal Kul, *Intermediate Studies of the Human Aura,* chap. 8, in Kuthumi and Djwal Kul, *The Human Aura.*
6. John 21:22.

CHAPTER 5 • **The Fire of Cosmic Purpose**
1. Words by Arthur Campbell Ainger (1841–1919).
2. See p. 369, n. 7.
3. Ps.1:1, 3.
4. Heb. 12:29.
5. *De-signs,* 'Deity *signs,* Deity's *sign*et, or Deity's *sign*ature'. The spiritual root of the word *design* shows that true art is intended to be an expression of God's magnificence and a tangible focus of the Divinity within the artist and every man, a pattern through which heavenly

virtue might penetrate and elevate the consciousness of the race.
6. Gen. 1:26–27.
7. Acts 17:26.
8. Rev. 2:11; 20:6, 14; 21:8.
9. Gen. 3:4.
10. Rev. 12:12.

CHAPTER 6 • **The Discipline of the Four Lower Bodies**
1. The Karmic Board is a court of eight ascended beings who dispense justice to this system of worlds, adjudicating karma, mercy and judgment on behalf of every individual. All souls pass before the Karmic Board before and after each incarnation on earth, receiving their assignments and karmic allotment beforehand and a review of their performance at its conclusion.
2. For more information about Saint Germain's embodiment as the Wonderman of Europe, see *Saint Germain On Alchemy,* pp. x–xxxi. See also Isabel Cooper-Oakley, *The Count of Saint Germain* (Blauvelt, NY: Rudolf Steiner Publications, 1970).
3. A detailed description of this journey of the soul may be found in Mark L. Prophet and Elizabeth Clare Prophet, *The Path to Immortality,* chap. 2.
4. I Cor. 3:19.
5. Phil. 2:5.
6. II Tim. 3:7.
7. Matt. 14:28–31.
8. *Unveiled Mysteries, The Magic Presence* and *The I AM Discourses* are published by Saint Germain Press.
9. Godfré Ray King, *The Magic Presence* (Schaumburg, Ill.: Saint

Germain Press, 1963), p. 243.

10. The Montessori method of education is intended to bring out the Christ potential of the child, as the child follows the direction of the inner teacher and selects in the classroom certain equipment and exercises that are appropriate for fulfilling the inner and spiritual needs of the child and bringing forth inner attainment. The combined freedom and order in the Montessori classroom is the true Aquarian-age education. This method of education for children was inspired upon Maria Montessori by Mother Mary. Mary said that this was the method she had devised with Elizabeth for teaching John the Baptist and Jesus when they were children.

For meditations for the development of the child from conception, see Elizabeth Clare Prophet, *Nurturing Your Baby's Soul.*

11. Luke 23:46.

CHAPTER 7 • Mastering the Flow of Energy

1. Rom. 12:21.
2. Gen. 1:28.
3. Phil. 4:7.
4. Matt. 13:24–30, 36–42.
5. The flames of God which may be invoked by those who desire to expand the Christ consciousness are many. Following is a list of those which have special importance for the evolutions of this solar system. Regardless of their color, all of the flames have a white-fire core of purity which embodies all of the attributes of God.

The flame of faith, power,

perfection, protection, and the will of God—blue; the flame of wisdom, intelligence, and illumination (focusing the mind of God)—yellow; the flame of adoration, love, and beauty—pink; the flame of purity (focusing the inherent design of all creation)—white; the flame of healing—emerald green; the flame of precipitation, abundance, and supply—Chinese green tinged with gold; the flame of ministration and service—purple and gold; the flame of freedom and transmutation (known as the violet singing flame)—violet; the mercy flame—shades range from pink violet to orchid and deep purple (visualizing a pink center around the white-fire core of the mercy flame will intensify the action of divine love within the quality of forgiveness); Mighty Cosmos' secret rays, five flames whose identity has not been revealed but which may be invoked with great personal and planetary benefit; the threefold flame of life (also known as the flame of liberty and the Christ flame because it focuses the balanced action of power, wisdom, and love, a prerequisite to Christhood)—blue, yellow, and pink, three plumes of the Trinity anchored in the heart of the God Presence, the Christ Self, and the body temple of man; the flame of cosmic worth—an accentuated, balanced threefold flame of power, wisdom and love; the resurrection flame—mother-of-pearl; the ascension flame—white; the flame of comfort (also known as the flame of the Holy Spirit)—white tinged with a delicate pink;

the cosmic honor flame—white tinged with gold; the flame of peace—golden yellow (often used in conjunction with the purple flame).

A simple method of visualizing the flames is to fix in mind the memory of a blazing campfire; retaining the concept of the action of the physical flames, see them take on the color of the God flame you desire to invoke. Now enlarge your image of the flames to fill your entire consciousness. Then visualize yourself stepping into the center of God's flaming Presence and feel his love enfold you as a thousand-petaled lotus—each flame a petal of God's all-embracing consciousness. *Prayers, Meditations, and Dynamic Decrees for Personal and World Transformation,* by Mark L. Prophet and Elizabeth Clare Prophet, will help you to sustain your visualization of the flames of God through the power of the spoken Word.

6. I Cor. 15:37–41.

7. "And when the day of Pentecost was fully come, they were all with one accord in one place. And suddenly there came a sound from heaven as of a rushing mighty wind, and it filled all the house where they were sitting. And there appeared unto them cloven tongues like as of fire, and it sat upon each of them. And they were all filled with the Holy Ghost, and began to speak with other tongues, as the Spirit gave them utterance" (Acts 2:1–4). "I indeed baptize you with water unto repentance: but he that cometh after me is mightier than I, whose shoes I am not worthy to bear: he shall baptize you with the Holy Ghost, and with fire" (Matt. 3:11).

8. Matt. 6:34.

9. II Cor. 12:7–9.

10. Matt. 5:28.

11. I Cor. 15:42–45.

12. James 3:17.

CHAPTER 8 • **Striving for Perfection**

1. Matt. 10:39.

2. In chapter 10 of *The Chela and the Path,* El Morya says, "To be a chela on the path of realizing a cosmic selfhood, you must train the mind to be free, to explore, and to discover self on many planes of being, to move with dexterity up and down the ladder of God's cosmic consciousness as the astronaut preparing for the walk in outer space, inner space. So you must become accustomed to penetrating life beyond the planet and then returning to the plane of practicality, of physicality, where you come to grips with keeping your accounts in order, keeping your house neat and clean, keeping your schedules, and keeping the balance in your relationship of employer and employee, husband and wife, father and son, mother and daughter.

"The farther you would go from your point of individuality in Matter, the more tethered you must be to that point. Self-discipline in the law of everyday living, obedience to the laws of God and man, exactness in detail, precision in the precepts of the Logos and of the Mother—these prepare your soul and your consciousness to expand and to reach out for the coordinates of the higher geometry of selfhood. Moving from plane to plane, the requirements of the law are more demanding; and thus the mastery of the self here below is necessary for the mastery of the self in the vast beyond" (p. 72).

3. Matt. 12:1–8; Mark 2:23–28; Luke 6:1–5.
4. Matt. 6:16.
5. Matt. 11:12.
6. Matt. 13:29.
7. John 1:14.
8. I Cor. 15:52.
9. John 6:68.
10. Matt. 7:24–25; 16:18; I Cor. 10:4.
11. Matt. 16:25.
12. Matt. 2:2.
13. Luke 12:32.
14. I John 3:2.
15. El Morya gives further explanation on the need to issue this challenge and to "try the spirits whether they are of God" (I John 4:1) in *The Chela and the Path,* chap. 16.
16. Rumplestiltskin is the name of a goblin in one of Grimm's fairy tales. He loses his temper when he is outsmarted by the heroine of the story.

Chapter 9 • Karma and Opportunity
1. Ps. 8:4.
2. Exod. 20:3.
3. Gal. 6:7.
4. I Cor. 8:5.
5. Isaiah 1:18.
6. John 14:13.
7. John 16:22.
8. John 10:10.
9. Acts 9:5.

10. Eccles. 2:11, 17.
11. I Chron. 13:7–10.
12. Gen. 19:1–26; Gen. 38:7–10; I Sam. 15; 31:1–4.
13. John 1:17.
14. John 14:12.
15. James 2:19.
16. Ps. 8:5.
17. Matt. 10:39.
18. Eph. 5:26.
19. James 4:8.
20. Col. 3:9, 10.
21. I Cor. 15:26.

Chapter 10 • Light and Darkness
1. Portia, December 31, 1974.
2. Ps. 1:2.
3. Gen. 3:1–19.
4. I Thess. 5:19.
5. *Mental karate* was the name given in the 1960s to methods for gaining power or influence over others through techniques of psychological manipulation.
6. Clara Louise Kieninger, *Ich Dien* (2005), p. 195.
7. Matt. 11:12.
8. Matt. 6:33.

Chapter 11 • The Energy of the Soul
1. Matt. 25:14–30.
2. Matt. 10:28.
3. James 1:17.
4. Gal. 6:7.
5. The City Foursquare is the New Jerusalem, archetype of golden-age cities of light that exist even now on the etheric plane (in heaven) and are waiting to be lowered into physical manifestation (on earth). Metaphysically speaking, the City Foursquare is the mandala of the four planes and the quadrants of

the Matter universe; the four sides of the Great Pyramid of Christ's consciousness focused in the Matter spheres. The twelve gates are the open doors to the twelve qualities of the Cosmic Christ sustained by the twelve solar hierarchies. Unascended souls may invoke the mandala of the City Foursquare for the fulfillment of the Christ consciousness, as Above, so below. The City Foursquare contains the blueprint of the solar (soul) identity of the 144,000 archetypes of the sons and daughters of God necessary to focus the Divine Wholeness of his consciousness in a given dispensation (Rev. 21:2, 9–27).

6. Scientists have detected energy waves around the Earth which they postulate were released at the birth of the material universe.

7. Luke 15:11–32.

8. Matt. 25:29.

9. Matt. 26:11.

10. James 1:17.

11. There are two different phases in the initiation of the dark night. In both the dark night of the soul, in which the soul's light is eclipsed chiefly by personal karma, and the dark night of the Spirit, in which the light of the I AM Presence is eclipsed by planetary karma as well as Christic initiation, the individual must deal with the tests unique to his lifestream and those common to all on the path of the ascension.

In the **dark night of the soul,** "the darkness that covers the land" is the weight of each individual's own returning karma as he is also learning to come to grips with world karma. Both types of karma eclipse for certain cycles the light of the soul and therefore its discipleship under the Son of God. When that personal karma is balanced by the soul, it must forge the Christ-identity, pass through the alchemical marriage (of the soul's union with the Christ Self), and be in a position, if required, to hold the balance for some weight of planetary karma. The latter occurs as the initiation of the dark night of the Spirit, which each initiate must face as the supreme trial of his Christhood. The dark night of the soul is the test of the soul's confrontation with its own karma of relative good and evil (the sin that can be forgiven); the dark night of the Spirit is the initiation of the soul's encounter with the Great God, Absolute Good, and, by that Good which he has become, of the vanquishing of Absolute Evil, its antithesis. The dark night of the soul is the tolerance of the Law, a period of grace for the soul to separate out from error and to transmute it; it is the prerequisite for the dark night of the Spirit.

Those who have been given the cycles necessary to pass through the dark night of the soul, but have not done so, must move on, regardless, to the initiation of the **dark night of the Spirit.** This is the initiation of the I AM Presence. It is the Self-limiting principle of the Law which does not tolerate the abuse of Christ by Antichrist. The latter initiation, given to saint and sinner alike, signifies that opportunity has run out for the individual to choose to be God. After hundreds of thousands and even millions of years of cycling through the wheel of rebirth, the soul-identity that denies the Presence of the Godhead dwelling in him bodily—His Word and His Work—is cancelled out by his own final decree, ratified by the judgment before the twenty-four elders at the Court of the Sacred Fire, in the second death (Revelation 2:11; 20:6, 11–15; 21:8).

The system of the Godhead for grace, mercy, and opportunity afforded to all for a season assures that all souls are given many lifetimes to repent of their evil works and be saved. It also assures that though mercy endures forever, Evil does not. The only hope for the perpetuation of holy innocence is that the evil word and the evil work (including that of the Evil One and his agents) can be and is terminated at the conclusion of abundant cycles of God's justice extended to all. See also "The Ascent of Mount Carmel" and "The Dark Night," in *The Collected Works of St. John of the Cross,* trans. Kieran Kavanaugh and Otilio Rodriguez (Washington, D.C.: ICS Publications, 1979), pp. 66–389.
12. "Our God is a consuming fire" (Heb. 12:29).
13. Matt. 18:3.
14. Gen. 1:26, 28.

CHAPTER 12 • The Nature of Individuality
1. Gen. 1:26.
2. John 10:7, 9.
3. I Cor. 15:50.
4. I Cor. 15:31.

5. Mark 1:11.
6. Saint Germain teaches students the science of precipitation in *Saint Germain On Alchemy.* At the end of chapter 7 he recommends the precipitation of an amethyst in the form of a Maltese cross as a first exercise for those who would study this science.

CHAPTER 13 • The Network of Joy
1. The author recommends the reading of *The Screwtape Letters,* by C. S. Lewis (New York: Macmillan Publishing Co., 1961) in connection with the series Understanding Yourself.
2. Luke 11:52.
3. "Just as the tides of the sea flow in and out, so the tides of the Eternal Sun radiate in ever-recurring cycles. When the incoming tide of the great solar light pours into your world, it is God conveying his grace and gifts to you. When the tide goes out, it is a time for you to convey to him your gratitude and your desire to become a very essential part of him. Those who are eager to receive the light that is incoming, with its buoyancy, its joy, its power, often do not recognize the moments when life does not seem to be with them— when the tides seem to be against them—as the moments when God is asking them to send love and supplication in his direction" (Helios, *Pearls of Wisdom,* vol. 13, no. 30, July 26, 1970).
4. James 3:11.
5. Matt. 7:9.
6. Acts 20:35.
7. Luke 1:52.

About The Summit Lighthouse

The Summit Lighthouse is an internationally recognized spiritual center for the advancement of inner awakening. Our international organization is a global family that is inspired, guided, and sponsored by those known as the ascended masters.

The ascended masters are the most beloved and trusted transcendent beings guiding our planet's material and spiritual evolution. Most of the world's religions are currently based on the revelations of one or more of these masters before their ascension. We openly embrace spiritual seekers from all paths of light including the mystical traditions of the world's religions.

The ascended masters and their messengers have given us over fifteen thousand hours of invaluable inner wisdom and insightful instruction, and they have provided the means for our direct initiation into higher consciousness.

For the ascended masters . . . no subject is off limits! Their teachings contain amazing truths and awesome answers on spirituality, alchemy, astrology, sacred geometry, spiritual science, karma, reincarnation, ascension, archangels (and fallen angels), and even those issues that are considered taboo or "out of this world."

Primary Goals of the Teachings of the Ascended Masters

The ascended masters challenge us daily to be bold, to dare to be who we truly are, and to face adversity with courage, patience, perseverance, honesty, integrity, inner love, discipline, and discernment—all for a greater sense of inner peace, fearlessness, stillness and silence, harmony, self-mastery, compassion, and wisdom.

These teachings help our souls get back to the origin of their individualized inner source of True Self Love—the Higher Self, or I AM Presence. Our point of contact with our Higher Self is the "Spark of Life" or "Sacred Fire of the Heart," the place where our consciousness expresses its true divine nature of unconditional love and happiness, universal oneness, and an authentic desire to serve others.

How Our Teachings Came into Being

Our teachings were all released through highly trained and trusted messengers, Mark L. Prophet and Elizabeth Clare Prophet. Mark was contacted by the ascended master El Morya at the age of eighteen and received training from him for many years before he was instructed to establish The Summit Lighthouse in 1958 in Washington, D.C.

With his ascension in 1973, Mark passed the torch for the mission to his gifted wife, Elizabeth Clare Prophet, who continued her service until her retirement in 1999.

The dictations of the ascended masters were regularly given in public. The ascended masters also inspired thousands of lectures delivered by the messengers. The content of the dictations are, by most human standards, beyond the mind's ability to construct in real time. They carry very powerful frequencies of light, awakening us to the highest truths we've ever experienced.

We leave it up to you to decide the value for yourself.

Moving toward Your Victory

No matter what path of light you are on, spiritual freedom is attained using tools that have been passed down in wisdom teachings through the millennia: meditation, selfless service, devotional music, prayer, mantra, and the science of the spoken Word. The masters bring an accelerated understanding of these principles, especially suited for the challenges of the modern world, including dynamic decree work and the use of the violet flame.

Next Steps

We are genuinely excited to meet you on the Path and hope you are too. We extend a warm welcome from everyone at The Summit Lighthouse, and we invite you to explore the teachings of the ascended masters at **www.SummitLighthouse.org**. Check out our free online lessons and hundreds of articles on a wide range of spiritual subjects. Browse through our online bookstore. And if you would rather talk to someone in person, please feel free to contact us today!

The Summit Lighthouse®
63 Summit Way
Gardiner, Montana 59030 USA
1-800-245-5445 / 406-848-9500
Se habla español.
info@SummitUniversityPress.com
SummitLighthouse.org

ELIZABETH CLARE PROPHET is a world-renowned author, spiritual teacher, and pioneer in practical spirituality. Her groundbreaking books have been published in more than thirty languages and over three million copies have been sold worldwide.

For more information about Elizabeth Clare Prophet's work, including her Pocket Guides to Practical Spirituality and her series on the Lost Teachings of Jesus and the Mystical Paths of the World's Religions, visit SummitUniversityPress.com.